The Armistead Family

1635-1910.

BY
Mrs. VIRGINIA ARMISTEAD GARBER
RICHMOND, VIRGINIA.

RICHMOND, VA.
WHITTET & SHEPPERSON. PRINTERS,
1910.

PREFACE.

A RECORD of the editor's branch of the Armistead family was begun in the summer of 1903, at the request of an elder brother, who came to Virginia for the purpose of collecting family data for his large family living in distant Southern States. Mrs. Sallie Nelson Robins, of the Virginia Historical Society, started the ball in motion when preparing his paper to join the Virginia Sons of the American Revolution. From this, the work has grown till the editor sends "The Armistead Family" to press, in sheer desperation at the endless chain she has started; powerless to gather up the broken links that seem to spring up like dragon's teeth in her path. She feels that an explanation is due, for the biographical notes, detail descriptions, and traditions introduced in her own line; which was written when the record was intended solely for her family. Therefore, she craves indulgence for this personal element.

Dr. Lyon G. Tyler's Armistead research in the *William and Mary Quarterly* is the backbone of the work, the use of which has been graciously accorded the editor. She is also indebted to Mr. Robert G. Standard and Mrs. Sallie Nelson Robins, of .the Virginia Historical Society; Mr. W. S'. Appleton's Family *of Armistead,* Bishop Meade's *Ola Churches and Pamilies of Virginia*, and various other authors of Vrginia history herein named. Obtaining correct data was a wearying undertaking; some phases of it amusing; charming letters.were receivêd and friendships started; sometimes, ignorance of, or indifference to knowledge of one's ancestry, prompted the remark "My father or grandfather was so democratic that he paid little attention to such matters." We wonder if they know that Thpmas Jefferson, that great apostle of democracy in Virginia, cared for "such matters."

There is on record a letter from Thomas Jefferson to John Adams, his London agent, in which he directs Mr. Adams "to search the *Herald's* office 'for the arms of my family.' I have what I am told are the family arms, but on what authority I know not. It is possible there may be none. If so, I would, with your assistance, become a purchaser, having Sterne's word for it that a coat of arms may be purchased as cheap as any other coat."

"What Mr. Adams found we cannot say, but thereafter upon the silver, china, paper of the Sage of Monticello, yea, even upon the fence that incloses his tomb, we find the three leopard's faces with the head of a talbot for its crest."

Craving indulgence for all mistakes, we send it forth, assuring the Armistead connection that we have done our best. We heard it said a few days since that only two men ever lived who never made a mistake—Enoch and Elijah, and they were translated.

MRS. A. W. GARBER,
211 E. Eranklin St., Richmond, Va.

A FOREWORD.

THE search for data and incidents, relating to the Armistead I family, has necessitated a great deal of reading, besides literal digging into the records of various counties and the Land Office, disciphering old tombstones, and visiting the sites of old homes and original grants. The drudgery, the weariness of it all, is forgotten, but the charm and romance of those early days linger with us, like some tender, bewitching dream, that we would fane keep fresh in the memory of those of the family, who may not have the same opportunity for the study of Virginia's Colonial history.

Before considering the country, or the conditions surrounding the early settlers, let us glance at the influences at work in England, that impelled the emigration of such stalwart, brave men.

The emigration to Virginia, at the beginning of the seventeenth century, was evidently the outcome of the restless spirit and craving for adventure that followed in the wake of the Reformation and the introduction of printing. These twin wires electrified the world. The rebound from the lethargy of dogma burst forth in the wild desire for change, for broadening the horizon of knowledge, and enlarging fortunes. The mystic, dreamland stories of early sea-rovers; later, the actual possessions of the Spanish crown in the Western Hemisphere, fired the heart of Sir Walter Raleigh, who had the bravery, daring and determination of a sea king, and the far-reaching vision of a statesman. The disasters of Sir Humphrey Gilbert, the mysterious fate of Sir Richard Greville's settlement on Roanoke Island, paralyzed the hopes of that generation. The spirit of adventure, zeal of the missionary, and lust of gold, reached high tide at the beginning of the seventeenth century. In the midst of this fever of unrest, Captain John Smith came back to England, a youth in years, just twenty-five, but a veteran in war and adventure. At the old Mermaid Tavern he and Bartholomew Gosnold, with other worthies of that day, would meet to talk over plans looking to a speedy fulfilment of their dream. King James at last authorized a voyage, and the first permanent English settlement in America at Jamestown was the mustard seed, from which has sprung the brains, energy and wealth of this vast United States of America. Edmund Spenser, in dedicating his *Facrie Queen* to Queen Elizabeth, linked Virginia with her other kingdom jewels, perhaps in compliment to his patron and friend. Sir Walter Raleigh, or did his vision penetrate into the future and see the marvelous

6

possibilites of this wonderland of the west? Aye, it was a very wonderland—"the Western paradise" so long dreamed of—to those pioneers, who, after an uncertain, stormy, mutinous voyage, landed first at Cape Henry, and next at the Indian town, Kecoughtan, "pleasantly seated upon three acres of land, half surrounded by the great River, the other part with the Baye of the other river falling into the great Baye, with a little Isle, fit for a castle, in the mouth thereof." "It was a Good Land, most pleasant, sweet and wholesome," but their orders were to settle inland, out of the way of the much dreaded Spaniards, so they sailed further up the river, and "moared their shippes" at Jamestowne.

From that time on, stalwart Englishmen literally hewed their way through dissensions, privations, treachery, famine and massacre, until they were firmly established in plantations or hundreds, all over Tidewater Virginia. It may be interesting to know, that up to 1633, each plantation or hundred was represented by a burgess; at that time the country was divided into eight shires "to be governed, as in England." In 1643 counties were formed. The thirteen counties, at the beginning of the Commonwealth, 1652, were Elizabeth City County, York, Warwick, Gloucester, Lancaster, Henrico, Charles City, Isle de Wight, Nansemond, Lower Norfolk, Northampton, Northumberland. Elizabeth City County was one of the eight original shires. Rapid changes were now taking place. Fine manor houses were being built instead of log houses; cultivated fields and rich harvests were in evidence. "The pioneer is now a burgess, a justice, a vestryman, a councillor, who rides in his coach and four; his land a valuable estate, which no creditor can claim for is it not entailed on his eldest son, who shall be lord of the manor after his father? On the banks of the James, the York, the Rappahannock, flourished a brilliant, prosperous society, whose centres were Virginia gentlemen, with their wives dispensing lordly hospitality."

Messrs. Standard, Tyler and Bruce have given to the public interesting and accurate facts of that time. It is plain from their research, that there was in Virginia, during the seventeenth century, a decided aristocracy; that "gentleman" had a definite meaning ; one who had a right to bear arms.

This class of Virginia gentlemen had a right to armorial honor from their ancestors. "Virginians were simply English people living in Virginia, tenacious of their rights and with a will and determination to defend them."

The history of the ballot in Virginia begins with that first legislative assembly in Jamestown in 1619. At first every plantation was entitled to suffrage, then counties and the parishes of the counties; voting was not only a right and duty, but was compulsory.

Rev. Hugh Jones, "Present State of Virginia in 1728," the intelligent professor of mathematics in William and Mary College, said; "They live in the same neat manner, dress after the same modes, and behave themselves exactly as the gentry in London ; most families of any note have a coach, chariot, Berlin, or chaise."

"The public or political character of Virginians corresponds with their private one; they are haughty and jealous of their liberties, impatient of restraint, and can scarcely bear the thought of being controlled by any superior power. Many of them consider the colonies as independent States, not connected with Great Britain, otherwise than by having the same common King, and being bound to her with natural affection" (Burnaby's *Travels in Virginia in* 1759).

In point of education, the Virginians, judged by the education prevalent in New England during the eighteenth century, were unquestionably better off than any other colony. The foremost merchant of Plymouth could not write his name. Nathaniel Morton, secretary of the colony, could write, but his. four daughters could not. "Records of Virginia and Massachusetts, marriage bonds, deeds, wills, letters, town and county records, etc., tell no uncertain story in favor of Virginians."

We are told by Hugh Jones "that planters, and even the native negroes, talked good English, without idiom or tone, and discoursed handsomely on most common subjects."

J. F. D. Smyth wrote in 1773; "The first class in Virginia are more respectable and numerous than any other province in America. These, in general, have had a liberal education, possess enlightened understandings and a thorough knowledge of the world, that furnishes them with an ease and freedom of manners and conversation, highly to their advantage in exterior, which no vicissitude of fortune or place can divest them of, they being actually, according to my ideas, the most agreeable and best companions, friends and neighbors that need be desired. The greater number of them keep their carriages, and have handsome services of plates, but they all without exception have studs, as well as sets of elegant and beautiful horses."

The Due. de Liancourt wrote that "in spite of the Virginia love for dissipation, the taste for reading is commoner there among men of the first class, than in any other part of America." John Davis wrote: "The higher Virginians seem to venerate themselves as men, and I am persuaded there was not one in the company who would have felt embarrassed at being admitted to the presence and conversation of the greatest monarch on earth. There is a compound of virtue and vice in every character; no man was ever faultless, but whatever may be advanced against Virginians, their good qualities will ever out-weigh their defects, and when the effervescence of youth has abated, when reason asserts her empire, there is no man on earth who discovers more exalted sentiments, more contempt for baseness, more love for justice, more sensibility of feeling, than a Virginian." * * * "The New Jersey man is distinguished by his provincial dialect and seldom enlarges his mind or transfers his attention to others; the Virginian is remarkable for his colloquial happiness, loses no opportunity of knowledge, and delights to show his wit at the expense of his neighbor." (Davis, *Travels in the United States*) Charles Dexter Allen, in his interesting work, *Ameriean Bookplates* (1894). notes these differences between the South and the North, that the former, "to which came men of wealth and leisure, with cultivated tastes, bringing books and musical instruments with them, retaining their connection with the far away home by correspondence and visits; sending their sons to the great universities to be educated, and to the law schools for a finishing course, and ordering their clothes, books and furniture and all the luxuries of life from England, was the first to use book plates. That the earliest comers to New England had a prejudice against coats of arms and trinkets of such like character, which their descendants soon forgot."

A few years ago, when Matthew Arnold was in this country, he was given a dinner at Washington, at which the only Southern gentleman present was Randal L. Gibson, of Louisiana. Being asked where in this country he found the best English spoken, he said: "Why in Virginia, which has the old English names for its counties and cities, and the best English speech."

LIBRARIES IN COLONIAL VIRGINIA.

Tyler says: "The careful examination of thousands of wills and inventories, enables the editor to say that books were not rare in Virginia, during the colony. Very few of the inventories of personal estates are without mention of them, though a failure to mention, is not always conclusive of their absence. * * * The backwoodsman in Virginia, in the time of Charles I., presented no worse picture than the English gentry, as represented by Macaulay."

The New England inventories cannot claim superiority. From the "Goodwins of Connecticut" we see that Ozias Goodwin had no books; William Goodwin, a Bible and two books." In Wentworth's Genealogy "fourteen out of thirty-five Massachusetts settlers made their marks in 1639.

"In his *Colonial Times on Buzzards Bay*, Mr. William Root Bliss shows us how illiterate the first immigrants to Plymouth were, and how much rubbish is collected in the Museum of Plymouth Hall in Plymouth. He shows that the first company of settlers, who landed at Plymouth Rock, eleven only are favorably known, the jrest are known unfavorably, or known only by name." In the New *York Critic*, November 25, 1893, Wheeden, shows that the wretched education obtained by the masses in New England, till a very late day, was a doubtful competency to read, write and cipher; the free schools were two months in winter, two in summer."

Some of the libraries of the Virginia gentry, notably those of William Byrd, Ralph Wormeley, Richard Lee, were astonishingly rich, many of their books being great folios, expensively illustrated. Col. William Byrd of Westover had three thousand, six hundred and twenty-five volumes — history, seven hundred; classics, six hundred and fifty; entertaining, six hundred and fifty: French, five hundred and fifty; law, three hundred and fifty; divinity, three hundred; scientific, two hundred and twenty-five; physics, two hundred. Two volume folios, *Reeords of London Company*, made at instance of the Earl of Southampton, are now in the Library of Congress.

"Library of Rev. William Dunlop: Several thousand volumes in most, arts and sciences; Hon. Philip Ludwell, Green Spring, books and library furniture appraised at £5,385. John Hood, a valuable library of entertaining and instructive books of the best editions : George Davenport had a large collection of law books; Joseph McAdams advertised in the *Virginia Gazette* A curious collection of prints and pamphlets, relating to all the transactions in Europe for years past; two hundred prints or pictures, representing all persons of note in Europe. Rev. Thos. Horrocks, a variety of valuable books and sermons, mostly celebrated authors. Library of John Semple, deceased; attoney at law, consisting of history law and novels, etc.

For sale at Jordan's Point, Prince George County, the personal estate of Richard Bland, the antiquary, including a library of valuable books. For sale at Dr. Alexander Jameson's, a library of books on various branches of literature. Rev. Charles Jeffrey Smith, New Kent, a large and valuable collection of books, 1771 *Virginia Gazette*. Library of Col. John Carter, of Lancaster County, classical, religious and miscellaneous, 1690. Library of Col. Daniel McCarty, of Westmoreland County, a valuable collection on all subjects. Charles Dexter Allen says: "There is more evidence of refinement preserved in Virginia, by means of tombstones, book-plates, records of libraries, than in any other of the colonies. Williamsburg was the first Colonial town to have a theatre (1716) and the first to have an asylum for the insane. Travelers were witness to the cultivation and numbers of first-class men in Virginia."

"The small land holders, or second-class in the social scale, answered to the English yeoman ; they lived in harmony with the aristocrats, as they may be called, having mutual regard and respect for each other. They stood shoulder to shoulder in the Revolution as neighbors, were associated and worked together for aims as dear to one class as to the other. They maintained a pride that lays at the foundation of true manhood." Mr. Tyler says there was no distinct line between the first and second class in Virginia; in public and in politics, they met on a plane of equality."

Henry A. Wise said in Congress: "Wherever black slavery exists there is found at least, equality among the white population."

Now as to cultivation and education, in *Virginia in Colonial Days*, Mr. Tyler quotes Mr. Jefferson as saying: "That the mass of education in Virginia, before the Revolution, placed her with the foremost of her sister colonies."

"Of the truth of Mr. Jefferson's remark there can be no doubt, after instituting a comparison with Massachusetts, who is generally admitted to have been the most enlightened of Virginia's Northern sisters. To both these colonies came very nearly the same elements of society in England. That Massachusetts had quite her share of disreputable characters, is apparent from the words of Rev. John White, one of the most active colonizers of Massachusetts, who, writing to John Winthrop, said that "the very scum of the earth was sent to New England." "It is well known that the climate of Eastern Virginia was most deadly to the new comers from England. In 1671, when negro laborers were beginning to be preferred, Sir William

Berkeley reported that four out of five white servants had hitherto succumbed to the inroads of disease." The class of servants who survived were undoubtedly those who suffered the least exposure — that is to say, the better class. Among these were many political refugees of family and education. It must not be forgotten that the word "servant" was in the seventeenth century, a much wider term than now; everybody in the employment of another was called "servant." Wards, secretaries, apprentices, etc., were "servants."

Mr. Bruce says: "The descent from convicts is a silly fable! that those best acquainted with Virginia records and genealogy have never found a family of such descent."

What is certain is, that life in Virginia, at that time was an ideal life, simple, wholesome and happy. "The planter in his manor house, surrounded by his family and retainers, was a feudal patriarch mildly ruling everybody; drank wholesome wine, sherry or canary, of his own importation; entertained every one; held great festivities at Christmas, with huge log fires in the great fireplaces, around which the family clan gathered, and everybody high and low was happy. It was the life of the family, not of the great world, and produced that intense attachment for the soil, which has become proverbial; what passed in Europe was not known for months, but the fact did not seem to detract from the general contentment. Journeys were made on horseback or in coaches, and men were deliberate in their work or pleasures. But if not so rapid, life was more satisfactory. The plantation produced everything and was a little community sufficient for itself. There was food in profusion ; wool was woven into clothing, shoes made, and blacksmithing performed by retainers on the estate. Such luxuries as were desired, books, wines, silk and laces, were brought from London to the planter's wharf, in exchange for tobacco, and he was content to pay well for all, if he could thereby escape living in towns."

During the winter large numbers of the planters went to Williamsburg to live, the vice regal capital, and here were held grand assemblies at the Raleigh Tavern, or the old Capitol, where the beaux and belles of the time, in finest silks and laces, danced and feasted. Or the theatre drew them, for the "Virginia Company of Comedians" had come over in the ship "Charming Sally," and acted Shakespeare and Congreve for the amusement of the careless old society."

If this state of things nurtured pride and the sentiment of self importance, many virtues were the result; honor, cordiality of manner, and abounding hospitality. The planter may have been a Nabob, but he was also a kind neighbor and warm friend. He was brave, honest, and spoke the truth; and under his foibles lay a broad manliness of nature, which gave him influence as an individual and a citizen."

Mr. Davis in his *Ancient Landmarks of Plymouth, Mass.*, says "that in the year 1793. a project to establish a school for girls was opposed because it might teach wives how to correct their husband's errors in spelling."

NOTE.—If any deed is recorded or discovered during Colonial times, without "Esquire" added to the surnames, it may be certain such families or surnames did not belong to families bearing coat-armor. "Esquire" means nothing now, in England or America, but it did mean much then when it was written "Armiger" before the Revolution. This "Armiger" descended from father to son, and carried rank with it, and in which case it involved the possession of coat armor. If on any tombstone, old deed, or old English charts, we find "Armiger." (or gentleman) attached to the name, it is certain that they bore arms as "Knights," the first rank which could claim any armor. "Esquire" did not depend on wealth, yet those who held it were considered more educated. We adopted this rule generally in our searching. E. C. M.

EDUCATION IN COLONIAL VIRGINIA.

The following is copied from *William and Mary Quarterly*, Vol. VI, No. 2. Beverley, who wrote in 1705, says: "There are large tracts of land, houses, and other things granted to free schools for the education of children in many parts of this country, and some of these are so large, that of themselves, they are a handsome maintenance, to a master. These schools have been founded by legacies of well inclined gentlemen, and the management of them hath commonly been left to the direction of the county court, or the vestry of their respective parishes."

"As early as 1617, King James had issued his letters patent, through the Kingdom for collecting funds for a college at Henrico in Virginia, and almost contemporaneously, money was raised for a school at City Point (then called Charles City), which was named the East India School, in honor of its first benefactors. The question of the Henrico College received discussion in 1619 in the assembly in

Jamestown, the first ever convened on this continent. But though the college and school were rapidly pushed, and a rector for the college, a master and usher for the school, and a manager for the college lands, and tenants were selected, and all but the Rector, sent over to the colony; the Indian massacre of 1622, by destroying at a blow, three hundred and fifty persons in the settlement, effectually crushed both the college and the school."

Private persons took up the design of a free school and some years after the massacre, Edward Palmer, of London, in his will (1624) left "all his lands in Virginia and New England, for the foundinge and maintenance of a University and such schools in Virginia as shall then be erected" * * *

A better fortune attended a few years later, the benefaction of a resident of the colony. Four years before John Harvard bequeathed his estate to the college near Boston, Benjamin Syms, of Virginia, left the first legacy by a resident of the American Plantations, for the promotion of education. By his will made February 12, 1634-35, he gave two hundred acres on the Poquoson, a small river, which enters the Chesapeake Bay a mile or less below the mouth of York River, with the milk and increase of eight cows, for the education and instruction of the children of the adjoining parishes of Elizabeth City and Kiquotan. Syms was evidently an Honest religious, and childless planter." The Virginia Assembly, in 1642-43 gave a solemn sanction to Syms, will * * * In 1647, early writer says: "We have a free school with two hundred acres of land, a fine house upon it, with forty milch kine, and other accommodations."

This school was soon followed by another, Thomas Eaton's gift of two hundred and fifty acres "at the head of Back River." Both schools were undoubtedly in operation at the time when Berkeley made his much quoted remark about free schools in Virginia. "I thank God there are no free schools and printing which I hope we shall not have these hundred years!'

Facts prove that Berkeley did not mean that there were no free schools (gratuitous), as is now meant by the term Free." Free school, then meant a school affording a liberal education. He had in mind such schools as Eton or Harrow, or the colleges at the universities in England. This supposition is confirmed by the fact that eleven years before (in 1660), the Colonial Assembly had passed an act for the founding of "a college and free schoole" to which object Berkeley, the Council, and members of the General Assembly, all subscribed. The

14

instruction of the Assembly to Dr. James Blair read: "That you shall endeavor to procure from their majesties, an ample charter for a Free Schoole and colledge, wherein shall be taught the Latin, Greek and Hebrew tongues, together with Phylosophy, Mathematicks, and Divinity; and in order to this, you shall make it your bisiness to peruse ye best Charters in England, where by Free schools and Colleges have been founded" * * *

In 1724, twenty-nine out of forty-five parishes, reported as to public schools. In six out of the twenty-nine, were public schools. Scattered all over the colony were schools of fair standing, and in many of them Latin and Greek were taught. Tutors were engaged in private families, many of whom were ripe scholars from the universities of Europe. Many sons of wealthy sent to England for their education.

Dr. James Blair's efforts in behalf of the "Free schoole and Colledge" in Virginia, met with hearty Co-operation from all classes of Englishmen, the Bishop of London, the Arch Bishop of Canterbury, and leading,merchants of London. Queen Mary lent a gracious ear, and at her request, even King Edward turned from affairs of state to listen to the appeal of his subjects in Virginia. On the second of Eebruary, 1693, there issued under the sanction of the seal of the privy council, the great charter of public education (in the Brittish archives).

Dr. Blair did not do things by halves. The College was the first corporation in America to be recognized by the royal will. It was the first English College to receive from the College of Heralds, in 1694, a coat of Arms. The college was to take rank in theory at least, with Oxford and Cambridge as "Their Majesties College of William and Mary." The corporation was not to be one, like Harvard's consisting of a "President and Tutors," but of a "President and Masters or Professors." The Eree schoole and Colledge" was to consist of three schools, viz.: Crammer, Philosophy and Divinity. In 1729, there were six professors, graduates of Edinburgh, Oxford and Cambridge. At Harvard at that time, there was only one regular professorship.

The influence of the College from 1729 forward, on public thought in Virginia, was enormous. Especially did it manifest its results in training that generation of Virginia statesmen, that left so deep an impress on the history of the world."

The efforts and acts of Virginians in furthering education, in the early days of the colony; cannot be too much emphasized. It was the catastrophe of an Indian massacre which alone prevented the founding of "The College and Eree schoole" some fifteen years before the first steps were taken in Massachusetts.

The Armistead family.

The progenitor of the family in Virginia was William Armistead, of Deighton Kirk, in the west riding of Yorkshire, England. He was the son of Anthony Armistead and Frances Thompson, and was baptized August 3, 1610, in All Saints', the only church in the parish. His name, William, suggests that she, Frances, may have been a daughter of William Thompson (sometimes spelled Thomson), a lawyer living at that time in Yorkshire, one of whose sons, Stevens Thomson, emigrated to Virginia and was attorney-general. Another son, Sir William Thomson, born 1658, remained in England. Deighton Kirk, in the northern part of west riding of Yorkshire, two miles from Wetherby, five and half miles from Knaresbrough, is near Wetherby Grange, a seat of the Thompson family. Wetherby Grange is one mile from Wetherby. Another seat of the Thompsons is Kirby Hall, nine miles from Wetherby. In looking over an old history of Yorkshire it is interesting to note the many familiar names: Thornton, Ambler, Lee, Howard, Starkey, Plumer, Randolph, Parker, Mallory, Savage. Thomas Savage was Archbishop of York, A. D. 1501, more of a courtier than prelate, had two palaces; and last but not least, Washington. As there has been some doubt as to the home of George Washington's ancestors, we quote the following:

"The mansion-house of Cave Castle is a large and noble structure, ornamented with a number of turrets, battlements, buttresses, etc., which give it an air of magnificence. The embellishments of the interior correspond with the grandeur of the exterior. It contains many spacious and elegant apartments with a very valuable collection of pictures by the best masters. Among these is a portrait of the late celebrated general, George Washington, the American hero, whose great-grandfather, John Washington, lived here and possessed a part of the estate, but emigrated from hence to America about the year 1657, and settled at Bridges Greek in the County of Westmoreland in Virginia, where the family have ever since remained." It is said there are few parts of England of the same extent that contain a greater number of noblemen's estates and gentlemen's seats than the West-riding of Yorkshire. It is one of the greatest manufacturing districts of England, the largest county, and of unusual historical interest.

17

Found in an old Armistead book in a junk shop by Dr. R. A. Brock, genealogist and historian. He had it photographed and published in "The Critic," the genealogical section of which was edited by him and Mr. Wm. G. Standard.

To return to the Armisteads. We learn from C. P. Keith's account of the Armistead family, "that Anthony Armistead, of Kirk Deighton, obtained a license to marry Frances Thompson, in the year 1608. "August 3rd, 1610, William, ye son of Anthony Armistead, of Kirk Deighton," was baptized in All Saints' Church. Search later discloses the fact that Anthony, the father, continued to reside there, having other children. Assuming that William, the emigrant, was born the year he was baptized, he was twenty-five when he emigrated to Virginia, in 1635, and obtained large grants of land in Elizabeth City County and subsequently in Gloucester, which was formed from York in 1642. He died before 1660, as in that year in York County, Virginia Records, his second son, John, was heir of his elder brother, William, who died childless. He, William, the emigrant, married Anne, and had issue:

I. William, who in a deed recorded in Elizabeth City County, November 20, 1695, is named as his "sonne and heire," and who died without issue before 1660, when John Armistead "as hey re and one of the Executors of Mr. Wm. Armistead, made a power of attorney in York Co." II. John; HI. Anthony; IV. Frances.

18

Were these children born in Virginia? In 1680, forty-five years after the. emigrant came to Virginia, John, his second son, is recorded as being lieutenant-colonel of horse in Gloucester; in 1688, was in the council; Anthony, in 1680, was captain of horse in Elizabeth City County, burgess in 1696-1699. It is uncertain where to place Ralph Armistead, who. in 1678, patented forty-eight acres of land in Kingston Parish, Gloucester, for transporting one person. It would appear from the latter clause that

he was an emigrant. Might he not have been a nephew of the emigrant? It is stated that the emigrant's father had other children who remained in England.

Mr. C. P. Keith, in his *Ancestry of Benjamin Harrison,* says: "There is a tradition that the Armisteads derive their name and origin from Darmstadt, Germany. The seat of the elder line in Virginia was called Hess. Without deciding when, or whether in modern times they crossed the German ocean, it is sufficient to say that they were Englishmen for generations before William Armistead came to America. The name, with varied spelling, frequently appearing in Yorkshire Records of the time of Queen Elizabeth."

Mr. George E. Tudor Sherwood, of London, England, has published a very interesting partial catalogue of a collection of wills preserved in England, among them the title, date and proof of seventy Armistead wills and administrations.

ARMISTEAD MSS.

"In the Eairfax manuscripts sold at auction in London, England, June 8th, 1898, there were two lots distinguished thus: 548 Yorkshire, thirteen Original Deeds on vellum relating to the families of Brerey, Eawkes, Vavasour, Armytstead, etc., and lords in Euiston, Burley, York, etc., from the time of Elizabeth, with signatures and seals."

In Burke's *Landed Gentry,* there is a pedigree of the Armistead family, of Crainage Hall ("descended from the 'Armisteads of Armistead', Yorkshire, who bear almost precisely the same arms as those on a pre-revolutionary book-plate of William Armistead, of Virginia"), beginning with Roger Armistead, of Armistead, Giggleswick, County of York, England, who-was the father of William A., living in 1650, whose son, Laurence A., born 1658, married 1682 Agnes, daughter of John Armistead, and died 1742. His descendent and representative, Rev. John R. Armistead, was living at

Crainage Hall 1878. Roger Armistead, of Knight Stayneford, in the County of York, was one of the first governors of Giggleswick school. In 1553, Thomas Armistead, son of Michael Armistead, of Shrewsburg, clerk, entered Magdalen College, Oxford, in 1677, fifteen, took his degree and forfeited his fellowship by marrying in 1693.

"574 Yorkshire (England) Twenty-eight original Deeds on vellum of the families of Barker, Kendall, Middleton, Armistead, etc., relating to lords in Burley and Ottley from the time of Queen Elizabeth, with signatures and seals."

From the foregoing data, it will be seen that the Virginia Armisteads were descended from English Armisteads.

A few weeks ago we visited the oldest seat of the family in Virginia—Hesse, in Mathews County, once Gloucester—and spent a most interesting day, wandering over the old place and house, asking questions of the caretaker and listening to the old stories told of it. The wife of the caretaker, feeble from illness, seated in a large chair outside of the simple home that had been built for them, gave us the clue to a most interesting find, namely, that there were letters and figures on one of the chimneys, high up. At last we sighted the place and made out A. o. 1674. The figures were very indistinct, the upper part of the seven gone, the four was like half of I and then a mark at right angle to it. Later, the sound of a threshing machine drew us to the barn, where, sitting on the well we saw an intelligent faced young man in his working clothes (the owner of the machine, we afterwards learned). We enlisted his eye service in deciphering the letters and figures on the chimney; did not tell him what we had made out. He read as we did, A. o. and 16, said the next figure looked like part of one. The testimony of two witnesses should establish the date of the building of Hesse. A. o. abbreviation of Anno 1674. The date of the building of the Burwell home. Carter's Creek, has been lately established by figures on the wall— 1684 or 1694. This seems to have been the custom among the early colonists. We have a note taken from some record, "that John Armistead, the Councillor, was dead before 1703; his third child, William, the oldest son was born about 1665, died 1711. We argue that John A., Councillor, built Hesse in 1674, and lived there with his wife Judith, and children, who were all mairried after that date. His eldest child, Judith, married in 1688; second child, Elizabeth, in 1687. It was the custom for fathers to build a home for the eldest son when married. There is a record that William and Anna Lee, his wife, were not living at Hesse; most probably at Oak Grove on Eastmost River, where his tomb is still to be found:

Here lyeth Interred
the of William Armistead
who departed this life the 13 day
of June 1711 age forty years.

As William and Anna, his wife, had seven children and he died in 1711, his father, John, in 1703, it is reasonable to suppose that William had his own home; besides, Henry Armistead, second son of John, who married about 1701, certainly residing at Hesse, the family seat of John his father. So Hesse may have been built in 1674 by John, the Councillor. The date of the patent of 500 acres on Pianketank River (Hesse) is September, 1659. In a chancery suit, 1797, the Hesse estate is spoken of as having 3,879 acres.

These are some of the names of the vestry of Kingston Parish, Gloucester County, beginning in 1677; "William Armistead, Kemp Plumer, Captain Thomas Smith, John Armistead, *William Armistead, of Hesse,* who married Maria Carter; Francis Armistead, Thomas Smith, Jr., Armistead Smith" (Bishop Meade).

The house at Hesse is of brick and beautifully located on a wide stretch of lawn, in full view of, and just opposite the mouth of the Pianketank, on a clean pebbly beach. As we walked to the end of the lawn, over the river, we expected it to slope somewhat; instead, it was precipitous, washed in swirls. Two large locust trees stood as sentinels midway between river and house, which has a cellar, with walls 2 feet 7½ inches thick. The first floor has two large rooms with four windows each, window seats and paneled blinds that fold back on the side; windows rather narrow with small panes set in heavy divisions. The mantels were of black marble or iron stone, a very hard marble, largely imported at that time for handsome tombstones. Each mantel had round pillars in relief, of iron stone supporting the shelf, the chimney-place faced with the same, the whole as solid as if lately built. The stairway, with hand-carved spindles and side-paneled structure, led up to a landing over the river-front door; then up to the second floor, where the spindle railing continued along the hall. A plaster partition at the side of the stairway, has made a hall;

originally, the stairway was in the room, making a very large reception hall or room. The doorways are all paneled, by reason of the thick walls; this called our attention to the plaster partition. The second floor is the same as the first, the garret is hip-roofed inside, two little windows in each gable, on either side of the chimney. The stairway faces the landside entrance.

Hesse. Gloucester Co Va

We ate our lunch sitting on a buttress of a brick wall that evidently supported a river-front porch. Erom where we sat the level sweep of the lawn, close cropped by sheep and cows, toucned the sparkling river line. Visions of those early days crowded our imagination; the stately Judith, as the bride of the handsome lordly master of Corotoman. The fair Elizabeth Armistead, plighting her troth to that man of culture and force, Ralph Wormeley, of Rosegill. "Rosegill, where the Wormeleys lived in English state" (Bishop Meade), was situated high upon the banks of the Rappahannock, a few miles from Christ Church. Ralph Wormeley presented to this church a communipn service of five pieces. These daughters of John Armistead must have been possessed of great beauty or rare qualities of manner or character, to have attracted two of the most conspicuous gallants of that time—King Carter and Ralph Wormeley, called "The greatest man in the colony."

John's two sons, William and Henry, also must have been men of high character and loveable qualities to have won the love of such wives as they had—Anna Lee, the daughter of Hancock Lee; and Martha Burwell, choosing Henry Armistead in spite of the fierce, lordly wooing of the explosive Governor Nicholson, and the devotion of the fearless Parson, Fouace, and a host of others. All these visions of Colonial days vanished when our companion of the twelve-mile drive to Hesse, came up to inform us that the owner of Hesse, down at the barn, could tell all about the house." His story was this: "A long time ago a German by the name of Hesse bought this place, and built a castle here, strong enough to protect him from the Indians—not that house, which is very old, but near to it. I can show you the old foundation bricks now overgrown with the sod." Which substantiates Dr. Lyon G. Tyler's information that a wing of the present house is lacking. The wing must have been built much later, for the simple lines and construction of the house are complete. We sat far off under the shade of locust trees that border the western limit of the lawn, and made the accompanying sketch. The story of Mr. "Hesse and his castle" rather accentuates the old German tradition—Hesse Cassel, Darmstadt, Germany.

Since writing the above we have had the privilege of reading many old Armistead letters, some written from Hesse, others to Hesse; one, from William Nelson, of King William, to William Cocke, of Cartersville, Cumberland County, dated February, 1798, speaks of the burning of the Hesse mansion. This was when the estate was leased to Mr. Vanbibber, two years after the death of that charming woman, Maria Carter Armistead, widow of William Armistead, of Hesse, who was the son of William Armistead and Mary Bowles. This William being the son of Henry, of Hesse, and Martha Burwell. The present house at Hesse must have been built on the old foundation, the chimneys standing.

We were impressed with the beautiful English in these letters, and the distinct, graceful penmanship. A glimpse into "Maria Carter, Her Book, 1763," was fascinating; the quaint expressions in stately measure, the quotations from authors of that day, so aptly placed, and the exquisite penmanship. Hesse at that time was called a "gay part of the world." Her father wjrites to her January 25, 1764, "to put a deaf year to the flattering speeches of the world."

Evidently Maria Carter Armistead was a beauty and belle of that charming old period. She married William Armistead in 1765.

We have in our possession an old book, possibly a plantation book, which runs from 1760 to 1780. It contains interesting entries in reference to John and Henry Armistead, Nathaniel Burwell, William Byrd, John Buckner, Carter Braxton, John Carter, William Churchill, John Clayton, Hannah Churchill, John Robinson, Nath. Littleton Savage, Captain Thomas Smith, William Shackleford, Edward Tab, Thomas Todd, Charles Tomkies, Warner Washington, Ralph Wormeley, William Nelson, Sir John Peyton, Mann Page, William Plummer.

On one page is the following:

9 yards of silk at 14/6.
12 yards of flowered silk at 16/6.
16 yards of sarsnet at 6/9.
10 yards of sattain, 9/6.
15 yards of Brocade, 10/6.
11 Scarves at 2/
14 yards of Genova velvet.
10 yards

This unfinished memorandum wafts to us the fragrance of lavender and old lace. We hear the click-click of the high-heel slippers across the hall; the swish of silken garments and the dainty maid vanishes up the broad stairway.

There is also in this book a full account of the law suit, *Price* vs. *Armistead*, before "the Honorable George Wythe, Esquire, Judge of the High Court of Chancery," involving part of the fortune of the wealthy Mary Bowles, who married William Armistead, of Hesse. His son, William, married Maria Carter, who speaks her mind in no uncertain terms in regard to Rev. Thomas Price, who was the second husband of her mother-in-law. That the Rev. gentleman lived with his wife, Mrs. Armistead at *Hesse*, eight months after their marriage "in a very expensive manner, having the entire command of everything in and about the house with at least seventeen servants"; that when he carried his wife to his own home he took Mr. Armistead s chariot almost new that cost one hundred and ten pounds, "a great deal of most valuable furniture, which they absolutely appropriated and never returned," and four house servants whom they kept several months!

The said Maria was afterwards the mistress of Hesse and knew whereof she affirmed.

The book bound in vellum is full of interest; the penmanship, in lines and formation, a model of neatness.

The following is copied from the *Baltimore Sun* :

"The Armistead family is one of the oldest, as well as one of the most distinguished families in Viginia, as also in America, The name Armistead, or Armitstead, was well known in England, during the reign of Queen Elizabeth, the representatives at that time being spoken of as stalwart Yorkshiremen. However, a very old tradition, is that the family came originally from Hesse Darmstadt; that they crossed the Seas with the hardy Norsemen, and settled in England.

"The fact that one of the principal seats of the family was called Hesse, was taken as an argument in favor of this theory, but Dr. Lyon G. Tyler thinks the tradition unsupported by fact; He says: T hazard the suggestion that as Col. Jno. Armistead was a warm friend of Lord Culpeper, Governor of Virginia, at that time he might very well have given the maiden name of Lady Culpeper, Marguerita Hesse, to his plantation on the Pianketank."

"Cranage Hall, County of Chester, is the present seat of the Armitsteads of England."

The following is taken from "Armorial Families Showing Arms borne by Legal Authority":

"Rev. John Armitstead, Master of Arts, Christ Church, Oxford, Patron and Vicar of Sandbach, of Cheshire, born May nth, 1829. eldest son of the late John Armitstead. Vicar of Sandbach, Masters of Arts, Justice of Peace; his wife, Susan Hester, second daughter of Rev. R. Massie, of Coddington, County of Chester. He succeeded his father, as Patron of Sandbach, in 1865, and 1877, upon the death of his cousin, Agnes Anestasia Armistead, to Cranage Hall.

Livery, drab coat, crimson waistcoat; Armorial bearings. Crest a dexter and sinister arm, embowered in armour, each hand grasping a spear, erect, proper; motto, *Pro Rege et Patria.*

He married the eldest daughter of Hon. William Henry Hornby, Ad. P. Seat, Cranage Hall. Holmes Chapel, Co. of Chester."

From the papers of Thomas Armistead, of Plymouth, N. C., the following:

There is a prominent sculptor, Robert Armistead, in London, whose name appears on the magnificent memorial statue of Prince Albert Consort, in that city as one of the artists engaged upon the work.

There is also Sir George Armistead, who represented Dundee, Scotland, in the British Parliament about 1888, and is I learn still living. He is an uncompromising liberal; was a friend of Parnell, the late Irish leader, and at a dinner given by him in London in 1888 succeeded in bringing together in private for the first time in their lives, Mr. Gladstone and Mr. Parnell, with Messrs. John Morley, Herbert Gladstone and other members of Parliament to discuss a more vigorous system of opposition to government measures; which was soon after adopted. He is a large manufacturer in Dundee and reputed to be of great wealth.

As a woman of the Armistead family, the editor has a pardonable pride in the following eulogy to the Armistead women, from the pen of Governor Henry A. Wise, in his *Seven Deeades of the Union*. It was written in reference to Mary Armistead of the Anthony branch. From our knowledge of eight or ten, in the present and preceeding generation, the characteristics, described by him, are still flowing, *strong, pure, and distinct,* through this line, like the Gulf Stream, in the midst of the ocean. "The daughters of this (the Armistead) family have been strikingly remarkable for their strength of character, and beauty of person; and the continuous line of male descendants has marked the name of hero after hero, on the tablets of their country's history. The "Star Spangled Banner" is blended with the name of Col. George Armistead, the defender of Fort McHenry. He was fighting the invader, while Francis Key was writing the anthem, "The Flag is Still There." His brother, Gen. Walker Armistead, won his laurels and lost an arm in the same brilliant battle. Two other brothers lost their lives in the assault upon Fort Frie; he who was lately killed at Gettysburg, leading a Confederate division against "certain death" was the son of Gen. Walker Armistead. Armistead T. Mason, through his mother, and Cary and William Seiden, through their mother, and Gen. Robert F. Lee, through his ancestress (great-great-grandmother, Judith Armistead), and President John Tyler, through his mother. Mary Armistead, all alike, in the maternal line, sprang from the root of the same family tree. * * * From all that is known and can be gathered from tradition, one of the prevailing causes of the greatness of the men of that period, was the lovely and noble character of the mothers of the men of that day. They were eminently strong, and yet pure, refined, chaste, delicate and modest. * * *

> * * * "happy he With such a mother! faith in womankind Beats with his blood, and trust in all things high Comes easy to him, and though he trip and fall He shall not blind his soul with clay."

THF LINE OF JOHN ARMISTEAD, THF COUNCILLOR.

John Armistead second son of the emigrant, is generally spoken of as "THE COUNCILLOR." He was sheriff of Gloucester county in 1675, member of the House of Burgesses in 1685, and appointed to the Council in 1687. After the accession of William and Mary to the Fnglish throne, John Armistead, Isaac Allerton and Richard Lee were dropped from the Council for refusing to take the oath of allegiance to the new sovereigns. In 1680, John Armistead was lieutenant-colonel of horse in Gloucester County and also one of the justices of that county.

The family name of Judith, whom John Armistead married, is uncertain, but the will of Christopher Robinson, part of which is herewith printed, might indicate that her name was Robinson.
He calls Col. John Armistead "My loving *brother-in-laiv*," and Judith, "My Loving Sister, Mrs. Judith Armistead."
The will of Christopher Robinson, January 27, 1692-3. * * * item; I give and bequeath to my loving (brother) Coll. John Armistead, and to my Loving Sister, Mrs. Judith Armistead to each of them, a Ring of Twenty Shillings value, for a remembrance of me. Item: I give and bequeath to my Loving Brother, John Robinson to be disposed of at his discretion in Rings to be given to my Friends and Relations for a remembrance of me; the same to be distributed to them in Cliesby in Yorkshire, where I was born."
"I give and bequeath to my true Friend Mr. William Churchill, * * * Executors of this my last will and testament, * * * I hereby Ordaine and Appoynt my loving *Brother-in-lazv*, Coll. John Armistead," etc.
In another record we read that Robert Beverley calls John Armistead brother.

John Armistead settled in Gloucester County, where his father had patented a considerable quantity of land. "He was son and heire" of William Armistead, late of Elizabeth City County, Cent.;" he confirms to his brother, Anthony, all land on Back River, in said county of which his father died seised." Issue of John Armistead and Judith his wife: Judith, Elizabeth, William and Henry,

JOHN ARMISTEAD

SECOND SON OF WILLIAM THE EMIGRANT.

1. Anthony[1] Armistead, Kirk Deighton, Yorkshire, England, married Frances Thompson, of that place. Issue: (2) William[2] married Anne * * . Issue: (3) William[3] (4) John[3] (5) Anthony[3] (6) Francis[3].

4. John[3] Armistead married Judith . Issue: (5) Judith4, (6) Elizabeth4, (7) William4 (8) Henry4

5. Judith4 Armistead, married Robert Carter.

6. Elizabetl4 Armistead, married, first, Ralph Wormeley, February 16, 1687; second, William Churchill.

7. William4 Armistead, married Anna Lee.

8. Henry4 Armistead, married Martha Burwell.

5. Judith4 Armistead, married Robert Carter, of Corotoman, Lancaster County. Her tombstone calls her the "eldest daughter of the Honorable John Armistead Esq., and Judith his wife. She departed this life the 23rd day of February Anno. 1699, in the-year of her age and the eleventh of her marriage, hav ing borne her husband five children—four daughters and a son, whereof Sarah and Judith died before, and are buried near her. Robert Carter, of Corotoman, Lancaster County, commonly called "King Carter," by reason his great wealth and influence, was the husband of Judith Armistead, eldest daughter of John Armistead of Gloucester now Mathews County where his father, William A., had patented a considerable quantity of land. On October 18, 1688, the said John was sworn of the Council. By close calculation O'f dates, we claim that Judith Armistead and Robert Carter were married about 1670. Robert Carter died "possessed of three hundred thousand acres of land, one thousand slaves, and ten thousand pounds sterling. He built Christ Church, Lancaster County, Virginia, which Mr. W. G. Standard says is "the most perfect example of Colonial church architecture now

remaining in Virginia." There are three round windows in the gables and twelve others which are six by fourteen feet; the high pews of solid black walnut with seats running around them are still (1906) solid and strong. There are twenty-five pews with a seating capacity of twelve each, and three, which will contain twenty persons each;" walls three feet thick. One of these pews near the altar and opposite the pulpit was for his family. In addition to the high backs and sides, Mr. Carter had placed a railing of brass rods with damask curtains "to prevent being gazed at." Tradition has it that the congregation did not enter the church on Sundays until the arrival of his coach when all followed him. (Bishop Meade's *Old Churches,* etc.)

John Carter, the father of Robert, was born in England, settled in Lancaster County in 1649, there in 1669, his son, Robert, then being only six years old. The mother of Robert Carter was Sarah Ludlow, John Carter's third wife.

Issue of Judith Armistead and Robert Carter: (I) Sarah, Judith, (3) Elizabeth, (4) Judith, and (5) John.

3. Elizabeth Carter, married, first, Nathaniel Burwell. Issue: Lewis, who was President of the Council of Virginia. Elizabeth Carter Burwell married, second, Geo. Nicholas, M. D. Issue, among others, Robert Carter Nicholas, Treasurer of Virginia. He married Anne Cary. Issue, among others, Elizabeth Nichols, who married Edmund Randolph, United States Secretary of the State.

The following from the facile pen of the editor of the *Times-Dispatch* Genealogical Column, will prove interesting to Robert Carter's descendants. These charming weekly contributions of Mrs. Sallie Nelson Robins, are bewitching bits of Colonial history and romance:

"John, the emigrant, was not commonplace or inert. He came to Virginia and settled in upper Norfolk (now Nansemond County), which he represented as Burgess in 1649, removed to Lancaster, and represented it in 1654. He was a vestryman (the most prominent men in the community always were), and the power of these Colonial vestries was enormous. He built a church where old Christ Church, in Lancaster, now stands. The vestry received it complete from his son, John, six months after the emigrant's death.

"John Carter's estate lay upon the Rappahannock, and he, indeed, chose the 'pick' of Tidewater Virginia. The house faced the Rappahannock where it is nine miles wide, full in sight of

Chesapeake Bay. On one side is Carter's Creek, a veritable little bay itself, and on the other is Corotoman River; so 'Corotoman,' this lordly estate, striking over an area of nine miles, was bounded on three sides by salt water. What a chance for fish, crabs and oysters — to be sure! From this spacious mansion house a line of cedars stretched to the parish church, about two miles distant, on the 'Corotoman' land, and these cedars (thinned, of course, by time) may be seen to-day. In themselves they are full of suggestion of the power and lordly ideas of our early planters. 'Corotoman,' builded by John Carter, passed to his oldest son, John, who dying early, and without issue, the estate passed from him to John Carter's second son, Robert. From Robert it went to Robert's oldest son, John, who married Elizabeth Hill, of 'Shirley.' John[3] left 'Corotoman' to his son, Charles[4], who lived there until the death of his mother, who had married, second, Bowler Cocke, and continued to live at 'Shirley.' At her death Charles[4] Carter removed to 'Shirley.' At his death he left 'Shirley' to his oldest son, John[5], and 'Corotoman' to his second son, George. 'Corotoman' was burned about this time.

"George married Lelia Skip with, and had Dr. George, of 'Corotoman,' and one daughter, Polly Carter, who married Dr. Joseph C. Cabell. Dr. George Carter married a Miss Corbin, and had one daughter, Parke, who inherited 'Corotoman.' She died unmarried, and left 'Corotoman' to her aunt, Polly Cabell. This Mrs. Polly Cabell died possessed of a very large estate, and her will is one of the most remarkable Virginia documents. The 'motif' of her will is the ever recurrent injunction that no lawyer should have anything to do with any part of her estate, but by the perversity of fate it is said the lawyer got three-fourths of it.

"George Carter, the last male Carter who owned 'Corotoman,' died before his wife, Lelia Skip with, and she married, secondly, Judge St. George Tucker. He was one of the lawyers who directed the sale of 'Corotoman' after Mrs. Cabell's death. She left no issue. Mrs. Polly Carter Cabell was the last Carter to own this famous estate. The house evidently was never rebuilt, an outhouse, probably a negro quarter, was there a few years ago. The magnificent site is now but a cornfield, and nothing in Lancaster, but the ragged cedars, the church and the tombs, toll of the magnificent estate of the Carters.

"There is something sad and dispiriting in the absolute absence of those who made it from a baronial state like 'Corotoman,' and when we see it without a mansion and cut up into little farms we can but wish that it had descended to the name, and that rebuilt and well kept it still owned a Carter master. 'Shirley' went to the Carters with Elizabeth Hill, and it is, and has been for years, the seat of the eldest branch of the family. It is only one of many Carter mansions, however, and only one besides has never passed from the family — 'Sabine Hall,' in Richmond County.

"The English ancestry of the Carters has not been positively defined. It is known, however, that one of the several wives of the first John was Anne, daughter of Cleave Carter, and it is most probable that she was also his cousin. The published lists of London marriage licenses includes one, on October 25, 1611, for "John Carter of 'Stepney,' Middlesex, to Jane Cleaves of All Hollows Barking, widow of John Cleaves, and this John and Jane are possibly the parents of John Carter,[1] of Corotoman.' This John had large ideas of the matrimonial privileges of a plan-, ter. He married only five times — first to Jane Glyn, second to Eleanor Eltonhead, who aforetime was the wife of William Brocas: third, to Anne, daughter of Cleave Carter; she died in 1662, and Carter was certainly married within the year; fourth to Sarah Ludlow, and fifth to Elizabeth Shirley, of Gloucester County, spinister, who survived him.

"The first, second and fourth are buried with him. Why the third was not we cannot tell.

"John Carter's will was made in 1669. The pedigree of his various wives is not clear, Sarah Ludlow was the daughter of Gabriel and Phillip Ludlow, Gabriel Ludlow was a lineal descendant of that William Ludlow, of 'Hill Deverill,' Wilts, who was butler to the King and member of Parliament, and who died in 1478.

"John Carter had two children by Jane Glyn, who died early, and are buried beneath his tomb, and another daughter, Elizabeth who married Nathaniel Utie. He had three sons and one daughter presumably by Sarah Ludlow; the daughter Sarah is buried with her mother in the very comprehensive Carter tomb, John, the eldest son by this marriage, married and had issue, but they all must have died early, as Robert inherited 'Corotoman, and all the emoluments vouchsafed at that time to an eldest son. He represents the ancestor of the noble army of Virginia Carters, who have been citizens of high standing in this and other generations, and his blood is commingled with almost every family in position and out of position in the State, John[1] Carter also had a son, Charles who must have died early. John[1] had a large fortune, but it was not approaching to the estate of Robert

II., master of 'Corotoman.' To read Robert Carter's will is to read a big bit of contemporaneous history. He was so powerful and wealthy that he is known as "King." There have been intimations (whether true or false, we cannot say) that his business methods were hard and grasping, but his magnificent tomb refutes all such sinister insinuations. His father, John[1], built Christ Church, but the capacity of this church was not equal to the increasing congregation. Lancaster County was on a boom in the time of Robert Carter, and he built the present beautiful and interesting edifice. There is nothing like it in Virginia, with its solid pews of black walnut, its ancient sounding board and perfect architecttural proportion. The Association for the Preservation of Virginia Antiquities has the honor of restoring this fascinating landmark. Outside the church is the tomb of Robert, the "King," the tomb which explains who and what he was. His father's tomb is in the chancel. Robert's tomb deposes: 'Here lies an honorable man !" Splendid preface to 'Rector of William and Mary — he sustained the Institution in its most trying times.'

" 'Possessed of ample wealth blamelessly acquired.' "

"'Entetrning his friends kindly, he was neither a prodigal or a parsimonious host.' "

" 'By his wives i.e had many children, on whom he expended large sums of money.' "

" 'At length, full of honors and years, when he had performed all the duties of an exemplary life, he departed from this world on the 4th day of August,' in the sixty-ninth year of his age. The unhappy lament their lost comforter, the widows their lost protector, and the orphans their lost father!' "

Magnificent conclusions! What more could he have done?

Robert[2] Carter, of 'Corotoman,' married, first Judith, eldest daughter of John Armistead, the councillor, and second, Elizabeth Landon, then a widow Willis, of the noble family of Landons. By these two marriages he had twelve children.

His children made brilliant marriages, proving the old adage that money mates money. They, male and female, were the 'catches' of the day. His oldest son, John, married Elizabeth Hill, heiress of 'Shirley.' He was Judith Armistead's child, as were Elizabeth and Judith. Elizabeth married Nathaniel Burwell, and became mistress of famous 'Carter's Creek,' in Gloucester County. She was the grandmother of Thomas Nelson, the signer. Her second marriage was to Dr. George Nicholas, and she was the mother of Robert Carter

Nicholas, Treasurer of Virginia. Judith married Mann Page, and became mistress of 'Rosewell,' the castle on the York, also in Gloucester County. Only a narrow creek divided the splendid homes of the sisters. To John[3], Robert[2] Carter left 'Corotoman.' The children by the second marriage followed the example of those of the first marriage. To Robert[3] was given 'Nomini Hall,' in Westmoreland, and married Priscilla Bladen. 'Nomini Hall' was a splendid estate, and in the diary of Philip Fithian, tutor of 'Nomini Hall' during the life of Councillor Carter, we get a splendid idea of customs there. They were generous, ceremonious and brilliant. 'Nomini Hall' is also no more. Robert[3] Carter was ancestor of Councillor Carter, who manumitted great numbers of his slaves, and changed his religious faith several times. To Charles®, son of Robert[3], and Betty Landon, Robert gave 'Cleve,' in King George County. It still stands in its stately, old time beauty on the Rappahannock River. Charles[3], following the family habit, married three times; first to Mary Walker, second Anne Byrd, and third Lucy Taliaferro.

His decendants are elaborately worked out on the Carter tree, which is open to students of genealogy at the Virginia Historical Society.

Landon settled and built 'Sabine Hall, which is in perfect preservation now, in Richmond County, and is still owned by a descendant. It has never passed out of the family, although its present owner, Mr. Carter Wellford, has Carter only for a given name. He inherited it through his mother.

Anne[3] Carter, King Carter's daughter by his second wife, married Benjamin Harrison, and became mistress of 'Berkeley. She was the mother of Benjamin Harrison, the signer. Her daughter, Anne, married William Randolph, and lived at 'Wilton.' Another daughter married Isham Randolph, and lived at 'Dingenness. His son, Charles, was general in the Revolution. Mary[3] Carter, another of King Carter's daughters, married George Braxton, and was the mother of Carter Braxton, the signer; and Lucy Carter, King Carter's youngest child, married Henry Fitzhugh, and became the mistress of 'Eagle's Nest.' At 'Shirley,' 'Rosewell,' 'Carter's Creek,' 'Berkeley,' 'Corotoman,' 'Nomini Hall,' 'Cleve,' 'Eagle's Nest,' 'Sabine Hall,' reigned the children of Robert[2] Carter. Only 'Shirley' and 'Sabine Hall' are now owned by the family. Later the Carters owned such lordly estates as 'Blenheim,' 'Oatlands,' and others less pretentious.

"When Robert[3] Carter, commonly called 'King,' died he left to each of his sons magnificent plantations. I should like to advise all who are interested in Virginia history to read King Carter's will. He died in his sixty-third year, and the record of his possessions is remarkable. To his oldest son, John®, he left historic 'Corotoman,' situated so proudly on the Rappahannock, in Lancaster County, from whose stately elegance a magnificent avenue of cedars led to his own Christ Church, one of the marvels of Virginia ecclesiastical architecture, now standing. To his second son, Robert³, he left 'Nomini' and much beside. To his third son, Charles³, he left lands in Lancaster and Northumberland, King George and Spotsylvania. Charles chose to reside in King George, and called his home 'Cleve.' One cannot forget 'Cleve' if one has seen it on a soft summer's evening, standing in its red and mellow glory amidst its embowering trees. The lawn, green and vast, dips gracefully to the Rappahannock a veritable rainbow of sunset hues. 'Cleve is square, staunch and imposing. It contains the inevitable hall and two rooms on each side — probably the very best sort of architecture for our climate. The first master of 'Cleve' was a good and public-spirited man, and he represented King George in the House of Burgesses, 1748-64. He was born in 1707 and he died in 1764, having lived fifty-seven years all told — by no means a great age, yet in that time he had married three times.

"He married, first, Mary Walker, when he was just twenty-one, and had Charles4, of Ludlow, who married Elizabeth Chis-well; Mary4, who married her first cousin, Charles Carter, of 'Shirley'; Elizabetl4, who married William Churchill, and Judith4, who married William Burnett Browne. In 1742, fourteen years after his first marriage, he married Ann Byrd, of 'Westover,' and had Ann4, who married, first, John Champe, and, second, Lewis Willis; John4, who married Philadelphia Claiborne; Maria4, married William Armistead; Sarah4, married William Thompson; Landon4, married, first, Mildred Willis, and, second, Mrs. Eliza C. Thornton; Caroline4, married Dr. Elisha Hall.

In 1763 Charles³ Carter married Lucy Taliaferro, and had one daughter, Anne Walker Carter, who married John Catlett, of Timber Neck. Landon* inherited 'Cleve' — another instance of the youngest son inheriting the home place. What a suitable home for these thirteen children was 'Cleve!'

"Landon's children were, by his first wife, Mildred5 Ann, who married, first, Robert Mercer, and, second, John Lewis; Lucy5, who married General John Minor; Robert Charles®, married Miss Beale; St. Leger5, married Elizabeth Lee; Eliza5, married William McFarlane; Thomas5; Frances5, married Josiah Tidball; Edward .Cleve5 and Anna Marie5. Another ample brood to -frisk over the reaches of stately 'Cleve!' St. Leger inherited the beautiful place, but unfortunately had no children, and at his death he bequeathed it to a nephew who lived in Mississippi. This gentleman seemed to have no reverence for ancestral things. The place was sold, the family silver was sent to a mint and turned into bullion; the portraits were scattered promiscuously, some serving their ignoble years as fire screens. Two portraits (groups) were taken to Missis'sippi between beds for protection, and a violent rain soaked the beds, and when they reached their destination a search for the portraits revealed peeled canvases, for the fine old pictures were hopelessly stuck to the bedticks. I have heard that there is one Carter picture still at 'Cleve,' most carefully preserved by Byrd Lewis, who now owns the place. The carelessness of Virginians about their portraits is one of the unexplained things. The last Byrd to own 'Westover' left the pictures on the walls when he sold it.

Happily, the place was purchased by Mr. Harrison, of 'Brandon,' and the pictures by him removed to that place. In the collection of the Robinsons, of Chelsea, a most beautiful portrait was used as a fire screen and scornfully called "The Governess." Succeeding generations did not know her name. The picture is so beautiful and so haughty—clad in satin and decked with orange blossoms—that we have decided in our own minds that it is none other but the portrait of Kate Spottswood, wife of Bernard Moore.

In this collection is Dorothea Spottswood, and why should not this haughty and beautiful creature be Kate? Why should Dorothea's picture hang at Chelsea and Kate, the mistress of the mansion, have no picture at all?

4. Judith Carter married Mann Page, Jr. (second wife). Issue: Alann Page, of "Rosewell," Gloucester County, who married, first, Alice Grymes; second, Anne Tayloe. Issue: John Page, of "North End," Gloucester, who married Jane Byrd; Robert Page, of "Broad Neck," Hanover, who married Sarah Walker.

6. Elizabeth4 Armistead, daughter of (4) John4 Armistead and Judith, married, first, February 16, 1687, Ralph Wormley, of "Rosegill," Middlesex County, Va., born 1650, matriculated July 14,

1665, Oriel College, Oxford, England. Burgess 1674; member of the Council 1677; Secretary of the State 1693; Collector and naval officer of Rappahannock 1692; one of the trustees of William and Mary College 1693, in the same year President of the Council. He was called the "greatest man in Virginia." His will is dated February 22, 1700; he died December 5, 1703. Issue; (I) John Wormeley, (2) Judith Armistead Wormeley, married Mann Page (first wife), August, 1712; died December 12, 1716. Issue of Judith and Mann Page; Ralph Page, died unmarried: Maria Page (called Judith after her mother's death), married William Randolph, of "Tuckahoe." Mann Page's two wives were first cousins, daughters of two sisters, Judith and Elizabeth Armistead, daughters of John Armistead, Councillor.

NOTE. — There is now on record in Middlesex County an inventory of Ralph Wormeley, Esq., who was "one of the wealthiest and most influential men in Virginia." The rooms in "Rosegill" mansion were, "the parlors, the chamber, the chamber over the said chamber, the chamber over the parlor, the nursery, the room over the Lady's chamber, the Lady's chamber, the entry, and Madam Wormeley's closet (a closet, a small room for privacy and retirement), besides kitchen, dairy, etc." Elizabeth A)rmistead Wormeley's grandson was Ralph Randolph Wormeley, Admiral of the British Navy. The tomb of Ralph Wormeley at "Rosegill" bears the date 1806.

6.   Elizabeth4 Armistead Wormeley, widow of Ralph Wormeley, married William Churchill, of Middlese: County, Va. Issue: Armistead Churchill, born July 25, 1704; died, 1757: married Hannah, daughter of Col. Nathaniel Harrison, of Wakefield, Surrey County. Priscilla, born December 21, 1705; died about 1757; married, first Robert Carter, of "Nominy"; second, John Lewis, of "Warner Hall," Gloucester. Elizabeth, born 1710, died at "Eltham," the Bassett residence, in New Kent, April 16, 1779; married, first, Col. William Bassett, of the Council; second, William Dawson,* President of William and Mary College, who died ten days after the marriage. Issue of Elizabeth Churchill and Col. William Bassett, *Elizabeth Bassett*, born December 13, 1730. She married Benjamin Harrison, the signer, and was the mother of President William Henry Harrison. The will of Col. William Churchill is dated November 18, 1710. "to his wife, Elizabeth, a gold watch and one thousand pounds sterling,

36

and her part of his negroes for life, and after her death to his son Armistead"; besides, he gave her "his new Calash I expect out of England." To his daughter Priscilla, one thousand pounds sterling; to his daughter Elizabeth, one hundred pounds, his wife to advance her fortune out of her own. To Armistead Churchill, his son and heir, he gave the bulk of his estate in Virginia and England, and made executors of his will, his brothers William and Henry Armistead, his friends Nathaniel Burwell, John Holloway and John Clayton. William Churchill appears as deputy sheriff in Aliddlesex County 1674 and member of the Council in 1705. According to his own deposition and will, he was born in 1649, North Aston, Oxfordshire, England. The arms of the family as represented on a wax seal attached to a deed of his son Armistead Churchill, identify him as belonging to the family of Churchill settled in the counties of Devon, Somerset and Dorset, during the reigns of King John, Henry the third, and Edward the first.

The children of Armistead Churchill and Hannah Harrison were William, Nathaniel, Armistead, Benjamin, Mary, Lucy, Priscilla, Judith, Hannah, Betty.

William of "Bushy Park," married Betty Carter of "Cleve." Their son Thomas married Eliza Berkeley of "Barn Elms." Their only child, Elizabeth, married her cousin, Thomas Nelson Berkeley, of Hanover.

Another son, Armistead, married Betty Blackwell and moved to Kentucky.

Mary Churchill married John Armistead, of Hesse, 1749.

Judith married, first, Churchill Jones; second, John Blackburn.

Betty married Major William Jones.

Nathaniel died young.

Benjamin (?).

There were several Priscilla Churchills. One, the *sister* of Armistead Churchill, who married, first, Robert Carter, of "Nominy"; second, married John Lewis of "Warner Hall," Gloucester; the other Priscilla was *daughter* of Armistead Churchill and Hannah Harrison, who married Williamson Ball. Their daughter, Margaret Ball, married John Walker Tomlin; their daughter, Mary Williamson Tomlin, married Gen. Corbin Braxton; their son, William Armistead Braxton* married Henrietta Garlick. Issue: Mary Armistead Braxton, Fanny Churchill Braxton, Corbin Braxton, Kate Braxton, who married Henry Lee Valentine, of Richmond. Issue: Corbin Braxton Valentine,

Catherine B. Valentine, Elizabeth Gray Valentine.

Corbin Braxton, son of William A. Braxton and Henrietta, his wife, married Louise Louther and has Emma T. Braxton, Catherine Span Braxton, Corbin Braxton, Jr.

In Middlesex records we find the following:

MARRIAGE BONDS.

Dec. 29th, 1759, Richard Span and Priscilla Churchill, dan. Armistead Churchill. Letter of consent of James Gordon to marriage of Richard Span, Feb. 9th, 1765, Williamson Ball and Priscilla Span, widow. Sec. William Churchill. Witness, Robert Elliot.

" 'Dicky' Span was married yesterday to 'Silla' Churchill, dau. Col. Churchill. The weather prevented the marriage on Saturday as was intended." – *From Diary of Col James Gordon,* Dec., 1759.

Lucy Churchill, daughter of Armistead Churchill and Hannah Harrison, married John Gordon, December 15, 1756. Issue: James Gordon (one of twelve children), who married Elizabeth Gordon. Issue, among others, William Fitzhugh Gordon, whose second wife was Elizabeth Lindsay. Issue, among others, James L. Gordon, married Mary Long Daniel. Issue, among others, Armistead Churchill Gordon, lawyer, poet and author, who married, 1883, Maria Breckenridge Catlett, of Staunton, where they reside. Issue, five children.

YOUNG.

Charles Carter, son of John Carter, who was the only son of Judith Armistead and Robert Carter, married Mary Walker Carter, of "Cleve," and had Mary Carter, who married George Braxton in 1763. Their son, Corbin Braxton, married Mary Williamson Tomlin; their daughter, Fanny Churchill Tomlin Braxton, married Col. John Brooke Young, of "Wesibrook," near Richmond, Va.; one of their sons, Armistead Churchill Young, married Sallie Munford Talbott (daughter of Charles Henry Talbott and Sallie Radford Alunford, his wife). Issue: Armistead Churchill Young, Charles Talbott Young.

The other sons are John Young, unmarried; Ormond Young, married Claudia Palmer, of Richmond; Aubrey Young, married Louly Walker, of Richmond, Va.; Fanny Braxton Young, married

Alason Miller, of Staunton; Mary Tomlin Young (now deceased), married James Anderson, of Richmond. Issue: Mary Tomlin Anderson.

ARMISTEAD, PAGE, CHRISTIAN.

William Armistead, the emigrant, married Anne. Their son, John, married Judith ; their daughter Judith Armistead, married Robert Carter, of "Corotoman"; their daughter, Judith Carter, when twenty-three, married Mann Page, of "Rosewell," Gloucester County. She was his second wife, his first wife was Judith Wormeley, her first cousin, daughter of Elizabeth Armistead, who married in 1887, Ralph Wormeley, of "Rosegill," Middlesex County, Judith Wormeley, his first wife, was seventeen when married.

Issue of Judith Armistead Carter and Mann Page was, among others, Mann Page, Jr., born about 1718, died young without issue. He had as his second wife, Anne Corbin Tayloe, of "Mt. Airy," Richmond County. Their son, Robert Page, born at "Rosewell" about 1751, removed to Hanover and married Elizabeth Carter, daughter of Charles Carter, of Eredericksburg. Their son, Mann Page, married Mary Chiswell Nelson, daughter of Col. William Nelson, of "The Dorrell," Hanover County. Their son, John F. Page, born 1808, married Lucy Nelson, daughter Wilson Cary Nelson. Their only child, Mary Mann Page, married about 1854, William B. Newton, of Norfolk. Issue; Lucy P. N., Willoughby N., Kate N.

Willoughby N. married Sue Booten. Issue, three children.

Kate Newton married Walter Christian, son of Judge Joseph Christian, of Charles City County. Issue: Joseph Christian, died young.

Lucy C. married Ambler Johnston, January G, 1910.

Mann Page's first wife, Judith Wormeley (daughter of Elizabeth Armistead Wormeley, who was sister of Judith Armistead Carter), married at seventeen, died in twenty-second year, left three children, the fourth died with her. There were no male descendants from this marriage as her two sons died unmarried, one in youth, the eldest born, later. The following is a part of what is on her tombstone:

"She was a most excellent and choice lady, who lived in the state of most holy matrimony for four years and as many months * * * an upright mistress of her family in whom the utmost gentleness was united, with the most graceful suavity of manner and conversation" *

* *

Elizabeth, daughter of Judith Armistead and Robert Carter, married, first, Nathaniel Burwell, of "Carter's Creek," in full view of York River. The mansion, as appears by figures on the wall, was built either in 1684 in 1694. The tombstones (very massive) on which the inscriptions are cut, are of iron stone or black marble. She, Elizabeth, was the mother of Lewis Burwell, President of the Council of Virginia. Her husband, Nathaniel Burwell, died in the forty-first year of his age, leaving three sons and one daughter, Elizabeth, who married President William Nelson, Yorktown, and was the mother of General Thomas Nelson, of the Revolution.

Elizabeth Carter Nelson, granddaughter of Judith Armistead and Robert Carter, was a woman of unusual piety. Bishop Meade says: "She was educated religiously by her aunt, Mrs. Page, of "Rosewell." Her private and public exercises of religion, her pious instruction of her children, her exemplary conduct in all things established the fact that she was a truly pious and conscientious woman."

Elizabeth, daughter of Judith Armistead and now widow of Nathaniel Burwell, married, second, Dr. George Nicholas. Her son, Robert Carter Nicholas, was distinguished at the bar in AVilliamsburg, in the House of Burgesses, in the Council, as Treasurer of the State, as patriot in the Revolution. But "higher than all this he was a sincere Christian and zealous defender of the church of his fathers." (Bishop Meade.) Robert Carter Nicholas died at his seat in Hanover, leaving five sons—-George moved to Kentucky, Lewis lived in Albemarle County, John moved to New York, AVilson Cary was in the Senate and House of the United States and Governor of Virginia; Philip Norborne, named for Lord Botetourt, his father's friend, and two daughters.

Judith Carter, daughter of Judith Armistead and Robert Carter, was the second wife of Alann Page; his father, mlatthew Page, married Mary Alann, of Timber Neck Bay, a rich heiress, and bequeathed an immense estate to his son Alann, who built the celebrated Rosewell," a grand English brick mansion, where richly carved mahogany wainscotings and capitals and stairways abound. (Bishop Aleade.) He owned besides "eight thousand acres in Frederick called Pageland, more than ten thousand acres in Prince William, four thousand five hundred in Spotsylvania, one thousand called Pampatike in King William, two thousand in Hanover, near two thousand in James City, besides other lands not mentioned."

(Bishop Meade.)

Mann Page was twenty-one and his first wife, Judith Wormeley, seventeen, when they were married. She lived after marriage four years and four months. In the old Page family Bible now in possession of Captain Thomas Jefferson Page, U. S. N., Mann Page in speaking of her death writes "the twelfth of December, 1716—the most unfortunate that ever befell me—my dearest dear wife was taken from me." From these two granddaughters of Judith Armistead have descended the Page family, of Virginia. Judith Carter, second wife of Mann Page, born about 1694, was twenty-three when married in 1717-18. Issue: Five children born at Rosewell—Mann, John, Robert, Carter, Matthew. She outlived her husband. It is a tradition that Thomas Jefferson drafted the Declaration of Independence in this mansion before going to Philadelphia. This is probable, as Jefferson was an intimate friend of Governor Page, and was frequently at "Rosewell." The lead weights from the window casements of this mansion were cast into bullets for the American Revolution. The whole roof was covered with heavy lead over the shingles.

John Carter, only son of Judith Armistead and Robert Carter, was educated at the Middle Temple, England, appointed Secretary of Virginia in 1722, and member of the Council in 1724. In 1723 he married Elizabeth Hill, daughter of Col. Edward Hill, of "Shirley," Charles City County, Va. His son, Charles Carter, did not leave "Corotoman," Lancaster County, until after the death of his first wife, Mary; her tomb shows that she died at thirty-four years old in the year 1770. *Charles Carter* moved to "Shirley" in 1776 and married *Anne Butler Moore*, granddaughter of Governor Spotswood. Their daughter, *Anne Hill Carter*, was the mother of Robert Edward Lee. (See *Lee of Virginia*.)

Anne Hill Carter, great-granddaughter of Judith Armistead, married Light Horse Harry Lee. Issue; Charles Carter Lee, Sydney Smith Lee, Robert Edward Lee. Anna Lee, Mildred Lee.

John Carter, son of Judith, had four children—Elizabeth, married Col. William Byrd, of "Westover," and had William and four others: *Charles*, married, first, Mary Carter: second. Anne Butler Moore. *Robert*, married Mary, daughter of Thomas Nelson. of York. *Edward Carter*, of "Blenheim," married Sarah Champe.

Charles Carter (son of John, son of Judith Armistead and Robert Carter, of Corotoman,) married second, Anne Butler Moore, and had

Ann, who married Light Horse Harry Lee ; Dr. Robert C., who married Mary Nelson; Kate Spotswood C., married Dr. Carter Berkeley; Bernard Moore C., married Lucy Lee; Williams C., married Charlotte Fouchee; Lucy C., married Nathaniel Burwell.

7. William* Armistead (John[3], William[2], Anthony[1]) was born in 1671 and died at Eastmost River in Mathews County, June 13, 1711, where his tomb still stands. He married Annna Lee, daughter of Hancock Lee and Mary, daughter of William Kendall, of Northampton County. Issue: (9) John5, (10) Mary5, (11) Judith5, (12) Anna5, (13) Joyce5, (14) Frances5. (9) John[3] Armistead married, first, Elizabeth Burwell; second, Susanna Meriwether, daughter of Thomas Meriwether, of Essex County, and had issue: John, William, Susanna, who married Moore Fauntleroy in or before 1735. Of these, John Armistead married Mary Churchill (marriage bond 1749) and had issue, Churchill Armistead, who married, in July, 1775, Miss Betsy Boswell, of the same place, probably a daughter of Major Thomas Boswell, whose daughter or sister, Jane, married, before 1760, John Seawell, of Glouce.ster County. The assessors books of Gloucester County in 1791 shows lands assessed to Churchill Armistead, William Armistead's estate, William Armistead, John Armistead, Jr., Dorothy Armistead, Robert Armistead, Richard Armistead, John Armistead, Isaac Armistead, and Currill Armitead's estate. In 1788 lands were assessed to William Armistead's estate, Churchill Armistead, and Currill Armistead's estate. In the *Virginia Gazette* for 1768 Dorothy Armistead and Robert Reade advertised as Executors of Captain Gwyn Reade. (10) *Mary5 Armistead* married, first, James Burwell; second, Philip Lightfoot, of York County. Issue: John Armistead, William. ((11) *Jndit5 Armistead* married George Dudley. James Burwell's will, proved September 15, 1718, at Yorktown, names wife Mary, daughter Lucy, son Nathaniel Bacon, brother John Armistead, sister Martha Burwell, sister Judith, wife of George Dudley, sister Elizabeth Armistead, sisters Anne, Joyce, Frances. (12) *Anma5Armistead* married 4th of April, 1725, Anthony Walke, born 1692, member for many years of House of Burgesses, son of the emigrant, Thomas Walke, who came from Barbardoes in 1662 and married Mary Lawson in 1689, daughter of Col. Anthony Lawson. (13) *Joyce5 Armistead,* daughter of William Armistead, of Eastmost River, married Mordecai Booth. A portrait of her is preserved in Gloucester County in the family of General William Booth Taliaferro, a descendant of Joyce Armistead, whose line runs: Thomas Booth, of

Lancaster County, England (born 1666, died in Ware Parish, Gloucester County, Va., October 11, 1736), married Mary Cooke and had Mordecai Booth, who married Joyce Armistead, and had George Booth, who married Mary Wythe Mason and had George Wythe Booth, who married Lucy Jones and had issue, Fannie Booth, who married Warner T. Taliaferro, whose issue was General William Booth Taliaferro.

8. Henry4 Armistead (John[3], William[2], Anthony[1]) married Martha Burwell, baptized November 16, 1685. Martha Burwell was the daughter of Major Lewis Burwell and Abigail Smith, his first wife (see will of Major Lewis Burwell, on record in Yorktown). Issue of Henry Armistead and Martha Burwell: (18) William5, (19) Lucy5, (20) Martha5, (21) Robert5. Henry Armistead is spoken of as residing at "Hesse," the family seat of John Armistead his father. His wife was the young lady with whom Governor Francis Nicholson became so infatuated. "swearing that if she married any one else he would cut the throat of the bridegroom, the minister and the justice who would give the license" She was one of Lewis Burwell's nine daughters. They were married about 1702 or 1703. In 1733 he was sworn county lieutenant of Caroline ; he died between July 17, 1739, and February 11, 1740, at which last date his son, William, succeeds him in the parish register, as owner of slaves in Christ Church Parish, Aliddlesex. (18) William succeeded his father,-Henry, at Hesse. In 1739 the *Virginia Gazette* mentions the marriage of Mr. *William Armistead*, son of Col. Henry Armistead, of Gloucester County, to a daughter of James Bowles, deceased, of the Council of Maryland, and granddaughter of Tobias Bowles, formerly a merchant in London in the Virginia trade. She was Mary Bowles, sister of Eleanor Bowles, who married, first, William, son of Sir William Gooch, Governor of Virginia. This William Armistead made his will in 1755, leaving issue; (22) William6, (23) John6, (24) Bowles®, (25) Henry®. Mary Bowles Armistead survived her husband and married, second. Rev. Thomas Price. (22)., William Armistead,[3] of "Hesse," studied at William and Mary College in 1755 when Secretary Nelson and Dudley Diggs are named in the bursars book as his guardian. He married in 1765, Maria Carter, daughter of Charles Carter, of "Cleve," and Anne Byrd of "Westover." The following interesting letters of that period are to Maria Carter from Mrs. Maria Beverley and the Hon. Williarm Byrd. The first part of the letter was defaced

written about 1764;

MRS. AIARIA BEVERLEY TO AIARIA CARTER.

* * Rebecca Burwell is soon to render Mr. Jacqueline Ambler happiest of Mortals. Miss Fairfax will shortly wed Mr. Warner Washington of Gloucester—what think you Molly of 45 for 21? Does it strike you as all together suitable? But can you hear of so Vast many of our Sex about to change their Estate, without enlisting yourself in this Number? I cannot think the young gentlemen of New England so Vastly depraved in their way of thinking as not to have made you many applications of that sort. I remember your Grandmother told me you had a great Variety of Suitors.

"Your Affectionate Cousin,

"BEVERLEY."

Judith Carter, sister of AIaria Carter, married William Burnett Brown, of Salem, Mass. Maria was visiting this sister. "Molly's" choice from her "great variety of Suitors" is told in the following letter:

"Westovcr, November the 26th, 1765.

WILLIAM BYRD to AIARIA CARTER:

"I was in great hopes, as well as your Aunt and Grandmother, that you would have given us the pleasure of your Company at Westover e're now—and I should have rejoiced in an Opportunity of conveying to you my Affection—Report in forms us that you are going to be married very soon; I wish it had been agreeable to you to give some of your friends here Notice of it, because we think ourselves interested in your Happiness; for my part I shall always be glad to contribute to it. Mr. Armistead is a young gentleman, entirely acceptable to us and we sincerely wish you both every blessing of the married State. Be pleased my dear Alolly, to present my best Compliments to him and accept yourself of our Love and tender Friendship. I and the rest of your relations here beg the Favour of you and Mr. Armistead to spend Christmas at Westover, where so many Young People are to make Merry. Our Coach shall attend you any where, at any time. I ever am,

"My Dear Niece
"Your Most affectionate Uncle,

"WILLIAM BYRD."

The following gossipy letters of that time are interesting. The first from Warner Lewis to Col. Landon Carter, of Sabine Hall, and dated September 18, 1765:

"My Dear Sir:

"This will be delivered to you by my nephew Will Armistead, who informs me that you are acquainted with his errand, which I hope meets with your approbation. I heartily wish my God Daughter Molly may like him, if she does, the sooner they are married the better. The house at Hesse is free from inhabitants by the Young Codds succeeding with our old acquaintance the W. D. W. It will give me great pleasure to see Miss Molly mistress of it. Armistead is a prudent young man, very good-natured, and I am sure will make her happy: You have been young yourself — for God's sake hurry on the match! If no objections. It will be to their mutual advantage to be soon settled, and I hope, once in my life, I may have a chance to spend a merry hour with you and your niece, on the banks of the Pianketanke.
"Yours most sincerely,

"WARNER LEWIS."

"William Armistead was the heir of Hesse, already alluded to on the Pianketank."

Letter of John Lewis, member of the Royal Council, then owner and occupant of Warner Hall, Gloucester County. It was probably from Williamsburg to Captain Lawrence Washington, just after the Carthagena troubles, under Admiral Verner:

"Virginia, *June 28th,* 1742.

"Captain Lawrence Washington,

"Dear Sir: Having the opportunity by a vessel of our own— I could not let it pass without letting you know that we are well. My son Warner is come from England, and I have taken him into partnership, by giving him half of all my vessels and cargoes. * * * Mr. Page is married to Miss Alice Grymes and Mr. Willis will S on be so to Miss Bettie Carter. Miss Howell, I believe is engaged to Mr. William Lightfoot. Mr. Moore, Mr. Baylor, Mr. Grymes, Mr. Burwell, and all the young ladies and gentlemen of any note are yet single, and like to be so, as far as I know. Mr. Thomas Nelson is come in, and gone to make his addresses to Miss Lucy Armistead, and it is generally thought it will make a match. Mr. Wormeley and Col. Charles Carter has lost their Ladys. Mr. Wormeley is making his addresses to Miss Bowles, of Maryland—how it may fare with him I cannot say—Miss Randolph is yet single, though many offers has been made her; it is reported, by some, that she stays for you, but not believed by many. * * * We have no news that can be depended upon from England, a great while. I cannot see what delight you take in such a life. I heartily wish you safe here with Honour, but I think it may be as deservedly acquired at home, in the service of his Country, County, Parish, and neighborhood, in peace and quietness.

"I am my dear Sir:
"your most affectionate Kinsman,

"JNO. LEWIS."

NOTE. — Betty (Elizabeth) Carter's outfit for her first season, 1739, when fourteen years old, received at "Corotoman," June 30, 1739: "a Cap, Ruffles, and tucker, 5s. per yard; one pair of white Stays; 8 pair white kid gloves; 2 pair colored ditto; 2 pair worsted Hose three pair thread ditto; I pair silk shoes, laced—I pair Morocco ditto; 4 pair Spanish ditto; 2 pair Calf ditto; I mask; I fan; I necklace; I girdle and buckle; I piece fashionable Calico; 4 yards Ribbon for knots; I hoop coat; I Hatt, I yard and half of cambric, A Mantua and Coat of Slite lutestring."

To return to the line of (8) Henry[4] Armistead (John[3], William[2], Anthony[1]) and Martha Burwell his wife. Their children were: (i) William, (2) Robert, (3) Lucy, married Thomas

Nelson; (4) Martha, married Dudley Diggs.

William Armistead, son of Henry and Martha Burwell, of "Hesse, in Gloucester County, married in 1738 Mary, daughter of James Bowles: died in 1755. She married 15th of September, 1765, Rev. Thomas Price. Children: William, John, Bowles,
Henry, dead in 1773, Judith, married 17th August, William Thomas.

Robert Armistead, of King George County, son of Henry and Martha Burwell, married Elizabeth, daughter of Charles Burgess, widow of Jeduthan Ball; secondly, Anne Smith. Children: (I) Henry, (2) Thomas, (3) Robert, (4) Martha Burwell, married Benjamin Dabney, of Gloucester.

William, son of William Armistead and Mary Bowles, married in 1765, Maria , daughter of Charles Carter, of "Cleve," in King George County. Children: (I) Mary A., born 1766, mar ried Thos. T. Byrd, of "Westover"; (2) Lucy B., born 1768, married Harvey; (3) William B., born October, 1770; (4) Jane, married William Cocke; (5) Anne Cleve, born October 2, 1773, married 14th March, 1793, John P. Pleasants, of Baltimore; (6) Judith Carter, born 29th December, 1774, married 16th April, 1797, Richard H. Moale, of Baltimore; married second, Robert Biddell; third, Richard Carroll. (7) Sarah, born February, 1776, married Fairfax Washington; (8) Charles Carter, born 1778; (9) Eleanor B., married William McAIechen, of Baltimore.

4.   Jane Armistead married William Cocke, of Bremo, and had William Armistead Cocke, of Oakland, who married Elizabeth Randolph Preston, daughter of Major Thomas Preston and Edmonia Randolph, daughter of Governor Edmund Randolph. They had issue: William Fauntleroy Cocke, killed at Gettys burg ; Thomas P. L. Cocke, Captain Edmund R. Cocke, and Preston Cocke, attorney now living in Richmond, Va.

3. William B. Armistead, born October 26, 1770, died before 1797, when his brother, Charles Carter Armistead became "son and heir."

24. Bowles7 Armistead, son of William[3] Armistead and Mary Bowles, was a student at William and Mary from 1763 to 1766, His will was proved in Culpeper Co., July 21, 1785. He heired all his father's land in Culpeper. He married Mary Fontaine, daughter of Peter and Elizabeth Winston Fontaine and had issue: (69) William Bowles Armistead, who died unmarried; (7o) Peter Fontaine Armistead; (71) Mary, married, first, C. Alexander; second, W. C. Seiden; (72) Elizabeth, married Ludwell Lee; (73) daughter, married

Terrell.

70. Peter Fontaine Armistead, son of Bowles Armistead and Martha Fontaine Winston, daughter of Isaac Winston, had issue, twelve children (nine of these were William B., Peter Fontaine, Patrick Henry, who married Miss Clanton, Isaac Coles, Eliza, Virginia, married Lanier, George Washington, Mary Anne, Martha, of whom there is now living Peter Fontaine Armistead, of Tuscumbia, Alabama, aged eighty years. His son, Fontaine Armistead, not now living, married the daughter of a distant relative, Geo'rge Graham Armistead, whose first wife was Alice V. Fontaine. They, George G. and his wife, Alice, were married November 7, 1831, and moved to Alabama. She was a daughter of Alice Berkeley and Fontaine, and granddaughter of Col. Edmund Berkeley, of "Barn Elms," Middlesex County. George Graham Armistead married, second, Jane, daughter of James H. Forsyth; lived at Florence, Ala. Children; (I) Hislop, captain Fourth Alabama Infantry, C. S. A., killed at Malvern Hill, July I, 1862; (2) Lewis Carter,Mary .Frances, married Young A. Gray, of Florence and of Texas; (4) Alice Fontaine died young; (5) A. D. Hunt, (6) George Graham, (7) Ellen Forsyth, married L. H. Aledberry, of Chicago (7) Lizzie Baker, married Peter Fontaine Armistead; (9) Arabella Dobbin, married Francis S. Bragg, of Arlington, Tenn.; (10) Jane married E. Y. Moore, of Chicago.

Robert5 Armistead (Henry4, John3, William2, Anthony1) was clerk of King George County Court in 1752-57, and married about 1750; first. Mrs. Elizabeth Ball. Issue (74) Henry A., of Fredericksburg, who married Winifred Peachy, daughter of Col. William Peachy. Henry's will, proved in Fredericksburg in 1787, names Elizabeth Burgess Armistead, Alice Annistead, brother Burgess Ball (colonel in Revolutionary Army) "my wife's father, William Peachy, my wife, Winifred, my brother, Thomas Armistead, friends, LeRoy Peachy and Benjamin Dabney. Married second, Anne Smith, sister of Rev. Thomas Smith and Col. Gregory Smith, and aunt of John Augustine Smith, President of William and Mary College. Issue by this marriage, (75) Thomas Armistead; (76) Martha Burwell Armistead, who married Benjamin Dabney, of Gloucester County, Issue, three daughters, of whom, Anne married her cousin Thomas Smith. (77) Robert Armistead married and is said to have had six children (*Quarterly*, Vol. IV., p. 102).

8. Henry4 Armistead (son of John A., of Gloucester, son of William A., emigrant), married Martha Burwell. Issue: (22) William5

A., (23) Robert, (24) Lucy, married second, Thomas Nelson; (25) Martha married Dudley Diggs.

24 Lucy Armistead married Thomas Nelson, second son and third child of Scotch Tom Nelson, of England.

Secretary Thomas Nelson was born at Yorktown, 1716; died there, 1782. He married about 1745, Lucy Armistead. Issue, no daughters, three sons — William N., Thomas N., Wilson Cary Nelson. William N. removed to "The Dorrel," Hanover County, married on November 24, 1770, Lucy Chiswell, daughter of Col. John Chiswell and Elizabeth Randolph; who was daughter of Councillor William Randolph, of Turkey Island. Lucy Chiswell, born August 3, 1752, died 1810, age 58. Children of William Nelson and Lucy Chiswell were many. The eldest son, Norborne Thomas Nelson, born at "The Dorrell," August 29, 1776, married 1801, first cousin, Lucy Nelson, of "Oak Hill," Mecklenburg County, and had many children, one of these, Catherine Page Nelson, married Thomas Barksdale Collier, of "Oak Hill," Haywood County, Tenn.; he was born in Mecklenburg County. When twenty-two years old, immediately after his marriage, he moved from Maury County, Tenn., in 1838 to Haywood County, where he became an extensive and successful planter. "He was a man of culture; his morality and integrity were of the highest."

Catherine Page Nelson Collier is spoken of as "one of the noblest, purest, best of women." Issue, among others, William Armistead Collier, of Memphis, Tenn., married Alice Treasvant. Issue: W. Armistead C., Thomas B. C., and a daughter, Alice, married Dr. Neeley, of Bolivar, Tenn. Issue, two children.

The descendants of John Chiswell will be intetrested in the following from Genealogical Column of *Times-Dispatch* :

CHISWELL.

In the old graveyard at Warner Hall, in Gloucester County, is a tombstone with this inscription;

MARY LEWIS,
First Wife of Warner Lewis, Esq.,
Daughter of John Chiswell,
of Williamsburg,
and Elizabeth Randolph,
of Turkey Island.

Died the first of November, 1776.
Aged 28 years."

The John Chiswell mentioned in this inscription was a commanding personage in 1766, and he died just ten years before his daughter by his own hand. He was son of Charles Chiswell, of Hanover, who died in Williamsburg.on.ril 8, 1738. The *Williamsburg Gazette* announces that Chiswell came to town on Wednesday in perfect health ; was taken ill of a pleurisy on Friday night, which was so violent that it carried him off on the Monday night following, and on Wednesday night he was decently interred in old Bruton Churchyard.

The *Gazette* further announces that "he was in great esteem among the gentlemen of this Colony, generally well beloved, and bore the character of a very worthy, honest gentleman." The press was not afraid of the word gentleman in 1737.

The custom of funerals by torchlight prevailed at one time in England, and was a mark of the high estate of the deceased. Evidently Charles Chiswell was buried by torches, and we can fancy the solemnity of the occasion—pine knots flaring, old Bruton rising in shadowy beauty, and the cadence of the burial service floating upon the awed silence of the Colonial capital.

Charles[1] Chiswell left one son, John[2], who married Elizabeth, daughter of the second William Randolph, of Turkey Island, and had three daughters—Susanna, who first married Speaker Robinson, and second William Griffith. By this last marriage he had one daughter, Nancy, who married John Lewis, of Eagle Point, Gloucester County, then called "Vue de l'eau," which name was transformed by the negroes into the most ridiculous contortions— "Bugelow," for instance.

French nomenclature does not especially appeal to the African mind. An old estate called "Level Green" was changed by the owner to "Beau Pre," and at once the negroes utilized their familiar exclamation "Do Pray!" while the printer preferred "Bean Pie."

Lucy[3], the youngest daughter of John Chiswell, married Col. William Nelson, oldest son of Secretary Thomas Nelson, of Yorktown, and had seventeen children.

To John Chiswell there hangs a tale—a weird, sensational tale. He was defendant in one of the most interesting murder trials of that or any other period. He killed Robert Routledge, a Scotch gentleman, in

Cumberland County; the County Court refused to give him bail, but William Byrd, John Blair . and Presley Thornton, well known members of the Virginia aristocracy—that close corporation to which Chiswell belonged—and members also the General Court, overruled the dictum already issued, and did bail Mr. Chiswell. His bond was £2,000 and theirs £1,000 apiece.

For their action the members of the General Court were bitterly attacked. We give the opinions of Chiswell's friends and Chiswell's enemies. Both constitute valuable commentaries on the feelings of the day.

The Rev. John Camn, then professor at William and Mary College, in a letter to a friend, written at the time, says; "Colonel Chiswell has committed a murder on the body of one Mr. Routledge. He was sent down by the examining court to take his trial in Williamsburg. Instead of his being lodged in jail, three judges of the General Court, led to it, no doubt, by Chiswell's connections, out of session, have carried their power so far as to stop him in his way to prison and admit him to bail, which is like, as well it might, to put the whole country into ferment."

It did put the country into ferment. The circumstances were these, colored to suit their fancy by adherents of both sides of the question:

On the night of June 3, 1766, Chiswell and Routledge were in the dancing-room of the tavern at Cumberland Courthouse. Colonel Chiswell was talking in an important manner, and somewhat liberal of oaths. Routledge gave a word of reproof. Chiswell then asked him if he ever swore. "Yes," answered Routledge, "by all the gods." "You fool!" said Chiswell, "there is but one." More heated conversation followed, and Colonel Chiswell called Routledge a "fugitive rebel" and a "Presbyterian fellow." Routledge had been drunk three times that day, and he was in no state of mind to stand anything. He snatched a glass of wine from the table and threw it in Chiswell's face.

This was an indignity that a man of honor had to resent, and Colonel Chiswell picked up a bowl of "bumbo" for Routledge's face; but some friends prevented him. Then he seized a candlestick for the same purpose, which was also defeated. Then he tried to hurl a pair of tongs, but these also were wrested from him. Enraged and baffled, he ordered his servant to go to his room and bring his sword.

The testimony for and against Chiswell varies somewhat. Mr.

John Blair deposed:

"That it was a most unhappy drunken affair and very culpable, yet there was no malice prepense. That the first assault was from the deceased, who threw a glass of wine in Colonel Chiswell's face, both much in liquor, which was returned with the bowl of punch; and so assaults on both sides were reiterated until Routledge took a chair to knock Chiswell down; on which he sent his man for his sword; but when brought to him naked he got his back to the wall and stood on his defense, pointing it out and calling several times to take Routledge out of the room; that accordingly one was taking him out of the room, and two men seized Chiswell's sword arm, and held it so strongly that it was impossible for him to move; that Routledge broke from the man that was carrying him out and rushed upon the sword that was pointed out, and was thus killed."

These accounts in Chiswell's favor and against him may be found in the *Virginia Gazettes* of June and July, 1766. A very irate person, who signs himself "Dikephilos," announces that Chiswell's friends would prevent the truth being published; but he, bent upon justice, gives his impression in a three-column letter, with diagram of the room in which Routledge was killed, with letters to denote every movement of the contending gentlemen.

The servant brought the sword, for his master assured him that he would kill him if he did not. Colonel Chiswell, taking the deadly weapon, swore that he would kill anybody who came near him. Then, in an imperious tone, he ordered Routledge from the room. Routledge was "desirous of remaining, and, hickuping, said that he had no ill will against Colonel Chiswell, and that he was sure Colonel Chiswell would not hurt him with his sword; and when some of the company proposed that Routledge should be carried off and put to bed, others said he ought not to be carried out, as he was not the intruder." Mr. Joseph Carrington attempted to take Routledge out, and Colonel Chiswell moved cautiously along the wall towards him, abusing Routledge roundly. While Mr. Carrington searched his pockets for a key to a room in which he proposed to put Routledge to bed, Colonel Chiswell continued his abuse, reiterating his opprobrious epithet, "Presbyterian fellow," and Routledge became enraged again, broke from Mr. Carrington, and ran towards the table near which Colonel Chiswell stood. Colonel Chiswell went instantly forward, and with his sword, or hanger, which was about two feet long, stabbed him through the heart across the table." Mr. Thomas

Swann was near by, and the sword in its way passed through his coat near the extremity of the third buttonhole from the bottom.

A gentleman tried to stay Colonel Chiswell's arm, but immediately Colonel Chiswell told him it was too late, adding, "He is dead, and I killed him." Mr. Routledge sank down in the arms of Mr. Carrington and expired.

Colonel Chiswell, unruffled, handed his sword to his servant. bade him clean it carefully with tallow, lest it rust, and added defiantly, "He deserves his fate, damn him. I aimed at his heart, and I have hit it." Then he ordered a bowl of toddy, drank freely, and became somewhat intoxicated before the arrival of the justice of the peace. This is the testimony of Routledge's side. "Dikephilos" thinks it natural that gentlemen of Colonel Chiswell's class should attempt to save a man of Colonel Chiswell's "figure," but he appeals to the public for justice. It is the beginning of a mass against class, of a clarion call to justice, unmindful of estate. "Philanthropos," on the 22d of August, 1766, in a fiery letter cries to the people: "Take heed what ye do, for ye judge not for man, but the Lord! Be strong, deal courageously, and the Lord shall be with you." It is indeed mass against class. This is testimony for Routledge.

The testimony of Colonel Chiswell's friends was contradictory. They differed materially from "Dikephilos," "Philanthropos," etc. They were Mr. Wythe, William Byrd, Ousley Thornton, John Blair, Thomas Mann Randolph, Richard Randolph, and many others.

Colonel Chiswell, "they affirmed," did order his sword, which was brought; he did order Routledge out of the room; he did call him "Presbyterian fellow" and "Scotch rebel;" he did hold his sword naked in his hand, but he did not advance, and Mr. Littlebery Mosby and Mr. Jacob Mosby had him so fast that he could not move the sword. But Mr. Routledge, who had been delivered by Mr. Joseph Carrington to a slave at the door, got so enraged at Chiswell's calling him "fellow" that he himself trushed upon the point of the sword. Chiswell did say "I have killed him," because he felt him upon the point of the sword which no other man could know. Virginia was shaken by the circumstances, contemporaneous papers bristled with it, the people awaited breathlessly for the decision of a case which would show how far an aristocrat could withstand the law — how far the law and public opinion agreed. Colonel Chiswell was first put in jail, where he preserved a careless and dignified demeanor, inquired after Colonel Swann, whose button hole his sword has pierced, and awaited developments which were somewhat unpopular owing to the decision of the three members of the General Court—Byrd, Thornton and Blair—to have him bailed.

On the 12th day of September this potential announcement appeared in the *Williamsburg Gazette*, "Yesterday Afternoon Colonel John Chiswell Arrived in Town." The trial was near. This gentleman went as usual to his'house, which still stands in Williamsburg. In October the trial was going on. Some witness swore that "it was out of Chiswell's power to advance— Routledge had cast himself upon the point of the sword"; others that Chiswell had cried, "So would I kill fifty others for the same offense." Joseph Carrington affirmed that "Routledge, stung at something Chiswell said, darted at him," and so it went. The people sneered at the partisanry of the Randolphs, Mr, Byrd and others.

The State was in a tense condition. The feeling for and against Colonel Chiswell was growing each way. He himself, intelligent and thoughtful, felt the tremendous consequences of his rash deed, and on October 14, 1766, he killed himself at his own house at Williamsburg. This notice came out in the *Gazette* of October 17, :

"On Wednesday last, about eleven o'clock in the afternoon, died at his house in this city, Colonel John Chiswell, after a short illness. The cause of his death by the judgment of the physicians upon oath were nervousness, owing to a constant uneasiness of the mind."

Blessed old *Gazette!* Throwing a veil of charity over an unfortunate deed, scorning to pander to vitiated tastes by dwelling upon a circumstance which would have been a dainty tidbit for our yellow journals—a tidbit to be shredded and chewed. Instead it merely announces the death of a distinguished and rashly impulsive gentleman, and calls suicide a "nervous fit owing to a constant uneasiness of the mind" —a very nice diagnosis.

23. John7, Armistead (William5, Henry4, John³, William², Anthony¹) was at William and Mary in 1755, when Thomas Nelson and Dudley Diggs are named in Bursar's book as "guardian." He received by his father's will all the land in Prince William County, and much stock in Culpeper and Caroline. He was executor of his brother, Bowles Armistead in 1785. He married Lucy Baylor, of New Market, Caroline County, March 17, 1764. Issue: (35) John8 Baylor Armistead, (36) William8 A., (37) Addison *Bowles8 A.*, (38) *George^ A.*, (39) *Lcwis8 G. A.*, (40) *Walker Kcith8 A.*, (41) *Mary A.*, born 1780, who married 1800, Landon Carter,* of Sabine Hall, Richmond County and had issue: Armistead Carter, who married DeButts. Issue: Frances, who married Rosier Dulany. (42) Frances8 A. married Dr. Gillis, of Alexandria, Va., and (43) Eleanor Bowles, born after her father's death, married Col. John Dangerfield, of Essex County, and had issue: Henry W. Dangerfield, who married Courtney Tucker Upshur. Issue: Emily Dangerfield, Armistead D., William D., George D., Lucy D., Annie D., Lar.don C., Mary C., who married Captain William Eleason, U. S. A.

35. John[3] Baylor Armistead (son of John A. and Lucy Baylor), captain U. S. Light Dragoons in 1799, and honorably discharged in 1800, married Anne B. Carter, of Prince William County, and had issue: (44) Robert9 Armistead, married Mary Carter; (45) John9 Armistead, married Anne Harrison; (46) Louisa" Armistead, married Taliaferro; (47) Mary8Armistead, married Kerfoot.

36. William[3] Armistead, of Prince William County, son of John7 Annistead and Lucy Baylor, married Anne Cary Norton. Issue: (48) Hebe Armistead, (49) Wilson Cary Armistead.; (50) Edmund Randolph Armistead; (51) Mary Armistead; (52) Willie Ann Armistead; (53) George Armistead.

37. Addison Bowles[3] Armistead, of Prince William County, son of John7 Armistead and Lucy Baylor, was made captain U. S. Army, September 30, 1806; died February 10, 1813, from wound received while engaged in defence of Savannah. He married Mary Howe Peyton, daughter of John Peyton, of Winchester, Va. Issue: (54) Mary Armistead, (55) Susan Peyton Armistead, married James Innis Randolph, son of Peyton Randolph, of Wilton. Issue: Innis Randolph, reputed one of the most brilliant writers of the South; served on editorial staff of *Baltimore American.* (2) Peyton Randolph, officer engineer in Confederate States Army, on the staff of his cousin, General Lewis Addison Armistead. There were twelve children by this marriage of Susan Peyton Armistead and Innis Randolph.

38. George8 Armistead (hero of Fort McHenry), son of John Armistead and Lucy Baylor, born at New Market, Caroline County, Va., April 10, 1780; died at Baltimore, Md., April 25, 1818; appointed second lieutenant U. S. Army, January 8. 1799; captain, November I, 1806; major, Third Artillery, March 3, 1813: was distinguished at the capture of Fort George, Upper Canada, May 18, 1813, and was brevetted lieutenant-colonel for the defence of Fort McHenry, September 12, 1814; married October 26, 1810, Louisa Hughes, sister

of Christopher Hughes of Baltimore, U. S. Charge d'Affairs in Denmark, Norway, Sweden. George Armistead died in Baltimore, April 25, 1818. Issue: (I) Mary Armistead, born in Baltimore, December 27, 1812; married, June 10. 1845, Bradford. She died 1885, he died 1852. (2) Margaret Hughes Armistead, born at Gettys burg, Penn., 15th September, 1814; married October, 1840, Lewis Howell, of New Jersey : (3) Christopher Hughes Armistead, born in Baltimore, April 21, 1816; (4) Georgiana Louisa Frances Gillis Armistead, born at Fort AlcHenry, 25th November, 1817; married 27th November, 1838, William Stuart Appleton; died in New York, 25th July, 1878; he died at Peperell, Alass., 7th Alarch, 891.

A clipping from *Baltimore Sun* is fittingly inserted just here. Miss Keys writes:

I wonder how many of the descendants of the 'Old Defenders' who have just celebrated the 12th of September remember the names of the heroes who made that day an epoch in the history of our people? Let us pause to do honor to Major George Armistead, the 'hero of Fort McHenry,' as he is styled, who on that day (September 14, 1814), saved the flag and so bravely and nobly held the fort against the British bombardment, he being the only man in the fort who knew that the powder magazine was not bombproof and that any moment should a shell strike it a horrible death awaited them all. But, thank God, a shell did not reach it, and Major Armistead by so gallantly holding the fort not only won for himself a glorious record, but, the historians tell us, saved the whole Atlantic seaboard from British invasion.

"The citizens of Baltimore, as an expression of their gratitude to Major Armistead for his gallant conduct, presented him with a silver bowl in the pattern of a bombshell, a set of goblets and a salver. This bowl is now in possession of his grandson, Mr. George Armistead. The historic flag, which was also presented to Major Armistead, is now the valued possession of Mr. Fben Appleton, of Boston, grandson of Major Armistead.

From a recent magazine:

"Francis Scott Key is the one to whom we are indebted for a song which will live as long as America lives. Like "Yankee Doodle" and "Hail Columbia!" this song too, had its birth in time of war and was inspired by the intensity of patriotism.

It was in the war of 1812, in the lattejr part of August, 1814, that Dr. William Beanes, an old resident of Upper Marlborougli, Maryland, was captured by General Ross of the British Army and held as a prisoner on the "Surprise," the admiral's flagship. The doctor was a personal friend of Key, who was then a young lawyer, living in Baltimore. On the second of September Mr. Key, in writing to his mother from Georgetown, said, "I am going to Baltimore in the morning to proceed in a flag vessel to General Ross. Old Dr. Beanes, of Marlborough is taken prisoner by the enemy who threaten to carry him off."

The English fleet was in Chesapeake Bay and Key was kindly received by Admiral Cochrane. General Ross had consented to the release of Dr. Beanes, but as a combined attack by sea and land had been planned to be made on Fort McHenry, it was stipulated that all of the American party should remain on the flagship until the fort was reduced.

"All during the night of that eventful thirteenth of September, the great guns of the fleet poured shot and shell upon the fortress. While standing on the deck of the flagship, Key could see by the flash of the cannon and the glare of the rocket, that the American flag was still waving victoriously. The fight was intense and persistent and the courage and endurance of the soldiers was taxed to the utmost. In the dawn's early light, as he beheld the Stars and Stripes rising above the smoke and waving triumphantly, amid such surroundings and in such a scene, Key wrote the words which will live.

The day after the bombardment he was taken ashore and that night, at a hotel in Baltimore, he revised it, making it substantially what it now is. The following day he showed it to his kinsman, Judge Joseph H. Nicholson, who was so delighted with it that he had it printed immediately and in a few hours, all Baltimore was reading the Star-Spangled Banner.

"A remnant of the flag which inspired the immortal lines on that memorable morning still exists. It is thirty-two feet in length by twenty-nine in the hoist and is said to be in a fair state of preservation. It is owned by Mr. Eben Appleton, of Yonkers, N. Y., whose grandfather. Col. George Armistead, was one of the heroic defenders of Fort McHenry in 1814.

"The original flag was made by Mrs. Mary Pickersgill, whose mother, Rebecca Young, made the first flag carried by the colonists in the war of the Revolution. Its original dimensions were forty feet by twenty-nine.

"Key was born in Frederick County, Maryland, in August, 1780, and was but thirty-four when he wrote the famous lines. He died January 11, 1843, and lies in a grave in Frederick, Md., over which floats every day of the year, the American flag, and it is revqrently renewed on each Memorial Day.

"The old English tune. "To Amacreon in Heaven" is inseparably associated with the 'Star-Spangled Banner,' and was composed in London sometime between 1770 and 1775 by John Strafford Smith, who was a member of an aristocratic society called The Amacreonites, and the regular fortnightly meetings were always opened with the song 'To Amacreon in Heaven.'

"No song is so used as this, and the memory of the author is forever kept green as daily at sunset, when the garrison flags of the United States are lowered, on all American soil and on every flag ship of every United States naval squadron wherever it may be, the band plays 'The Star-Spangled Banner.' "

39. Lewis Gustavus Adolphus[8] Armistead, son of John Armistead and Lucy, first-lieutenant and captain of riflemen ; killed September 17, 1814, in a sortie from Fort Fire, Canada, during second war with Great Britain.

40. Walker Keith Armistead, born at New market in 1783; U. S. Military Academy at West Point, 1803, as second lieutenant of Engineers, captain 1806, major 1810, lieutenant-colonel 1812, chief of engineers with army in Canada, colonel in 1818, colonel Third Artillery 1821, brevet brigadier-general 1828; married in 1814, Flizabeth, daughter of John A. Stanley, of Newbern, N. C.; died at Upperville 13 October, 1845; she died in September, 1861. Children: (I) Lucinda Stanley Gillis, born at Alexandria ist of November, 1815; married 13th May, 1835, Joseph G. Carr, of Fauquier County; died 3rd of January, 1850. (61) Lewis Addison, born at Newbern 18th February, 1817; (64) Mary Walker, born at Newbern, 1831; married 8th of June, 1843, J. Travis Rosser, of Petersburg; died at Alexandria, December, 1857; (66) Flizabeth Frank; (67) Virginia Baylor; (68) Cornelia, married Major Washington Irving Newton, U. S. A.; (62) Frank Stanley, U. S. Military Academy, 1856; second lieutenant Tenth Infantry, first lieutenant 1861, resigned 1861; colonel C. S. A.; died in Kentucky 18th April, 1888; (63) Edward Bowles, born at Upperville 26th April, 1837, and Walker Keith, sergeant Sixth Virginia Cavalry, C. S. A.

General Lewis Addison Armistead, born at Newbern, North Carolina; educated at West Point; killed on the heights of Gettysburg, July 3, 1863, after he had penetrated, with heroic bravery far into the lines of the Federal troops. He entered the Sixth U. S. Infantry in 1839. In the Mexican War he was brevetted captain and major for galantry at Contreras, Cherubusco and Malinadel Rey. At Chapultepec he was one of the storm party and was wounded. He was made captain March 3, 1855. In 1859 he commanded a detachment against the Indians, defeating them. On the breaking out of the war in 1861, he resigned from the Federal army, and was made colonel of the Fifty-seventh Virginia Infantry, and in the same month (April) was made a brigadier general in Confederate States Army (Tyler, *Quarterly*, Vol. VL).

We have the following from another source:

"Lewis Addison Armistead entered West Point as a cadet, but on account of some youthful escapade was retired from that institution in 1836, just before graduation. The youthful escapade was the partial cracking of Jubal Farly's skull with a mess-hall plate. In 1839 appointed from citizen's life, second lieutenant in U. S. A., and assigned to the Sixth Regiment, commanded at that time by General Zackery Taylor, afterwards President. He served during the latter part of the Florida War under his father. General Walker K. Armistead, and early in 1861 he resigned his commission in U. S. A., and in company with General Albert Sidney Johnston and other officers, who had resigned, crossed the plains and offered his services to Virginia. He was mortally wounded at Gettysburg while advancing in front of his line with hat upon the point of his sword, after having taken first line and guns of the enemy and planting his flag upon their stronghold. He was taken in charge by Major-General Hancock, his old companion in arms, and sent to the Fleventh Corps Hospital at Gettysburg, where he died of his wounds the next day. Walter Harrison, A. A. G., and inspector-general of Pickett's Division, says of him: 'As a firm disciplinarian and executive officer, in addition to his high qualities for personal courage and judgment, he had no superior in the service. The Philadelphia Veteran Brigade, his adversaries on that fatal field, erected a memorial to him on the Gettysburg battlefield with the inscription: "On This Spot brave Armistead fell."

General Lewis Addison Armistead married Cecelia Lee Love, daughter of Richard H. Love, of Fairfax County, Virginia. Issue:

Walker Keith Armistead, born at St. Davids, Ala., 11 December, 1844; married 12th April, 1871, Julia Frances Appleton, daughter of Samuel Appleton, of Boston, and granddaughter of Daniel Webster, died at Newport, R. I., 28th March 1896. Issue: Lewrs Addison Armistead, Daniel Webster Armistead, and Keith Armistead, who accidentally shot himself when thirteen years old. Daniel Webster Armistead married in the summer of 1807, Miss Fitch, of Pittsburg.

NOTE.— Ludwell Lee married, second, in 1797, Flizabeth, daughter of Bowles and Mary Fontaine Armistead. Had six children. He resided at Shooters Hill near Alexandria.

Ludwell Lee married, first, 1788, his first cousin, Flora, daughter of Philip Ludwell and Flizabeth Steptoe, of Stratford, and had three children: (I) Fliza Matilda Lee, born September 13, 1791 ; died 22nd January, 1875; married 1811, Richard H. Love, of Fairfax County. Issue: Cecelia Matilda, married 1844, Major Lewis Addison Armistead, U. S. Army.

62. Frank Stanley Armistead, son of Walker Keith Armistead, entered Virginia Military Institute at sixteen; here two years under Thomas J. Jackson, graduated and went West. Was in the Rocky Mountains when the wa'r broke out in 1861. In feeble health, he traveled over 3,000 miles—part on mule, part walking to enter the Confederate service as private; was promoted and served to the end. Settled at Fort Smith, Ark., afterwards moved to Charleston, Arkansas.

63. Bowles Fdward Armistead, captain Company A, Sixth Virginia Regiment Cavalry, C. S. A., married first, 15th October, 1867, Susan Lewis Marshall, daughter of Fielding L. Marshall, of Fauquier County, Va., and great-granddaughter of Chief Justice Marshall. She died July, 1868, and he married, second, 23rd November, 1871, Flizabeth Lewis Marshall, daughter Henry Marshall and great-great-niece of the Chief Justice: Issue (i) Mary Morris Armistead, born 2nd January, 1873; married November 9, 1898, Aubrey Clarence Gochnauer. Issue, son Pembroke and Mary Armistead. (2) Henry Marshall Armistead, born 15th May, 1874. When nineteen he moved to Little Rock, Ark.; in 1895, graduated from the law department of the University of Arkansas; after which he was admitted to the bar, and is now a prominent and successful practitioner; also a member of the bar of the Supreme Court of United States, where he has appeared several times. November 2, 1903, he married Elizabeth,

daughter of Hon. George W. Murphy, attorney-general of Arkansas ; they have two children living—George M. born February 10, 1906; Henry M, November 10, 1907. (3) Lewis Addison Armistead, born 2nd January, 1876; (4) Stanley, born 9th September, 1877; (5) John Baylor Armistead, born 22nd January, 1879; (6) Eleanor Bowles Armistead, born 18th April, 1881; (7) Elizabeth Marshall Armistead, born 30th August, 1884; (8) Robert Morris Armistead, born 26th August, 1886; (9) Virginia Baylor Armistead, born 18th April, 1888; (10) Courtenay Warner Seiden Armistead, born August, 1890.

Walker Keith Armistead, son of Walker Keith Armistead and Elizabeth Stanley, born 1835 Fortress Monroe; died in Richmond, Va., September 3, 1904; served all during the Confederate War, first sergeant Company A, Sixth Virginia Cavalry.

Christopher Hughes Armistead, son of (38) George8 Armistead and Louisa Hughes, born in Baltimore, April 21, 1861; married in Fredericksburg, March 2, 1841, Agnes Campbell, daughter of Samuel Gordon, of Kenmore, died in Baltimore, February 14, 1876; she died January, 1880. Children, who were all born in Baltimore, are: (I) Susan Gordon, born July 21, 1842: married. November 21, 1867, Cuthbert Powell Grady. (2) Louisa, born September 18, 1844: died November 24, 1847;

(3) Agnes Gordon, born September 12, 1847; married January 9, 1877, Alexander Gordon. (4) George, born August 27, 1849; unmarried. (5) James Ryan, born April 30, 1851; died February 8, 1894; (6) Frances Carter, born November 17, 1855; unmarried. (7) Marion Gordon, born December 9, 1857; married January, 1877, Clarence C. Whiting. (8) Samuel Gordon Armistead, born July 27, 1860; married October 21, 1869, Ella Howell, of Philadelphia. Issue, Geo'rge Armistead.

The children of Mairion7 Gordon Armistead and Clarence C. Whiting: (I) George Armistead Whiting; (2) G. W. Carlyle Whiting; (3) Agnes Gordon Whiting; (4) Marion Dulany Whiting.

1. George Armistead Whiting married Susanna Butler (a great-great-granddaughter of Eleanor Custis). Issue: Eleanor Custis Whiting and George Armistead Whiting.

2. G. W. Carlyle Whiting married Nathalie Conteé Thomas.

The Whiting family line runs thus: Col. John Carlyle, the first of his name in Virginia, built in Alexandria, the famous Carlyle mansion in 1755. It was General Braddock's headquarters. Colonel Carlyle took an active part in the French and Indian wars; married in

1748, Sarah Fairfax, daughter of Hon. William Fairfax. Their second daughter, Anne Fairfax Carlyle, married Henry Whiting, of Gloucester; their son, Carlyle Fairfax Whiting, married Sarah Manly Little in 1838; their son, George Carlyle Whiting, married Mary Anne DeButts Dulany; their son, Clarence Carlyle Whiting, married Marion Gordon Armistead.

The children of Agnes Gordon Armistead and Alexander Gordon: Margareet Gordon, Alexander Gordon.

The children of Susan Gordon Armistead and Cuthbert Powell Grady, married in 1867 (Master of Arts, University of Virginia at the age of twenty; entered the Confederate army as private, promoted to colonel; Professor of Latin, Washington and Lee University, Lexington) : (I) Susan Ryan Grady, mar ried Henry Fay Green, of Baltimore; (2) Agnes Gordon Grady, married Edward Porter Alexander (son of General E. P. Alexander, Chief of Artillery C. S. A., Longstreet's Division). Issue: Jenny Powell Armistead.

APPLETON-ARMISTEAD LINE.

Georgiana Louisa Frances Gillis Armistead married William Stuart Appleton, of Massachusetts. This Appleton family has always been one of the most prominent of New England in literary, social, mercantile and political affairs.

William Stuart Appleton was the son of Eben Appleton, who was the brother of Nathan Appleton, LL. D. and author, United States Senator, manufacturer; he with others started the first loom-power for weaving cotton in the United States. With another brother, Samuel, he amassed wealth in the manufacture of cotton. Samuel was a noted philanthropist, spending the most of his income for benevolent and scientific purposes; he was a great traveler for more than twenty years, visiting various parts of the world. His daughter, a beautiful, accomplished girl, Frances Elizabeth, was the second wife of Longfellow, the poet. Georgiana Louisa Frances Gillis Armistead was the daughter of Colonel George Armistead and Louisa Hughes, born at Fort McHenry, November, 1817; married 27th November, 1838, William Stuart Appleton. Their children :

1. Louisa Armistead married F. T. Knight, of Boston. Issue, one child, Theodora Irving, who married George Knight Budd Wade. Issue: Ruth Wade.

2. William Stuart Appleton died.

3. Sarah Paterson Appleton died.

4. George Armistead Appleton died when thirty-four.

5. Eben Appleton married Isabel Slade, of New York; one child living, married William Morton, of Baltimore, Md.

6. Georgiana Louisa Frances Armistead Appleton married George M. Hunter, of Baltimore, Md.; several children, among whom is Isabella C. H., of New York City.

7. Edith Stuart Appleton married her cousin, William Sumner Appleton, of Holbrook Hall, Newton Centre, Mass. Issue: Eleanor Armistead Appleton, William Sumner Appleton, Majorie Crane Appleton, Dorothy Everard Appleton, Gladys Hughes Appleton. Eleanor Armistead Appleton married R. H. F. Standen, of BalHnderry, Mullingar, Ireland; several children.

8. Margaret-Armistead Appleton married George Livingston Baker of Boston. Issue; Six children — (i) George L. Baker, (2) Christopher Hughes Baker, died; (3) Edith Appleton Baker, married Dirk H. A. Kolff, of Java Island; (4) Caroline Frances Baker, married Harry T. Church, of Goshen, N. Y.;
(5) Mildred Armistead Baker, married Brady Green Ruttencutter, of Parkersburg, W. Va.; (6) Appleton Lawrence Baker.

9. Caroline Frances Appleton, died.

10. Alice Maud Appleton married John Clarke Kennedy, of London. Issue, two sons.

The parents of William Sumner Appleton, of Holbrook Hall (who married his cousin, Edith Stuart Appleton), were Nathan Appleton and Harriet Coffin Sumner, his wife.

75. Thomas Armistead married Miss Marchant of North Carolina. He was captain of the First Virginia State Regiment from April 6, 1776, to January, 1780, in the Revolution. Issue: (78) Martha Burwell, married Fowler, and lived in Baltimore; (79) Abiah, married William Mitchell and had issue, Alfred Mitchell, of Richmond, and William Mitchell, of Texas. (80) Anne Smith, married Barton, and had Armistead, died in New Orleans, and a daughter who married Hutchings, of Williamsburg, Va., and had issue two daughters, one of whom married a West India planter, the other, Moody, of Williamsburg. (81) Catharine, born March 25, 1787, married, first, William Pierce, of James City County (issue: two children, one of whom, Emily, married Robinson Arnold, and had issue, Catharine Armistead) ; married, second, Everard Hall, a distinguished lawyer

of Norfolk, Va. She died in Richmond, June 2, 1864.

ARMISTEAD, CARTER, WICKHAM.

Judith Armistead, eldest child of John and Judith Armistead, married, in 1688, Robert Carter. Their youngest child, John Carter married Elizabeth Hill, of "Shirley." Issue: Edward C., Charles C.. Elizabeth Hill C. Edward Carter, of "Blenheim," married Sarah Champe. Charles Carter, of "Shirley," married, first, his cousin. Mary Walker Carter. Charles Carter married, second, Anne Butler Aloore, of "Chelsea." Issue, among others, Anne Hill C., Williams Lee C., (Dr.) Robert Carter. Anne Hiil C. married General Henry Lee (Light Horse Harry), and had, among others, (General) Robert Edward Lee. Williams Lee Carter, of Hanover, married Charlotte Fouchee: their daughter, Charlotte Lee, married George Wickham; their daughter, Charlotte Wickham, was the first wife of W. H. F. Lee, son of General Robert E. Lee.

Dr. Robert Carter, of "Shirley," married Mary Nelson, of York, daughter of Governor Thomas Nelson and Lucy Grymes, his wife. Issue: Hill C., Anne C., Lucy C., Thomas C. Hill Carter (1796-1875) married Mary Randolph.

Anne Carter married William Fanning Wickham, of "Hickory Hill," Hanover County. Their son (General, C. S. A.,) Williams Carter Wickham, married Lucy Penn Taylor. Issue: Henry T. Wickham, Anne Carter Wickham, Julia W., died young, William F. W.

Henry T. Wickham (general counsel for C. & O. R. R.) married Elise Barksdale. Issue: Williams C. W. and George W. Anne Carter W., married Robert H. Renshaw. Issue: Williams C. W. R.. Frank R., Robert H. R., Julia R. William F. Wickham married Anne Ould. Issue: two sons and a daughter. William F. Wickham, deceased.

The first John Wickham, "eloquent, witty, graceful, married, first, Miss Fanning, daughter of an Englishman. Issue: William Fanning W. Edmund W. married Lucy Carter.

John Wickham married, second, Elizabeth, daughter of Dr. McClung and Elizabeth Seiden, his wife. Issue, among others, Littleton Wickham, married Miss Ashby, of South Carolina; Judge Ashby Wickham was their son.

William Fanning Wickham married Anne Carter, and had Williams Carter Wickham.

Dr. McClung moved from Elizabeth City County to Richmond in

1783. He was a noted physician.

Old Dr. Fouchee had some charming and beautiful daughters; one married Williams Lee Carter; another, Mr. Richie, of *The Enquirer*. Dr. Fouchee's was called the "home of the Graces," — *Riehmond in By-Gone Days*.

John Armistead (son of emigrant William) married Judith, and had, among others, Judith, who married Robert Carter. Their daughter, Elizabeth C., married Nathaniel Burwell, of Carter's Creek; their only daughter, Elizabeth, married President William Nelson, of Yorktown. She was a woman of deep piety and high ideals. Their son, Robert Nelson, married Susan Robinson; their son, Peyton Randolph Nelson, married *Sally Berkeley Nieholson;* their son, Wilmer W. Nelson, married Sally Browne Catlett; their daughter, Sally Berkeley Nelson, married Colonel Wm. Todd Robins, now deceased; their children are Ruth, married Thomas Gordon, lawyer of Richmond; Elizabeth, married Mr. Lunn, of Pittsburg, Pa.; Warner, a graduate of West Point, and an officer in U. S. A.; Nelson and Polly.

Sallie Berkeley Nicholson was the daughter of Dr. Robert Nicholson and Elizabeth Digges. The latter was the daughter of Dudley Digges and Elizabeth Wormeley, who was the daughter of John Wormeley and Elizabeth, his wife. John Wormeley was the son of Elizabeth Armistead and Hon. Ralph Wormeley Elizabeth Armistead was the daughter of Hon. John Armistead of Hesse, who was the son of William A. the emigrant.

William, the emigrant, had son John, who married Judith. They had two sons, William and Henry. Henry married Martha Burwell, and had William, who married Mary Bowles; they had Bowles, who married Mary Fontaine, daughter of Peter and Elizabeth Winston Fontaine; they had Peter Fontaine Armistead, who married Martha Henry Winston, and had twelve children. Martha Henry Winston was the daughter of Isaac Winston and Lucy Cole, the great-grandson of Isaac Winston, the emigrant. Issue of Peter Fontaine A. and Martha Winston, his wife: (I) Mary, died young; (2) William Bowles; (3) Isaac Winston; these never married; (4) Kate Winston A., married Captain Robert McFarland, C. S. A., Florence, Ala.; (5) Peter Fontaine A.; (6) Henry Cole A.; (7) George Washington A., married Mattie Reynolds, 1871; (8) John Anthony A., died single; (9) Martha Henry A., married Dr. E. C. Reid; (10) Dora Virginia A., married R. T. Bugg; (11) Walker A., never married; (12) Robert Lee A., married

Mary Bacon Steele.

5. Peter Fontaine Armistead married Elizabeth Baker Armistead, daughter of Colonel George Graham A. and Jane Forsyth, his wife, September, 1878. Mrs. E. B. Armistead, now a widow, lives in Arlington, Tenn. Their children: Gus. Henry A., James Baker A., George G. A., Peter Fontaine A. Louis Carter Armistead, son of Colonel George G. A. and his first wife, Alice Fontaine; his daughter married Mr. E.E. Throckmorton, of Tuscumbia, Ala.

6. Henry Cole Armistead married Mary Catherine Adair Armistead, December, 1872. Issue: Isaac Fontaine, married Mary Brown, 1901 ; Henry Cole, married Mattie Lee A., 1906; Nannie Barry, married Fred B. Arnett, 1908; Mary Susan, married Ed. H. Pendleton, 1904; Clara Henry, single; Elizabeth Baker, died in infancy; Kathleen Adair, single; Dora Virginia Lanier, single; Robert Lee, single; Wm. Bowles, single.

Frances Armistead, only daughter of William Armistead, the emigrant, married, first, the Rev. Justinian Aylmer, of Jamestown. "The Rev. Justinian Aylmer, born in 1635, was probably the Justinian Aylmer who matriculated at Trinity College, Oxford, July, 1656, and became B. A. October 24, 1657. The pedigrees of Aylmer and Hone and the connection of those families in Virginia, render it reasonably certain that he was a grandson of Theophilus Aylmer, archdeacon of the diocese of London, 166i. He was minister of Hampton Parish, York County. A little later he was minister of Jamestown, but died not long after, and widow, Frances, married Lieut.-Col. Anthony Elliott, of Elizabeth City County, who died in 1666; and she married Capt. Christopher Wormeley." (*Cradle of the Republic.*) In January, 1666, the will of her second husband, Col. Anthony Elliott, was recorded in Middlesex County. It mentions three sons—William, Thomas, Robert. Executors—William Elliott and John Armistead. In November, 1666, probate was granted Captain Christopher Wormeley in place of William Elliott and John Armistead, "as having married the relict of Rev. Justinian Aylmer," of Jamestown. This lady departed this life on the 25th day of May, 1685, was buried at home in their garden the next day.

There is an entry in the old Middlesex register: "Captain Wormeley's wife's son, Aylmer, Dyed the 16th and was Buried the 18th January in the Chancell near the South end of ye Communion Table, 1669." This boy died sixteen years before his mother, and most probably took his last rest beside the ashes of his father, the Rev. Justinian Christopher Wormeley, requested before he died to be buried in the garden between his first wife, Frances, and his last wife, Margaret. His second wife was the widow of Colonel John Carter, Jr.

WORMELEYS.

The first of the name in Virginia were two brothers, Christopher and Ralph, descended from Sir John de Wormeley, of Hadfield County, of York, England; knighted in 1312.

(i) Christopher Wormeley, acting Governor of Tortugas Island, in 1631-'35, when, owing to some negligence of his, the Spaniards captured the island, and he was compelled :o flee. He reached Virginia in 1635 and received grants of land, 1,450 acres, on Charles River Co. in 1638; member of Council 1637; died in 1649. His brother Ralph[1] W., was heir of his brother Christopher Wormeley's 4,545 acres. Ralph W., born 1620; died 1665; married Agatha Eltonhead of Eltonhead, Northampton Co. He was member of the Council in 1666; one of those proscribed by Bacon in his proclamation against Gov. Berkeley. Issue of Ralph W. and Agatha E.: Christopher, Ralph, Aylmer. Col. Christopher Wormeley married Frances Armistead, daughter of William A., emigrant, issue one daughter, Judith, and perhaps others. "Frances Wormeley wife of Col. Christopher Wormeley died May 25, 1685, and was buried in the garden next day." Judith Wormeley, born May 25, 1685. February 16, 1687, Ralph Wormeley, brother of Colonel Christopher Wormeley, married Elizabeth Armistead, neice of Frances Armistead Wormeley. Their eldest son, Ralph, died. John, the next son, married Elizabeth, and had Sarah and Judith, twins (Sarah died), Elizabeth, Sarah, Mary, Ralph, Agatha, John.

Ralph inherited "Rosegill" from his father, John. "Rosegill ' is one of the most magnificent estates in Virginia. The house is three stories high; it faces on an immense lawn that slopes to the Rappahannock, which is several miles wide at this point. The hall, perhaps the grandest in Virginia, occupies the whole river front, with a stairway at either end; into this opens the dining-room, drawing-room, library, sitting-room, paneled in mahogany and oak. It was to this home that Ralph Wormeley took his bride, Elizabeth Armistead.

SMITH — Arm ISTEAD-TABB-TODD.

It is said that Thomas Smith, son of Thomas and Armistead Smith, comes of the Lawrence Smith line. The first Lawrence Smith, of Abington Parish, had oldest son John, member of the Council. Lawrence, the second son, removed to York, and was the ancestor of Elizabeth Smith who married 187. Robert Armistead. Charles, another son, moved to Essex County; died about 1710, when his widow, Dorothy, Augustine Smith, and R. Buckner gave bond in Essex County. They had a daughter Dorothy.

The line runs thus :

The first Lawrence and John Smith, of Gloucester, are said to have been sons of Thomas Smith, son of Arthur Smith, who emigrated to Virginia in 1622 and settled in Isle de Wight County. His brother, Alexander Smith, settled in Middlesex County, 1634. These brothers, Arthur and Alexander, were nephews of Sir Thomas Smythe, President and Treasurer of the Virginia Company, and also of British East India Company. His father, Sir Thomas Smythe, of Osterhanger Castle, County of Kent, England, married, in 1552, Alice Judd, daughter of Sir Andrea Judd, Lord Mayor of London.

1. John Smith, of Purton, Gloucester County, Speaker of the House of Burgesses, married Anne Bernard in 1662. Their only son, (2) John S., married Mary Warner, February 17, 1680. Issue: (3) John S., Mildred S., Mary S., Augustine S of "Shooters Hill," Elizabeth S., Philip S., Anne S.

2. John Smith married Anne Alexander in 1711. Their son, John S., was born 1712; married (?) May not Captain Thomas Smith, of Kingston Parish, Gloucester County (who married Dorothy Armistead in 1755) have been the grandson of (4) John S.?

The destruction of Gloucester County records by fire in 1820, makes a gap that cannot be filled, except by records in Bibles, and unfortunately the Bible of Captain Thomas Smith was burned or lost in some way.

The search for Dorothy Armistead has been as exhausting and futile as the gap in the Smith line. The tradition that she was of the Hesse family has come down from father to son or daughter, to the present generation. John Armistead the Councillor had only two sons, William and Henry. Henry inherited Hesse. He married Martha Burwell about 1702 or 3, and had two sons, William and Robert, whose children and grandchildren are recorded in this volume. There is no Dorothy among them. We find Dorothy frequently among the Ralph Armistead line, which we give below, but none of the Dorothy Armisteads agree with the date of her marriage to Thomas Smith, which was about 1753. Her second son, Armistead, was born 1756.

Ralph Armistead patented in 1678 forty-eight acres of land in Kingston Parish. He may have been a nephew of the emigrant.

This Kingston branch of the Armisteads intermarried with the Gwyns, of Gwyn Island* (which is opposfte Hesse, on the Pianketank), the Reades and the Buckners.

The following are entries from Kingston Parish register, Mathews, formerly Gloucester County;

Anne, dau. of Robert and Catherine Armistead, born Oct. 17tn, F6.

Anne, dau. of John and Anne Armistead, b. April Ist 1769.

Ralph, son of Richard and Elizabeth Armistead, born June 1oth, 1769.

Francis, son of Currill and Margaret Armistead, b. Dec. 8th, 1772.

Wm., son of William and Mary Armistead, b. Oct. 26, 1769.

Dorothy Reade, dau. of Geo-, and Lucy Armistead, born May 23rd, 1775.

Mr. Starkey Armistead and Miss Mary Tabb were married June 19th, 1773.

The following notes are inserted here:

Daniel C. Armistead, b. 1851, of Norfolk, is the son of George Reade Armistead, b. 1808. George Reade A. was the son of Francis Armistead and Elizabeth Buckner, who were married in 1798. Four of their sons were Thos. Buckner, Geo. Reade, John Patterson and Francis, and daughter Lucy.

Francis Armistead, son of George Reade A. and Lucy Palmer, his wife, b. 1773.

Dorothy Reade Armistead, dau. of George Reade A. and Lucy Palmer, his wife, b. May 23rd, 1775.

Francis Armistead, of Mathews, married Dorothy Reade, Feb. 2nd, 1766. Dorothy Reade was the widow of Captain Gwyn Reade, eldest son of Benjamin Reade, who, in 1691, deeded the site of Yorktown.

The assessor's books of Gloucester County, in 1791, show lands assessed to Churchill Armistead, Wm. Armistead's estate, John Armistead, Jr., *Dorothy* Armistead, Robert Armistead, Richard Armistead, and Currill Armistead's estate.

In *Virginia Gazette*, 1768, Dorothy Armistead and Robert Reade advertised as executors of Captain Gwyn Reade.

The marriage of Thomas Smith and Dorothy Armistead is settled both by tradition and the following:

Mathevvs County, Kingston Parish Register:

"Armistead, son of Thomas and Dorothy Smith, was born Dec. Ist, 1756.

"Teste

THOMAS JAMES,
K. R."

Captain Thomas Smith, of "Beechland," married his first wife, Dorothy Armistead, about 1753. Their first son was Thomas, the next Armistead. These two brothers were students at William and Mary in 1776, and with several others founded the Phi Beta Kappa Society at that college, the first Greek letter fraternity in this country. Thomas Smith married, second, December 26, 1771, Ann Plater, of an old Maryland family. No children by this marriage. During her widowhood she made her home with her husband's eldest son's widow, Rosamond Lilly Deans Smith. Her portrait, in blue velvet, was given to Mrs. William Hubard, and has descended to Mrs. John Lloyd, her daughte.

Capt. Thos. Smith's will (*William and Mary Quarterly*, Vol. VI., No. 4), dated Kingston Parish, Feb. nth, 1789, names sons Thomas and Armistead; daughters, Susannah S. and Elizabeth Buckner, and Anne Armistead's children.

Teste: Anthony Morton.
Richard Armistead.

His daughter Anne, who married — Armistead, had died, leaving children. Richard Armistead was Anne's husband's brother, as we found elsewhere.

Armistead Smith married Martha Tabb, of Seaford, Gloucester County, January 13, 1780. She was the daughter of Edward Tabb and Lucy Todd, his wife. The children of Armistead Smith and Martha Tabb:

1. Harriet[2] Smith married Captain William Todd, November, 1798.

2. Lucy[3] Armistead Smith married Thomas Tabb, of Toddsbury,

December 15, 1803. Their daughter, Maria[3] Tabb, married William H. Hubard, an artist of note. Their daughter married Rev. John Lloyd, of Southern Virginia Diocese.

John[3] Tabb (son of Thomas Tabb and Lucy Armistead Smith, his wife,) married Margaret, and had Margaret, Lucy, Maria, and John.

George[3] Tabb (son of Thos. T. and Lucy Armistead Smith, his wife,) married Mary Randolph, and had Ellen T., who married Lane; Kate Tabb, who married --Robinson. Continuing, the children of Armistead Smith and Martha Tabb, his wife:

3. Thomas[2] Armistead Smith, of Woodstock, unmarried.

4. Elizabeth Cary[3] Smith married Christopher Tompkins, May 8, 1806.

5. Philip[3] Armistead Smith, while taking a sea voyage for his health, was shipwrecked off the Isle of Pines, and confined in a dungeon until released by the United States Government. He soon died.

6. Edward[3] Tabb Smith.

7. Pauline[3] Smith.

8. William Patterson[3] Smith.

William Patterson[3] Smith married Marian Andrea Morson Seddon, daughter of Thomas Seddon and Susan Pierson Alexander, his wife. Issue: Martha Tabb S., first wife of Col. Wm. Todd Robins, of Gloucester County, Va.; Anne Seddon Smith, married Col. Isaac Howell Carrington, of Richmond, Va.; Thomas Armistead Smith, of Glen Roy; William Alexander Smith; Maria n Morson Smith; Sallie Bruce Smith, married Wm. J. Alann, of Fauquier.

Elizabeth Tabb (daughter of Edward Tabb, and sister of Martha Tabb, who married Rev. Armistead Smith,) married John Patterson, of England, founder of "Poplar Crove," Mathews County, Va. They had Maria , second wife of Christopher Tompkins, and Elizabeth, first wife of Thomas R. Yeatman. This Jolrn Patterson was pronounced one of the most cultured, elegant men of that time.

Anne Seddon Smith (daughter of William Patterson Smith and Marian Seddon, his wife,) married Col. Isaac Howell Carrington, of Richmond, Va., son of Paul S. Carrington and Emma Cabell, his wife. Issue of above marriage:

Heyward Carrington, died when sixteen.

Nannie Seddon C., died in infancy.

Marian C., died in infancy.

Malcolm Carrington.

Mary Coles Carrington.

Seddon Carrington.

Margaret Cabell Carrington.

Mrs. Carrington has beautiful crayon portraits of her father, Patterson Smith, and his parents, Armistead Smith and Martha Tabb, his wife, done by Sharpless, the distinguished English artist. Also, an oil portrait of Mr. Patterson Smith's two beautiful daughters, Anne and Martha, with their brother, Thomas Smith, of Glen Roy, Gloucester, seated between them. This was done by Wm. H. Hubard. Mrs. Carrington has two life-size St. Memin's of Col. Robert Gamble, her husband's great-grandfather, and of Judge Wm. H. Cabell of the Supreme Court of Virginia and Governor of Virginia.

Ralph Armistead, who came to Gloucester 1678, and must have been closely related to John A., the Councillor of the Hesse estate, as he settled in Gloucester, had a son Francis Armistead, who was to be uncle Francis' heir in case his uncle's children, John, one year old, and Elizabeth, two years old, should die. (*Quarterly*, Vol. VI.)

May not this Francis have been the father of Dorothy Armistead who married Thomas Smith about 1753? Her second son, Armistead, was born 1756. Dorothy Armistead must have been born about 1733.

Thomas Smith (eldest son of Thomas Smith and Dorothy, his wife,) married Rosamond Lilly Deans, of Mid Lothian, Gloucester County, a very beautiful and wealthy girl. No children by this marriage. She married three times.

TODD FAMILY.

The emigrant, Thomas Todd, patented land in Elizabeth City County in 1664. He settled later in Gloucester County, and built "Toddsbury," that quaint and beautiful colonial home, still one of the show places of Gloucester. Anne Todd, granddaughter of the emigrant Thomas, married Mordecai Cooke, of Wareham, Gloucester, son of the first Alordecai, who was called "staunchest of all the King's men of Gloucester." He it was who declared he would take a wife of the maids to be sent for wives to the colony in 1621. The story of one of these maids has been woven into a fascinating romance, "To Have and To Hold," by Mary Johnston. Sir Alordecai swore he must have his choice. When the news came of the arrival of the ship's cargo he was chasing a red fox, and yelled, "The red fox first, then the maid !" but he dispatched a messenger to the captain of the ship, promising two hogsheads of the fairest Virginia tobacco if he would "batten the hatches and keep the maids close till the fox was caught." Joan Constable was his choice; a beautiful Jewess with auburn hair.

Thomas Todd, of Toddsbury, the emigrant, married Ann Gorsuch. Issue: Thomas Todd, married Elizabeth. Thomas Todd was Justice of the Peace of Gloucester, 1698-1702. His daughter, Anne, married Alordecai Cooke, of Wareham. His son, Thomas, went to Maryland, married Elizabeth, and had Thomas, of Todd's Neck, Baltimore County, Maryland, who married Eleanor Dorsey.

Elizabeth Smith, of Shooter's Hill, born April 25, 1701, married Christopher Todd, of Toddsbury. Their daughter, Lucy Todd, married Edward Tabb. Their daughter, Martha Tabb, married Armistead Smith.

The children of Edward Tabb and Lucy Todd are: Alartha, married Armistead Smith; Philip, of Toddsbury, married Marv Alason; Thomas, of Seaford; Elizabeth, married John Patterson (born 1760); Paulina (born 1766); married G. W. Booth; Mary, married John Wyatt.

To Bishop Madison of Virginia:

"Ware, *July 2nd,* 1792.

"Right Reverend and Dear Sir:

"This will be presented you by the Rev. Armistead Smith, who is a candidate for holy orders. He has acted as a probationer in the churches of Kingston much to the satisfaction of the audience who will gladly receive him as their minister if you should think proper to ordain him. The inconvenience the inhabitants of this Parish have labored under from a succession of unworthy pastors who were strangers, prate powerfully in favor of Mr. Smith who is a native of the place, of known and approved conduct among them from his infancy.

"Further requests are before you. Right Rev. and Dear Sir— T still only add that if you think proper to introduce Mr. Smith into the church, you will meet the wishes of a numerous and expecting people, destitute of a spiritual guide.

"With sentiments of real regard, I am Right Reverend Sir, affectionately and sincerely yours,

"JAMES MAURY FONTAINE."

"The Right Rev. Dr. Madison, Bishop of Virginia:

"*Sir,* — The Parish of Kingston having become vacant by the late death of the Rev. James McBride, we whose names are herewith subscribed being members of the Vestry of the Parish of Kingston and anxious for the prosperity of the Protestant Episcopal Church, do conceive it our bounded duty forthwith to announce it to you as its divine Head and benefactor in order that this vacancy be supplied. We sincerely lament that we have so long experienced its gradual decline since the death of the Rev. James AIcBride. Yet fondly hope under the favor of Heaven and you our guardian, friend and protector, together with the joint exertions of a virtuous clergy again to see its day of prosperity return. It concerns us truly to relate that we have been too often unfortunate in its appointment of clergymen heretofore to fill the sacred office, and having attributed its decline to our want of a thorough knowledge of their breeding, general conduct and fitness to serve us — to supply them this defect in future and to guard against its dreadful consequences, we shall presume to nominate and recommend Mr, Armistead Smith for holy orders, who is a gentleman independent in his circumstances, is well known to us and was born and bred amongst us and is exemplary in his conduct. In the private walks of life we highly esteem him for his steady regard and attachments to the interests of our Church, we have the greatest confidence in his sobriety, integrity, moral rectitude. We strongly recommend him to your notice. He being then the object of our choice, we sincerely hope that no obstacles be thrown in his way in procuring the needful to enable him to make himself useful to ourselves and a numerous people in the discharge of his sacred duties. With the greatest regard we are your obedient and humble servants.

> "THOMAS SMITH,
> "JAMES JONES,
> "JOEL FOSTER,
> "ROBERT CARY,
> "GEORGE ARMISTEAD,
> "THOMAS SMITH, JR.,
> "THOMAS TABB."

Copied from the tombstone of the Rev. Armistead Smith at Toddsbury, Gloucester County. The families of Tabbs, Todds and Smiths are buried here.

Sacred to the Memory of
REVEREND ARMISTEAD SMITH
of Mathews County
who after having faithfully served God
in the Gospel of His Son
departed this life
September 12th 1817
age 60 yrs 9 m. 12 days
If sincerity in friendship — a heart glowing
with true piety, benevolence and charity have
a claim to everlasting regard, the
memory of the deceased will
be fondly cherished

BOOTH, BUCKNER, READE, ARMISTEAD.

There were Booths who came early to Virginia and settled in York and Gloucester Counties. Thomas Booth, from Barton, Lancastershire, England, where he was born in 1663, settled on Ware River, Gloucester County, where he died in 1736. He was the son of St. John Booth, who was son of John, the son of George Booth. George B. was also the father of William B. who was the father of George, first Lord Delamere, who was the father of Henry Booth, Earl of Delamere (*Macaulay's His.*). Thomas Booth, emigrant, married Mary, daughter of Alordecai Cooke, of Mordecai's Mount. Their tombs, with Arms, are at Jarvis Farm, Gloucester County, Va. They had ten children.

Adam B. manried Thomas Reade. Isabella B-, born 1704, married, first. Rev. John Richards; second. Rev. John Fox. Elizabeth B. married Davis. Mary B. married John Perrin. Dr. George B. married Frances . Alordecai married Joyce Armistead. Booth B. married Mary Alason Wythe; his son, George B., born 1772, married, first, Pauline Tabb;

second. Mary Jones. Issue: Frances B. married Warren T. Talliaferro and had William Booth Talliaferro, major C. S. A..

Thomas Booth, student at William and Mary, 1699-1701, justice and sheriff 1732, will made and probated in Hanover County, St. Paul's Parish, married first, *Anne Buckner,* and had George, known as George of Poropotanke, who married Mary Talliaferro, Issue: Thomas Booth, sheriff in 1795 married, first, *Mary Ann Allen,* daughter of Richmond Allen.

BUCKNER.

There were two emigrants of the name—John, in Gloucester, and Philip, in Stafford,—presumably brothers. John Buckner is believed to have married a Miss Cooke, and had William Buckner, of Yorktown; Thomas and John Buckner, of Gloucester, and Richard, of Essex, who married Elizabeth Cooke. Of these, Major Thomas, of Gloucester, married Sarah, daughter of Captain Francis Morgan; issue, among others, Anne Buckner, who married *Thomas Booth; issue: George Booth, of Poropo tanke.*

KINGSTON PARISH ARMISTEADS

It is recorded that Ralph Armistead patented lands in Kingston parish in 1678. Mr. Tyler says he might have been a son of the emigrant, William Armistead; if so, why was he not mentioned in deeds and will with his other three sons? It seems more probable that he was a nephew or cousin of the emigrant, who came in 1635. Copying from Mr. W. S. Appleton's record of the "Family of Armistead": "Francis Armistead, of Mathews Court House, wrote, in 1894, that he was eighty-four years old, and son of Ralph A., who died about 1820, age about sixty-five, and that his father had brothers, Robert, William and John. From Kingston parish register we learn that Ralph, son of Richard and Elisabeth A., was born June loth, 1769; evidently the father of Francis."

These Armisteads of old Kingston parish intermarried with the Gwynnes, of Gwynne's Island, and the Reades. (See Gloucester Cary section for this Armistead line.)

From the Kingston records we have "George Reade Armistead married Lucy Palmer; issue: Francis Armistead, born 1773, married Elisabeth Buckner (niece of Armistead Smith) in 1798; issue, ten children. Four of the sons were: Thomas BUCKNER Armistead, George Reade Armistead, John Patteson Armistead, Francis Armistead; daughter, Lucy Armistead.

Thomas Buckner Armistead married "the beautiful Harriet Allen Booth" about 1830. Issue: only one child, Thomas Buckner Armistead, born July 18, 1832, at Myrtle Grove on East River, Gloucester County, who married Mary Jane Walthall, of Mecklenburg County, Va., October 18, 1858, daughter of Francis Lockett Walthall and Sarah Frances, his wife. Issue: Mary Jane, Sarah, Catherine, Nina, Frederika Mott, Thomas Buckner Armistead died when young, and Margaret Booth Armistead. who married Louis John Heindl, of Richmond, Va., January 14, 1892. Issue: Constance, Louis Armistead, Margareet Booth, Mary Caroline (died), Thomas Armistead, Frances Buckner, Louise Chesrown, William Sclater, Francis Walthall, Christopher Tompkins.

Harriet Allen Armistead married William John Tucker, of Frederick, Maryland, now living in Atlanta, Ga. Issue: William Armistead Tucker.

Frances Wilson Armistead married Edwin Courtney Shield, from Richmond, Va. Issue: Mary McCabe Shield.

Tomasia Buckner Armistead married, January 14, 1901, Robert Browning Rood, born at Great Barrington, Mass., now living in Berkshire Hills, Mass. Issue: (1) Robert Pelton Rood, born January 24, 1902;~died October 28, 1906; (2) Armistead Rood.

Nannie Louise Armistead married Elias Chesrown, of Pittsburg, Pa., November 24, 1898; died March 2, 1906, leaving a daughter, born March I, 1906, named Virginia Louise Armistead Chesrown.

Francis Walthall Armistead married Marie Fisher from Staten Island, June, 1906.

The father of Thomas Buckner Armistead, only son of Thomas Buckner Armistead and Harriet Allen Booth, died when he was six days old; his mother, who was famed for beauty and wealth, married, second, Dr. , who proved most unworthy. He sold whatever property he had power over, and left her while they were living in Washington. She died when her son was only twelve years old. His uncle, Thomas Booth, took charge of him and raised him as his own child, at "Rosewell," in Gloucester County. Thomas Booth bought "Rosewell" for ten thousand dollars about 1834; lived there thirty years, and then sold it for twenty thousand dollars to Mr. Tabb Catlett, whose wife was a cousin of Thomas Buckner Armistead.

To the "beautiful Harriet Allen Booth" was left an estate of two hundred acres, on York River, by an old bachelor named Banks, who said "she was the most beautiful woman in Eastern Virginia." This estate had its residence, quarters, outhouses, stock of all kinds, servants, carriage and horses.

READE.

Mildred Windebank, daughter Sir Thomas Windebank, married Robert Reade, Esq., of Yorkshire, England. Their son, George Reade (Honorable), who came to Virginia in 1637, married Elizabeth Martain (Martian), of Belgium, daughter of Captain Nicholas Martian. Issue: Mildred R., Elizabeth R., Robert R. Benjamin R., Margaret Reade.

Mildred Reade married, about 1665, Col. Augustine Warner, of Warner Hall, Gloucester; Speaker of the House, 1675; member of Council until his death in 1681.

Elizabeth Reade married Captain Thomas Chismon about 1675. Issue: (later.)

Margareet Reade married Thomas Nelson. They were the grandparents of General Thomas Nelson.

Robert Reade married Mary Lilly, granddaughter of John Lilly and Dorothy Wade, daughter of Armiger Wade and his wife, the heiress of Malson of York.

Benjamin Reade married Lucy Gwynn, of Gwynn's Island. Issue: Gwynn Reade, of Kingston Parish, Gloucester County (now Alathews) who married Dorothy . After Gwynn'.s death, Dorothy married Francis Armistead on February 2, 1766.

Mildred Reade, daughter of Benjamin Reade and Lucy Gwynn, married John Gwynn.

In 1610 Captain Owen Gwinn is in the list of "Lords, Esquires, and Gentlemen" who came to America under the third charter in 1611. He had been knighted. Married Grace Williams. Their son, Hugh Gwinn, was burgess in 1652 to 1690; prominent as vestryman 1652 to 1677 with Gwinn Reade, Captain Thos. Smith, and others.

CHARLOTTE, PRINCE EDWARD AND CUMBERLAND ARMISTEADS.

After our correspondence with Mr. Louis L. Armistead, of Lynchburg, when it was settled that his ancestor and William Blair

Armistead's were brothers and that Dr. Jesse Armistead, of Cumberland, was a cousin of his father, it was apparent that the three above mentioned were descendants of one progenitor. The tradition is inerradicable in the families of the two first, that their ancestors came from Gloucester County and from Hesse. This latter was proved a mistake. In our dilemma we appealed to Dr. Lyon G. Tyler (always so generous with his information) in, regard to the descent of Dr. Jesse Armistead's grandfather, John, and he unhesitatingly wrote that he believed he was descended from Ralph Armistead, who patented land in Gloucester 1679. (*Quarterly*, VII., p. 184.) He thinks the line runs thus: "Ralph A. (patented lands in 1679) had John (inventory recorded in Essex County, 1703) ; John had Francis and Ralph A, (will pro. in 1719. Francis A. was the father of John (will proved 1768), who was father of James A., the father of Dr. Jesse A."

We continued our search and felt like exclaiming, "Eureka!" when we came across the following statement in Mr. William Stuart Appleton's brochure of the "Armistead Family": "Francis Armistead wrote, in 1894, that he was ninety-four years old and son of Ralph A., who died *about* 1820, *about* sixty-five, and that his father had brothers — Robert, William and John," The three names we were hunting — Robert and William of the Charlotte County lines, and John of Cumberland County. After comparing dates, we feel convinced that the line of John A., of Cumberland (will proved in 1669), is as stated by Dr. Tyler, and that Robert and William are the above Robert and William, brothers of Ralph, and son of the Ralph who was brother f Francis, as stated by Dr. Tyler. To state it more plainly, Robert and William, of Charlotte County, were nephews of John, of Cumberland, whose will was proved in 1669. And so at last the *Gloueester* tradition is fulfilled, and all the information collected coincides. For further items in regard to Ralph Armistead line, see "Armistead Smith" and "Booth-Buckner-Reade" sections of this volume.

Descendants of William Armistead, of Charlotte Co., VA.

1. William Armistead[1] married Peggy Morris, daughter of Samuel Morris and Mary Lewis. Issue. 2. William[2] A., and perhaps others.

2. William[2] Armistead married Mary Lewis Cobbs, daughter of Captain Robert Cobbs and Anne Poindexter.

Captain Robert Cobbs (born 1754, in Louisa County, removed in 1795 to Campbell County) was the only son of Samuel Cobbs and Mary Lewis, his wife.

Captain Robert Cobbs married Anne Poindexter, daughter of John Poindexter, of Louisa County, Va. Issue, nine children; one, Mary Lewis Cobbs, married William Armistead, of Charlotte County, Va., 1806. (Mary Lewis Cobbs born June 11, 1787.)

The following data is taken from the Lewis-Cobb Genealogy Book:

"Ambrose Cobbs, emigrant, born about 1590, came to Yorktown, Va., about 1613. (I) Robert Cobbs, son of Ambrose C., born about 1620; (2) Robert Cobbs, son of Robert C., born 1660.

"Thomas Cobbs, John Cobbs, Robert Cobbs, appear on records of Henrico and Goochland from 1736 to 1750 — sons of (2) Robert Cobbs, born, respectively, 1706, 1708, 1710 — heads of the three lines of the name in the United States.

"The fact that Robert Cobbs, the second of the name in America, born 1620, was Justice of the Peace and High Sheriff, is proof that he was a man of importance, as these positions could be held at the time by none but the best class of citizens. Justice of the Peace in 1650 was a position equally as honorable and important as Judge of the Supreme Court at this day."

Issue of William Armistead and Mary Lewis Cobbs: (1) John (Dr.) Oliver A., born 1807; died, 1873; lived near Lynchburg; married Elizabeth Jennings, of Charlotte County, Va., about 1830. Issue: Mary Susan A., Sarah Anne A., Emma A., Bettie A., Henrietta A.

(2) William Blair A., son of William A. and Mary Lewis Cobbs, born at Turnip Creek, Charlotte County, Va., 1811, was left an orphan when very young, and raised by his uncle, William Cobbs, near Lynchburg, Va., at "Poplar Forest," once the home of Thomas Jefferson. He removed to Nashville, Tenn.; married Mary Robina Woods, daughter of Robert Woods, of Nashville, Tenn., and Sallie B. West, his wife, of Frankford, Kentucky. The home of Robert Woods was "Westwood," three miles south of Nashville, Tenn., on the Franklin Pike. He had two brothers, James and Joseph. All three moved from Virginia to Nashville, Tenn., and were among the first bankers established there. Issue of (2) William Blair Armistead and Mary Robina Woods; (1) Roberta[3] A., born May 10, 1844; married Duke R. Johnson, November 15, 1869. Issue:

William Ormsby Johnson, born October 5, 1870; died April 23,

1886.

Duke Robert Johnson, born July 20, 1873.

James Woods Johnson, born August 23, 1875.

Edward Lee Johnson, born June 29, 1878; died April 27, 1880.

Marion Johnson, born November 13, 1887.

(2) Robert Lewis³ A., born May 7, 1847; married Nancy Minor Merriwether Humphreys, of Clarksville, Tenn., April 21, 1875. Nancy Minor Merriwether Humphreys, daughter of Robert West Humphreys and Mary Merriwether, of Montgomery County, Tenn. Issue of (2) Robert Lewis³ A. and Nancy M. M. Humphreys, as copied from Robert Lewis Armistead's family Bible:

(I) Robert Lewis4 A., Jr., born January 31, 1876, Clarksville, Tenn.

(1) Robert Lewis4 A., died June 5, 1897, Clarksville, Tenn.

(2) Carl Merriwether4 A., born November 15, 1877, Nashville, Tenn.

(2) Carl Merriwether4 A., married, August 29, 1906, Martha Jane Foster.

(3) Ellen Barker4 A., born August 31, 1879, Clarksville,

(3) Ellen Barker4 A., married, January 19, 1904, Rev. Henry

B. Searight, of Sumner County, Tennessee.

(3) Ellen Barker4 A. Searight, died December 17, 1904, in Acworth, Ga,

(4) Nancy Minor Merriwether4 A., born September 14, 1881, Clarksville, Tenn., married, June 6, 1907, Dr. Ellis Saunders Allen, of Louisville, Ky., formerly of Newbern, Ala,, where his father, a cotton planter, lives.

(5) West Humphreys4 A., born September 24, 1884, Clarksville, Tenn.

(6) William Cobbs* A., born December 30, 1886, Pass Christian, Aliss.

3. William Blair Armistead, born June 14, 1849, married, August 31, 1875, Elizabeth Hadley Clock, born May 5, 1857. Issue of William Blair Armistead, JR., and Elizabeth Hadley Clock:

(1) Mary Robina4 A., born May 31, 1874.

(1) Mary Robina4 A., married, January 20, 1892, J. Washington Aloore, born March 31, 1867. Issue:

Elizabeth Clock, born November 5, 1892; died November 8, 1896.

J. Washington Aloore, born April 29, 1895.

William Armistead M., born April 7, 1901.

Mary Hadley M, born January 25, 1903.

Sarah Frances M., born March 10, 1906.

2. William Woods4 A, born February 27, 1885.

4. Julia Woods[3] A., born September 7, 185—, Nashville, Tenn., married, October 3, 1876, Major Thomas AlcDonough Andrews, born in Williamson County, Tenn., October 15, 1841; served four years in the Confederate army; was with General Forest through four campaigns; with President Davis when captured. Admitted to the bar at Franklin, Tenn., in 1870. Issue of Julia A. and Thomas Andrews:

(1) Garnett Stith Andrews, born at Nashville, Tenn., December 12, 1887. A. B., University of Nashville, 1903; LL. B.. Vanderbilt, 1906.

(2) Forest West Andrews, born in Nashville, Tenn., October 21, 1880. A. B., University of Nashville, 1904; LL. B., Vanderbilt, 1906.

(3) William Van Roy Andrews, born in Nashville, Tenn., January 17, 1883.

(4) Julia Louise Andrews, born at Church Hill, Mississippi, January 13, 1890.

6. James[3] Woods Armistead married Kate Washington, daughter of Thomas Laurence Washington and Mary Knox Gale. Issue of James[3] Woods A. and Kate Washington: Mary Knox A., Laurence Washington A., John Oliver A., Kathryn Woods A.

5. Mary Theora Armistead, born December I, 1854, in Nashville, Tenn., married, December 6, 1872, James William Hughes, son of Rev. John F. Hughes, of Columbia, Tenn., born at Alt. Pleasant, Tenn., June 12, 1847. Ex-Confederate soldier; joined First Tennessee Regiment Infantry, November 1, 1861; paroled as a member of Ninth Tennessee Cavalry, Forest Command, May 10, 1865, at Gainesville, Ala., having been in the army over three years and six months before he arrived at the age of eighteen. By profession a druggist at Columbia, Tenn., and Birmingham, Ala., until 1897, when he was appointed Postmaster at Birmingham in September, and remained Postmaster till February, 1905. In politics a Republican, was delegate to National Republican Convention, 1892-'6, 1900-1904. Issue ot Mary T. A. and James W. Hughes:

(1) Mary Lavinia H., born August 19, 1874, died August 6, 1875-

(2) James William Hughes, Jr., b. February 13, 1877; married, June 12, 1901, Callie Kobb Richardson, daughter of Lucien J. Richardson, of Montgomery, Ala. Issue: (1) Mary Frances Hughes, born October 26, 1904.

(3) Blair Hughes, born October 5, 1879; married November 5, 1906, Eloise Chesley McCaw, daughter of William Robert McCaw

and Eloise Chesley, of Lexington, Ky.'

In our search for the ancestor of William Armistead, of Charlotte County, we were informed of the near relationship of Mr. L. L. Armistead, of Lynchburg, Va., to this line, and that he might throw light on this subject, which he did most graciously in several interesting letters, though eighty years of age or more. His concise style, memory, and good English were noticeable in this day of careless letter writing. He states that his grandfather, Robert A., and William Blair A.'s grandfather, William A. were brothers, and married sisters, the daughters of Samuel Morris, of Hanover, a leader of dissenters about the time of the Revolution; one of the founders of the first Presbyterian Church in Hanover, of which Samuel Davies was the first pastor. Robert Armistead was living in Hanover at this time, and probably William Armistead, as both married Morrises. Besides, that noted patriot and Presbyterian, Caleb Wallace, went from there to Charlotte County as pastor of the Charlotte Church. It was he who wrote those petitions of Hanover Presbytery, which are among the great papers of American history. He became the first Chief Justice of the State of Kentucky. It is presumed that it was through the influence or friendship of William A. that Caleb Wallace went to Charlotte County, where William A. settled. It is stated by Mr. L. L. Armistead that Robert A., his grandfather, was a resident of Hanover County, bringing his wife, Morris, with him to Charlotte. The father of L. L. Armistead was Samuel, son of Robert A. and Morris, his wife. Samuel Armistead married twice—first, a daughter of General Joseph Martin, of Henry County, Va., who was commissioned by the United States to treat with the various Indian tribes in the Southern States. The issue of this marriage three sons: *Henry*, AI. A., *Joseph* AI. A., and *Samuel* A. Henry A. married Marcia Lambeth, a widow; nssue; Samuel A. and three daughters. Joseph A. married Martha Phillips, of Yazoo River, and County, Mississippi. Her father, Maj. Wm. Phillips, distinguished himself in the battle of New Orleans under Andrew Jackson; war of 1812. Issue of this marriage, two sons. The younger died in infancy; the elder, William P. Armistead, belonged to the Eighteenth Alississippi Regiment; was noted for his bravery during the war. Samuel Armistead married Frances Cobbs, of Campbell County, Va.; issue: a daughter.

Samuel Armistead, son of Robert A. and Morris, his wife, married, second, Nancy Madison, daughter of Henry Madison, and White, of Charlotte County. He died when ninety-four years old.

Nancy Madison was the youngest of eleven children. Issue of this second marriage: (1) Katherine Penn A., married Benjamin Wyatt, of Charlotte County, Va. (2) Martha A., married D.W. Williamson, of Charlotte Co. (3) Lucy Claiborne A., married Bryce A. Martin, of Henry County. (4) Harriet Pendleton A., married Thomas D. Williamson, of Charlotte County. (5) Sarah Madison, married Hezekiah Font, of Charlotte County. (6) Justina C. A., married Rev. Robert C. Anderson, of Prince Edward County. Issue: five sons and five daughters; only one died. Of the sons, three are lawyers, two of whom, Samuel and James L., are successful practitioners in Richmond, Va.; one a clergyman, one a physician. Their mother is eighty-four, and in good health (1910).

7. James Aladison A. (deceased five years ago) married twice—first, the widow Slaughter, a cousin; second, Fanny Steptoe. No issue.

8. Louis L. Armistead married Nannie Bryce Mitchell, daughter of Rev. Jacob D. Mitchell, D. D. The eldest child of this marriage, Harriet M. Armistead, married Rev. J. A. McMurray, pastor of Floyd Street Presbyterian Church in Lynchburg, Va. Issue: two children—Lewis Armistead McAlurray, Charlotte Boyd McMurray.

The son of L. L. Armistead and Nannie Bryce Mitchell is jacob D. Mitchell Armistead, Ph. D., Professor at Agnes Scott College, Decatur, Ga.

In *Quarterly,* VII., page 184, it is stated that Rev. Jesse Scott Armistead was the son of James A., who was the son of John A., of Cumberland County, whose will was recorded there March 27, 1769, and names children—William, John, Francis, Thadeus, and daughters—Sarah Russell, Elizabeth Bradshaw, Hannah Armistead, Mary, Fanny, Nancy, wife now with child (James). Son-in-law, Josiah Bradshaw, and son, William Armistead, executors.

John Armistead, of Cumberland County, lived on or near Muddy Creek, about halfway between the Courthouse and Cartersville. His son, James, born about 1768, married Nancy Miller. Issue:

1. The oldest, a daughter, married Taylor. Issue:
a daughter, who married Jones, of Alabama, and had three sons—James Armistead Jones, United States Senator from Alabama; William Armistead Jones, and Jones.

2. Ann Armistead married Mr. Payne. Several sons and daughters.

3. Arianna A. married Watkins, from Appomat tox. They had several children. One daughter married one of her Jones cousins.

4. Dr, Thomas Armistead married Martha Wilson, of Cumberland County. Issue: three daughters and one son.

(1) Elizabeth, unmarried.

(2) Nancy Aliller Armistead married Mr. Aliller. Issue; two daughters—Lou married Mr. Bolling, of Southwest Virginia; Martha married .

(3) Fanny Wilson Armistead married Lowman.
Issue: Elizabeth Lowman.

(4) James A. Armistead married Jennie Aladison, of Cumberland County. Issue: Lou A., Martha A., Ellen A., (Dr.) Thomas A., James A., Blanche A., Jennie A., Aladison A. Dr. Thomas Armistead married Miss Shelburne, of Richmond, Va. Lou A. married AIcRae. Alartha A. married Morton. Ellen A. married Guerrant. Blanche A. married Mr. Morton, of Farmville. Jennie A. married Cralle.

5. Jesse Scott Armistead (Rev.), a distinguished Presbyterian divine, married Martha Storres Trueheart. Issue: (1) Nancy Aliller Armistead, (2) Eliza Truehart Armistead, (3) Maria Page Armistead, (4) Charles James Armistead.

(1) Nancy Aliller A. married Dr. Philip Blanton and had (Dr.) Charles Armistead Blanton, Jessie Blanton, Prescott Blanton, Maria Page Blanton. Dr. Charles A. Blanton married Elizabeth Wallace; issue: Windham B., Wallace B., Elizabeth B. Jessie Blanton married William Johnson; no issue. Prescott
Blanton married Kate Faris, of Alontgomery, Ala.; they have two sons and two daughters.

(2) Eliza Trueheart Armistead married Archibald Bolling. Issue: Stanhope B., Blair B., Windham B., Martha B.; all unmarried. .

(3) Maria Page Armistead married John Bolling. Issue: Maria Page Bolling, married E. S. Walker.

6. Anderson Armistead, of Lynchburg, afterwards Baltimore, Md., married, first, a Langhorne. Issue: (1) Nannie Armistead, (2) James Armistead; married, second, Miss Rowan. Issue: (3) John Armistead, (4) Alice Armistead.

(1) Nannie Armistead married, first, Edward Longhorne; second, George Longhorne.

(2) James Armistead married , and had eight children; the two youngest, Lewis A., Keith A.

(3) John Armistead married Miss Poore.

(4) Alice Armistead married Hanson.

7. John Armistead.

8. *William Armistead.*

James Armistead married Judith Ann Blanton, sister of Dr. Philip Blanton, who married Nancy Miller Armistead. James Armistead and Judith Ann Blanton had (1) Lucy Ann Armistead, married Mr. McGehee. (2) James Munroe Armistead, married Carrie Dielle, of Plattesburg, New York; issue: Add'.e Armistead, William Armistead, Therese Armistead, Ann Armistead. Therese Armistead married Mr. Charles Covington, of Florida; Ann A. married Parker, and had one son, Rutledge P. (3) AVilliam Anderson Armistead married Frances Anne Flippen (daughter of R. Flippen and Manerva Clatilde Palmore) and had a family of children, all of whom died except Nannie Palmore Armistead, who married James Dobson Crump, of Richmond, where they now (1910) reside. Issue of this marriage: Armistead Cochran Crump; Wilbur Palmore Crump died as he neared young manhood, greatly beloved, a handsome youth of fine qualities; and a daughter, Lora Crump. Armistead Crump is now a physician practicing in New York City.

James Armistead, above mentioned, who married Judith Ann Blanton, was evidently the grandson of James, who was father of Dr. Jesse Armistead and son of 8. *William A.*, the brother of Dr. Jesse A. Unfortunately, there are no records to prove this— only tradition, names and dates—which indicate very surely.

John Armistead, of Cumberland County, Va., who lived on or near Muddy Creek (will recorded March 27, 1769), married Nancy and had John (mentioned in will), who married , and had son John A., born March 4, 1774; married Keziah Anderson, born June, 1777. It is presumed he married in Cumberland County, as Anderson is a name of that section, and a family name in James Armistead's family. James and John being sons of the John whose will was recorded in 1769.

John Armistead emigrated to Oglethrope County, Georgia, in 1798, thence to Walton County, Georgia, 1820, where he remained until his death, November, 1856. The children of John and Keziah (his first wife) were Elizabeth A., born April 2, 1799; William A., born July 17, 1801; John A., born March 5, 1803; Nathaniel A., died young; James A., born October 23, 1807; Frances A., born January 20, 1810; Susannah A., died young; Nancy A., born October 9, 1814; Keziah M. A., born September 23, 1816. John A. married, second, Mrs. Amy Owens, widow of Captain Owens, United States Army. Children of this marriage: Jesse A., born March 16, 1820: Thomas R. A., born

September 18, 1821 ; Vigil A., born August 27, 1823; Almarine A., born Aug. 27, 1825; Jabez Jubal A., born December 8, 1828.

Marriages of children of first wife: Elizabeth A. married Ezekiel Daniel; died in Mississippi, 1865. William A. married Susan Malcolm; died in Atlanta, Ga., 1871. John A. married Elizabeth Falkner. Nancy A. married A. W. Weaver.

Marriages of children of second marriage: Jesse A. married AI. F. Cubreath, 1841. Thomas R. A. married Drucilla Beard, 1841. Virgil A. married Lucy A. Chick, 1844. Almarine A. married Mr. Street. Jabez Jubal A. married Mary Chick, 1850.

FAMILY RECORD OF JABEZ JUBAL ARMISTEAD,-YOUNGEST SON OF JOHN ARMISTEAD.

(Sent by Deseendants.)

Jabez Jubal Armistead was born in Walton County, Ga., December 8, 1828.

Mary Osborne Chick was born in Walton County, Ga., June 12, 1829.

Jabez Jubal Armistead married Mary Osborne Chick in Walton County, Ga., April 24, 1850. Mary O. Chick's mother, Sallie Chick, was a native of England. Her father, James Chick, a planter and slave owner, was of Puritan descent.

Children of Jabez Jubal and Mary Osborne Armistead:

Frances Almarine, born in Walton County, Ga., March 8, 1851.

Ezra Powell, born in Walton County, Ga,, November 28, 1852.

Charles Henry, born near Albany, Dougherty County, Ga., November 1, 1856.

Edward Ceymour, born in Lauderdale County, Aliss., September I, 1859.

Jabez Osborne, born near Brandon, Rankin County, Aliss., November 24, 1862,

Minnie Carrie, born near Beauregard, Copiah County, Miss., March 12, 1866.

Robert Virgil Lee, born near Lake, Scott County, Miss., April 27, 1870.

Mary Osborne Chick, wife of Jabez Jubal Armistead, died in Newton, Newton County, Miss., September 1, 1889.

Jabez Jubal Armistead and Virgil Ann Gage were married in

Quitman, Clarke County, Miss., April 22, 1896, Rev. A, B. Coit officiating minister. Virgil Ann Gage, born May 1, 1858, was the daughter of Matthew Gage and Patience Williams Sanders, of Holmes County, Aliss.

Jabez Jubal Armistead died in New Orleans, La., June 28, 1901.

FAMILY RECORD OF EZRA POWELL ARMISTEAD.

Ezra Powell Armistead was born in Walton County, Ga., November 28, 1852.

Jennie Floyd Bonner, daughter of William Henry Bonner and Martha Caroline Wilson, of Garlandville, Aliss., was born December 19, 1860.

Ezra Powell Armistead and Jennie Floyd Bonner were married in Garlandville, Jasper County, Miss.

Children of Ezra Powell and Jennie Bonner Armistead:

Charley Bonner, born in Newton, Newton County, Miss., June 14, 1881.

Ruth, born in Newton, Newton County, Miss., at midnight, March 11, 1883.

Mary Osborne, born in Newton, Newton County, Miss., November 17, 1885.

Jennie Bonner, wife of E. P. Armistead, died in Newton, Newton County, Miss., April 15, 1889.

Ezra Powell Armistead and Ella Loper, daughter of Captain Frank Loper, were married in Newton, Newton County, Miss., October 16, 1890.

Children of Ezra Powell and Ella Loper Armistead:

Frank Loper, born in Newton, Newton County, Miss., July 6, 1892.

Kate Powell, born in Newton, Newton County, Miss., July 10, 1894.,

Ezra Powell Armistead died in New Orleans, La., July 25, 1895.

Ella Loper, widow of E. P. Armistead, died in Newton, Newton County, Miss., October 17, 1900. '

Marriages.

Ruth married Orrin Smylie McPherson in Newton, Newton County, Aliss., June 26, 1901.

Charley Bonnor and Louise Ophelia Williams were married in Collins, Covington County, Miss., November 3, 1903.

The children of Thomas R. Armistead and Drucilla Beard, his wife (married 1841): John, Almarine, James, Kimbriel R., Thomas, Mary, Frances, Charley, Rufns, Jesse, George, Lucy. Thomas and Drucilla moved to Desoto County, Alississippi, and lived there until his death, in 1892. Their oldest son, John Armistead, born 1845, Married Nancy Wells, 1866; moved to Memphis 1882, and lived there until his death, in 1904. Children of this marriage are: John L. A., Robert M. A., Mrs. H. N. Divine, and Mrs. Simon Dundee (Minnie A.), of Alemphis, who has kindly furnished the above information of her line.

In addition to Mrs. Dundee's statement is the following from Thomas Macon Armistead, of Atlanta, Ga., all of which verifies that John Armistead, of Cumberland County, whose will was recorded March 27, 1769, was the son of Francis A. The line runs thus: Francis A. had (1) John A., who marrried Nancv; they had (2) John A. who married Elizabeth, and they had (3) John A. who married Keziah Anderson. (3) John A. was born March 4, 1774; Keziah Anderson, his first wife, was born June 19, 1777. Mrs. Amy Owens, his second wife, was born November 8, 1783.

James Anderson Armistead, son of (3) John Armistead, married Emily Strong Colley, daughter of Rev. Joel Colley, a Baptist minister, who was a Virginian by birth. They had the following children:

Mary Keziah, born March 22, 1836.

Joel Colley, born January 16, 1838.

John James, born September 26, 1839.

Sarah Adline, born September 11, 1841.

Thomas Alacon, born September 21, 1843.

William, born April 10, 1846.

Zachariah Jabez, born June 9, 1847.

Susan Francis, born June 2, 1850.

Amanda Emily, born July 9th, 1851.

Emma Elizabeth, born September 26, 1853.

Frank Colley, born January 10, 1856.

Egbert Anderson, born February 4, 1859.

Of the above, four are still living: Joel C., Thomas M, Egbert A., and Amanda E., now Airs. H. L. Shipley. All live in Atlanta, Ga., except Egbert A. Armistead, whose home is in Social Circle, Walton County, Ga.

James Anderson Armistead spent his entire life upon the farm, and was noted throughout the country for his high character, agricultural knowledge and love for fine stock. He died November 22, 1891, and was buried in the family burying ground at Alcova, Ga.

"This indenture made on the fifth day of January, one thousand seven hundred and eighty-nine between John Armistead and Elizabeth his wife of the County of Cumberland of the one part and Samuel Atkinson, Jr., of the said County of the other part. WITNESSETH:

"That the said John Armistead and Elizabeth his wife, for and in consideration of the sum of forty-eight pounds fifteen shillings current money of Virginia, to them in hand paid by the said Samuel Atkinson, Jr., the receipt of which is hereby acknowledged, have granted, bargained and sold and do by these presents grant, bargain and sell unto the said Samuel Atkinson, Jr., a certain tract or parcel of land lying and being in the said County on Snow Quarter Greek, containing by estimation fifty-nine and an half acres more or less, being part of a larger tract devised to him, the said *John,* by the last will and testament of *his father John Armistead,* deceased of record in the Court of the said County, bounded by the lands of James Austin and Samuel Atkinson, Senio:r, and by a new line running from corner pointers in the said John Armistead's west line between the said Samuel Atkinson, Senior and William Armistead, South fourteen degrees, East to a white oak bush and pointers in *Francis Armistead's* line and by the lands of the said Francis together with all the appurtenances belonging to or in any wise appurtaining to the said tract or parcel of land and premises, etc.

"IN WITNESS WHEREOF the said John Armistead and Elizabeth his wife have hereunto severally set their hands and affixed their seals the day and year first above written.

"JOHN ARMISTEAD (L. S.)

"Sealed and delivered in the presence of
"M. CARRINGTON
"ELIZABETH CRIDDLE
"SAMUEL ATKINSON.

"At a Court held for Cumberland County the 27th day of January, 1789.

"This indenture was acknowledged by John Armistead a party

thereto and ordered to be recorded.

"Teste,

"TSCHARNER WOODSON, Deputy Clerk.

"A Copy
   "Teste

"(Signed) R. O. GARRETT
                                        "DeputyClerk.

"May 6, 1907."

TABB EXCURSUS.

Humphreys[1] Tabb, married Joanne. Issue: (2) Thomas[3] Tabb. (2) Thomas[3] Tabb married Martha. Issue: (3) Humphreys[3]; (4) Thomas[3]; (5) John[3]; (6) William[3]; (7) Edward[3]; (8) Elizabeth[3].

4.   Thomas[3] Tabb married Elizabeth Moss. Issue: (9) John[3]; (10) Thomas4: (11) Henry, and others.

9.   John* Tabb married, first. Mary Sclater. Issue: (17) Thomas5; (18) John5; (19) Elizabeth5; (20) Rachel5; (21) William5; (22) Joanna5; (23) Sarah; (24) Martha; (25) Mary, married Westwood Armistead. (9) John Tabb's will dated November 26, 1761.

(10) Thomas* Tabb married Mary Armistead, daughter of Anthony Armistead (son of Anthony and grandson of William[1] Armistead). He left six children according to will proved in 1736, who, according to the Bible and the will of the widow, Mary Armistead Tabb-Wills-Armistead (she was married three times), were: (29) Elizabeth5, born 1726: (30) John®, born November 15, 1728; (31) Thomas5, born December 18, 1730; (32) Mary, born December 24, 1732; (33) Rachel, born February 1. 1734; (34) martha, born April 27, 1738. Mary Armistead Tabb married, second, mathew Wills, of Warwick. Third marriage about 1762 to Robert Armistead, of Elizabeth City County.

(10) Thomas4 Tabb, who married Mary Armistead, was brother of (9) John* Tabb, whose daughter, Mary, married Westwood Armistead.

(1) Humphrey[1] Tabb patented a thousand acres in Elizabeth City County in 1637-'38-'56. In 1651 he had a grant for 1,000 acres in Northumberland County. He was burgess for Elizabeth City in 1652. Died before 1662, as in that year the grant of 900 acres on Harris Creek Elizabeth City County was reentered in the name of Thomas

Tabb, "son and heir of Humphrey Tabb, deceased."

3. Humphrey[3], "eldest son" of (2) Thomas[2] Tabb, dying without issue, left 3.313 acres to William Armistead, his executor.

(9) John* Tabb was captain, colonel, justice, sheriff, member of House of Burgesses from Elizabeth City County. His will dated November 26, 1761. He married Mary Sclater, daughter of Rev. James Sclater, of Charles Parish, York County. His daughter, (52) Mary Tabb married Westwood Armistead.

4. Thomas[3] Tabb, grandfather of (52) Mary Tabb, who married Westwood Armistead, was brother of (5) John[3] Tabb, who married Martha Hand. Issue: (49) Thomas Tabb, of Amelia, "Clay Hill," one of the richest merchants of Virginia, and (50) Edward Tabb, of Gloucester, Va. Thomas Tabb, In his will, proved 1769, gives to his daughter, Mary Marshall T., wife of Col. Robert Bolling, of Dinwiddie County, ten thousand pounds, current money.

Mary Armistead, who married (10) Thomas Tabb4, was the daughter of (83) Anthony* Armistead and Anne, his wife.

(83) Anthony4, son of (3) Anthony[3] and Hannah Ellison.

(3) Anthony[3], son of William the emigrant.

(169) Westwood5 Armistead, who married Mary Tabb, was the son of (83) Anthony* Armistead and second wife, Elizabeth Westwood.

Edward Tabb, of Gloucester County, married Lucy Todd, of Toddsbury, Gloucester, and had Martha, who married Rev. Armistead Smith, and Elizabeth, who married John Patterson, of Poplar Grove, Alathews County.

ANTHONY ARMISTEAD LINE.

KIQUOTAN, OR KICOUGHTAN, ELIZABETH CITY COUNTY, VA.

Before speaking of Kiquotan, or Elizabeth City County, where the Armisteads first settled, we will again quote from Governor Henry A. Wise's *Seven Deeades of the Union,* in regard to the Peninsula, of which Elizabeth City County is a part:

"It is a land of genial climate, of generous soil, of majestic rivers, of fruitful fertility of fields, and of forests of richest frondage. Above all, distinguished for its men and women. It was settled by a race or stock of families the like of which will rarely be seen again—so manly, refined, so intelligent, so spirited, proud, self-reliant, independent, strong, so fresh and free. The family names of this Peninsular known to honor and fame are countless — the Armisteads, Bollings, Byrds, Blairs, Burwells, Amblers, Carters, Cloptons, Christians, Carys, Dandridges, Digges, Fontaines, Gregorys, Harrisons, Coles, Innesses, Mallorys, Nicholases, Randolphs, Pages, Nelsons, Kennons, Griffins, Barrons, Sclaters, Shields, Dudleys, Tuckers, Tylers, Tabbs, Tazewells, Wallers, Peachys, Saunders, Wythes, Lightfoots, Semples, Bassetts, and others no less known, from whom have sprung names of note in every Southern and Western State, as well as in other parts of Virginia.

"There was no place on earth where the word 'domesticity — sacred to the household gods — meant more than on the plantations of the Peninsula. To guest and family alike, they were homes of unaffected, liberal, cordial welcome.

"The mother of these domestic scenes, when an affair of State came on, was a queenly woman — commanding, stately, whether at the table or in the salon, at the dinner, or in the dance; she could talk of stately matters with bewitching wisdom, or play her smiling, classic wit or humor, like a fairy, and command men to do her homage, due only to dignity, sense, sweetness, and grace. There were duties as well as pleasures; they could arrange the warping bars, turn the spindles, wind the skein, darn the stockings, and, walking over floors of waxen cleanness, see to pantry and laundry. Ruling and providing for a large retinue of servants, the seamstresses kept busy cutting out and making clothes, ministering to the sick. The plantation, a little kingdom in itself." * * *

"Kicoughtan was the original Indian name. In 1619, when William Capps and William Tucker represented it in the House of Burgesses, they were commissioned to sue that body for a change of name. Elizabeth City was the name given in honor of the daughter of King James I. The legal name of Hampton dates from 1705; named in honor of the Earl of Southampton. We find a permanent English settlement at Kequotan as early as 1610. The Parish of Elizabeth City is the most ancient in continuous existence, while Hampton itself is the oldest continuous settlement in America, and has earned, because of its struggles and vicissitudes, the soubriquet 'Game Cock Town.'

"The oldest free school in the country still exists in this Parish, without a break in its history since 1634 — the Syms-Eaton School. There is in the keeping of this Parish, and in constant use, a communion service which was made in London, England, in 1618.

This service was given by Mrs. Mary Robinson, of London, to a church endowed by her in Smith's Hundred, Va., later called Southampton Hundred. The first church in Hampton was built on the Glebe land, now a part of the Tabb estate, in 1610; the site is marked by a clump of trees just north of the road between Hampton and Old Point.

"The ancient town of Hampton, when an Indian settlement, contained 'eighteen shanties situated on about three acres of land — now the Soldiers' Home — a beautiful point jutting out into the Elizabeth River," which made a little bay or inlet between another point — now Old Point Comfort.

"Extending back from the water were Indian cornfields, two or three thousand acres in extent, cut into convenient peninsulars by the many bays and creeks that made into the mainland; 'a pleasant plaine, with wholesome aire, having plenty of springs of sweet water with pasture and marsh and apt places for vines, corn and gardens.'"

In the year 1619 were brought over the three old pieces of communion plate now in use in St. John's Church, Hampton. They bear the hall mark of 1618. This plate has been in use longer than any other communion plate in the United States. In 1620 the first Guest House or hospital was erected. These houses were one hundred and eighty feet long, sixteen broad, with twenty-five beds for the shelter and recuperation of newly arrived immigrants after a weary sea voyage.

Probably the most interesting papers that have been preserved of the early colonial period are "The lists of the living and dead in Virginia, February 16, 1624, and the musters of the inhabitants in Virginia, 1625." The list of 1624 gives a total of three hundred and forty-nine for Elizabeth City. After a lapse of nearly three hundred years, to call the name of nearly every man, woman and child in the parish, with the date of their arrival and the name of the ship in which they came, brings us in close touch with those early days. "But the toll of English lives that was paid is appalling," Alexander Brown says: "Before 1631 more than three thousand English had died; among them as honorable people as any in our annals." The foundation of the first church, erected in 1610, was unearthed in 1910 by Mr. J. Heffelfinger, whose historical address at the three hundredth anniversary of St. John's Church, Hampton, July of the same year, adds a chapter of unusual interest to the history of Virginia. The dimensions of the foundation are fifty-three feet six inches long, by twenty-three wide. Old Pembrooke was the next church built, and then St. John's, a flourishing church with five hundred and sixty-six communicants. The sites of the first two are owned by St. John's.

(The above facts are gleaned from Mr. Heffelfinger's address.)

William Armistead landed here in 1634-35, and settled here or near by, as we hear of him as vestryman in 1646. In the History Building at Jamestown Exposition (1907) the Elizabeth City vestry book was opened at the following entry;

'I, William Armistead, do promise to be conformable to the Doctrine and Discipline of the Church of England, as by Law established.

"WILL^M ARMISTEAD."

Evidently, both Williams were vestrymen of the first churcn, 1610, as the Pembroke Church, one mile west of present St. John's, was "new in 1667, while the old one was still standing" (Rev. Reverdy Estill, D. D., rector of St. John's). The present St. John's dates from 1727. From 1646, William Armistead, to 1848, Westwood Armistead, there have been vestrymen of the name in the parish, to say nothing of parishes in other counties, all which indicates that they were from the first loyal supporters of the Church.

THE VESTRIES OF COLONIAL TIMES.

"The vestries were the depositories of power in Virginia. They not only governed the churches, but made laws in the House of Burgesses, levied taxes, etc. The Councillors, too, were vestrymen. In the history of the vestries we have the origin not only of that religious liberty which later developed in Virginia, but also of the determined stand taken by the Episcopalians on behalf of civil liberty. The vestries, the intelligent moral strength of the land, had been trained up in defense of them rights against Governors, Bishops, Kings, Queens, and Cabinets."

"The vestries were the ruling men of the parishes—men of property and education. In communications to England, the clergy spoke of them as aristocratic bodies—twelve lords or masters of the parishes. Even Mr. Thomas Jefferson and Mr. Wythe were vestrymen—'they *must he among the rulers.*'"

The principal seats of the Anthony Armistead family were on Back River. In 1697, Col. John Armistead, of Gloucester County, made a deed (which is on record in Elizabeth City County) in which styling himself "brother and heir" of William A., deceased, and "son and Heire" of William Armistead, of Elizabeth City County, Gent., "he confirms to Anthony Armistead, his brother, all land on Back River, in said County, of which his father died seised." "Willocks" was the name of one of the estates, a very large tract, only the burying ground of which is now in the possession of this family.

Anthony Armistead, brother of John A., and son of the emigrant, had three sons, William, Anthony, and Robert. To William was given that part of the estate on an arm of the river known as "The Brick House" tract. He probably built the house, as his descendants lived there till about 1861; about 1850 it was known as "The Haunted House," as gruesome tales were told of the place.

A private road divides "The Brick House" estate from "Willocks" and "The Mill" (a tide mill) which was one of the places owned by Anthony A. "Willocks" faces on the county road; the land lays on plateau gradually rising higher, and sloping on up, including a woods, which was once a forest, until it slopes again to the broad water front of the river, flowing into the bay. This was the country home of 178 Robert Armistead and Elizabeth Smith, his wife; he also owned a home in Hampton, at the corner of King and Queen Street. Besides, he owned "Bay Tree Plantation," or "Back Creek," several miles from Yorktown; this he bought of Thomas Smith, father of his wife. Here several of his children were born (see Bible record).

NOTE.—Father often told us of "The Mill" place during the War of 1812—he was the youngest child, only four years old, so it was more from what the older ones told him, than what he remembered himself—of how everything was manufactured on the place. There was a cooper shop, a shoemaker's shop, a weaving room, spinning wheels, carpenter shop where rush and split-bottom chairs, etc., were made; the mill, always busy. As we stood on the bridge this summer over the inlet where the tide rushes in to the mill, and looked at the heavy blocks of stone—part of the foundation of the mill—memory was bu.sy with the past; the wooings and weddings; once two weddings within a week; the births, the deaths, the merry goings-on in the servants' quarters, the tum-tum of the banjo, the weird singsong moaning over the dead; the harvest song in the field. All the concomitants of plantation life passed in review. The old house was gone! The present one is built on the foundation of the old one, or certainly the old English-made bricks were used in the building, for we made a close examination of everything relating to the olden days.

As before stated, Anthony Armistead, son of the emigrant, had three sons — William, whose descendants inherited "The Brick House" tract; Anthony, "Willocks" and "The Mill," and Robert, who inherited "Buckroe" an original Armistead patent. (This information comes from Major Edward Armistead Semple, the surveyor of the county.) It is beautifully situated on the Chesapeake Bay, indented by an arm of Mill Creek, near where the old dwelling stood; nothing left now but the Englishmade brick foundation, over grown with bushes and vines. We brought one of the bricks away with us. It was, and still is, a very large tract; now a fashionable summer resort on the bay side, laid out in villa sites; many attractive summer homes are already built. An electric car line connects it with Hampton.

Robert Armistead, of Buckroe, was the ancestor of Mary Armistead, who married Governor Tyler. Buckroe is spoken of as early as 1623-'4; at that time it was a name designating a section of country containing a number of plantations; later the name was confined to one plantation.

The Mill plantation was known as "The Mill" as early as 1695, as is shown by land office records: "Captain Anthony Armistead in 1676 patented 928 acres on northwest side of Back River; in 1695, 150 acres on the head of his own land, ac 'The Mill,' thence and adjoining the land of Captain Henry Jenkins; Captain William Armistead, 1696, 130 acres adjoining his father, besides 750 other acres, Back Creek and Bay Tree Plantation, near Yorktown; the former spoken of in family Bible, the latter in a deed of Thomas Smith to Robert Armistead." Mr. T. T. Hudgins, clerk of the court at Yorktown, writes the following:

"Bay Tree Plantation is in the lower end of Crab Neck, York County, and extended in colonial times from Back Creek to Chisman's Plantation, and fronted on Chesapeake Bay, hence the name 'Bay Trees,' and is now so called. The bay front of the farm was and now is studded with pine trees. Temple farm is about one mile southeast from Yorktown, with a frontage of three-quarters of a mile on York River; Wormeley's Creek is on the south-east of it. There is neck of land called Goodwynne's Neck, between Temple Farm and Bay Tree Plantation, distant from each other about three miles."

All this tract. Temple Parm and Bay Tree, or Back Creek

Plantation were owned by Lawrence Smith; Elisabeth Smith's girlhood home, as several of her first children were born there.

Anthony Armistead was County Lieut, under Lord Effingham (Lord Howard) Governor of Virginia; he married Hannah Ellison, daughter of Dr. Ellison, of James City County. Dr. Ellison was leading Burgess in 1656-'59-'60-'6i-'62-'63, witn rank of Captain. "We find among the lawyers of York County 1646, William Hockaday, Francis Willis, Thomas Bushrod, and Dr. Robert Ellison; all these were trusted and tried men." The will of Dr. Henry Waldron, 1657, bequeaths "all my Library and Books, whatsoever in this country, and my horse together with my chests of physical means" to Captain (Doctor) Robert Ellison of James City Co.

On the fly leaf of one of the record books (1671-1676) In York County clerk's office, is written in large, bold hand: "Hannah Armistead IS One of ye handsomed Girls in Virgin Hannah For Ever!" Probably, Hannah daughter of (5) Anthony Armistead and Hannah Elliason. He died before 1728. Their daughter, Judith Armistead, married John West of West Point, Va., son of Maj. John West, who was the son of Captain John West, brother of Lord Delaware. The license for their marriage was obtained in Elizabeth City October 15, 1698, and there is a deed, dated July 18, 1698, of Captain Anthony Armistead and Hannah, his wife, to their "Son-in-law, John West, for 200 acres in New Kent (King William) given to said Hannah by her father. Mr. Robert Ellison, of James City County, deceased. Issue of Judith Armistead and John West: Charles West, who inherited 4,000 acres in Pamunkey Neck, adjoining Delaware, commonly called West Point.

VIRGINIA LINE.

The son of Sir Thomas[1] West, Lord Delaware, was Hon. Col. John West[2], 1590-1659, Governor and Captain-General of Virginia, born in Hampshire, England; B. A. Magdalen, Oxon, 1613; member Colonial Council of Virginia twenty-nine years, 1630-1659 [on his mother's side he was descended through the Plantagenets; the Segraves; Thomas Mowbray, Duke of Norfolk; John Howard, Duke of Norfolk, who fell on Boswell Field; Thomas Howard, Duke of Norfolk and Earl of Surrey, victor at Flodden Field; Mary Boleyn, daughter of Sir Thomas Boleyn and sister of Queen Anne Boleyn; and the Carys from King Edward] ; married Anne , and had one child.

20. Col. John[3] West, of "West Point," Va., born at "Bellefield," Chyskiack, Va., 1633 (the first English child born on York River), died 1691, senior justice Colonial General Court; sat on court-marial which tried the rebels in Bacon's time; member House of Burgesses; married Unity, daughter of Major Joseph Croshaw [member House of Burgesses, 1659-'60; J. P.; major of militia, etc., etc.], of "Poplar Neck," York County, Va., and had:

John4, Nathaniel4, Thomas4 and a daughter Anne4, who married Henry Fox.

Col. John* West married Judith Armistead.

Elizabeth Elliason, mother of Hannah Elliason, who married Major Anthony Armistead, is mentioned as one of the sponsors for William Randolph, baptized September 12, 1659, in James City. This register is written on the margin of the Randolph Bible "in John Randolph's hand."

(82) William Armistead4, son of (5) Anthony[3] and Hannah, of Elizabeth City County, was Burgess in 1693-1702, and major of the militia. He married several times before November 20, 1696; first, Hannah Hines, born July 1, 1673 (New Pocosin Register), daughter of Thomas Hines and Hannah his wife. In 1696 Hannah, "wyff of William Armistead, made a power of attorney to her father-in-law, Anthony Armistead. Maj. Armistead married lastly, Rebecca Moss, dau. of Edward Moss of York Co., whose will was proved in 1716. Maj. Armisteads will dated Jan. 5th, 1716-15, proved Feb. 15th, 1715-16, shows that he had seven sons and two daughters (one infant my wife now bears), Hannah (as shown by other records), named in her grandmother, Hanned Elliason Armistead's will, was the first wife of Miles Cary, of Pear-Tree Hall. Their issue as appearing in Judith Robinson's will, (1) John Cary, born about 1745; died 1795; married first, Sally Sclater ; second, Susannah Armistead, dau. of Gill Armistead of New Kent. (2) Robert Cary. (3) Rebecca Cary, who married Rev. Aliles Seldon. (4) Elizabeth Cary, married Benjamin Watkins. Second daughter, Judith, born after her father's will, named in her grandmother's will, married John Robinson, jr. Her will dated March 6th, 1768, proved Jan. 27th, 1769, names her sister, Hannah Armistead Cary's children, and her son Starkey Robinson."

(1) Anthony Armistead, of Yorkshire, England, married Frances Thompson. Issue; (2) William Armistead[2] married Anne. Issue: (3) William, (4) John[3] (5) Anthony[3], (6) Frances[3].

5. Anthony[3] Armistead married Hannah Ellison. Issue; (82)

William4 A., (83 Anthony4 A., (84) Robert4 A., (85) Judith4 A., (86) Hannah4 A.

(83) Anthony4 Armistead married, first, Anne. Issue: Elizabeth A., Mary A. married Thomas Tabb. Alarried, second, Elizabeth Westwood. Issue: (169) Westwood5 Armistead married Mary Tabb. Issue: (172) Westwood6 A, (173) Elizabeth A. (174) Mary A. (172) Westwood6 A. married Mary Jenkins. Issue: (178) Robert7 A., (179) Westwood* A. died unmarried. (172) Westwood A's will, made Jan. 18, 1782, proved June 22, 1786, names only two sons. (173) Elizabeth Armistead, sister of (172) Westwood A., married Thomas Smith of York County, about 1760. Issue: Elizabeth Smith and Mary Smith. Elizabeth Smith married her cousin (178) Robert Armistead; Mary Smith married Mr. Young of Scotland. Issue: Thomas and Charles.

(169) Westwood Armistead who married Mary Tabb, had one son, (172) Westwood A., and two daughters, (173) Elizabeth and (174) Mary. Elizabeth A. married Thomas Smith of York; Mary A. married Dr. Matthew Pope of Yorktown, surgeon in the English Army. During the Revolution he became surgeon in the American Army.

NOTE. — During the Revolutionary War the editor's grandmother, Elizabeth Armistead, was visiting her cousin, Robert Armistead, in Hanover County, who niarried Louisa Westwood. Their home was on Elk Creek. General Tarletan made a raid in the neighborhood, and hearing that Dr. Pope was at the home of Mr. Armistead, entered the house. Our grandmother, about twelve years old, was coming down the stairway and halted midway at the approach of the officers. They demanded: "Where is Dr. Pope?" She calmly replied, "I do not know." One of the officers took out his pistol, and pointing it at her, said: "You do know! and if you do not tell me, I will shoot you!" Looking him fearlessly in the eye, she replied: "I do not know; but if I did, I would not tell you!" They eyed each other for a second, then turning his pistol, he fired it in the ceiling, saying: "You have a d sight of courage!" and left the house. This story is told just as the editor's father told it to her.

After the death of his wife, Mary Armistead, Dr. Pope married Betty, daughter of Philip Grymes of Brandon, Aliddlesex County. There were no children by either marriage.

Will of Dr. Matthew Pope of Yorktown, bequeaths to his brother, John Pope of Goudhart, County of Kent, England, to his sister Anne Pope, to his sister Elizabeth Pope, to Mary, second daughter of

General Nelson of York, house, furniture, lots. in Yorktown; two negroes to Philip Nelson; two negroes to Elizabeth, wife of Mann Page of Gloucester; to Dr. Augustine Smith of Yorktown, his surgical instruments; the rest of his estate to his wife, Betty Pope, and her heirs; proved 1792.

The portrait of Dr. Pope's first wife. Mary, hung on the wall of one of the chambers at our home in Hampton. We children had a kind of fear of our father's "Aunt Pope" because her eyes seemed to follow us, to be watching us; a slim, stately young dame, in green satin, pointed waist, square neck gown. A spirited high-bred face, with arched eye brows, broad white forehead, from which her hair was piled in lofty pompadour. The portrait had been sabre thrust by the British. When our father hurriedly left Hampton at the beginning of the War in 1861, the portrait was cut from the frame and taken to Williamsburg. Later, when we lived in Richmond, he took it to Elder, the artist, to remount; amid the exciting scenes of that period it was forgotten, and when called for it could not be found.

(172) Westwood Armistead (Westwood5, Anthony4, Anthony[3], William[2], Anthony[1]) married Mary Jenkins. (172) Westwood was under age at his father's death, in 1756. His father, (169) Westwood A. married Mary Tabb, and had only (172) Westwood and two daughters, Elizabeth A. and Mary A. Mary Jenkins, wife of (172) Westwood A. was the daughter of Henry Jenkins and Mary Curie. Mary Curie and William Roscoe Wilson Curie were the children of Wilson Curie and Priscilla Aleade, who was a daughter of Andrew Aleade and Susannah Everard. whose romantic marriage is so quaintly told by Bishop Aleade, Vol. I., p. 292. William Roscoe Wilson Curie was a distinguished patriot of the Revolution.

DESCENDANTS OF (178) ROBERT ARMISTEAD AND ELIZABETH

SMITH.

(1) Anthony Armistead married Frances Thompson of Kirk Deighton, Yorkshire, England. Issue: (2) William A., the emigrant.

(2) William A. married Anne . Issue: (3) Wil liam[3] A., (4) John[3] A., (5) Anthony[3] A., (6) Frances[3] A.

(5) Anthony[3] Armistead married Hannah Ellison. Issue, among others: (83) Anthony[3] Armistead, who married Elizabeth Westwood. Issue, among others: .

(169) Westwood4 Armistead, who married Mary Tabb. Issue :

(172) Westwood5 Armistead, (173) Elizabeth5 Armistead, (174) Mary³ Armistead.

(172) Westwood Armistead married Mary Jenkins. (172) Westwood A. made his will January 18, 1782, proved June 22, 1786. It names wife Mary Jenkins and only two children: (178) Robert A. and (179) Westwood, died unmarried. A student at William and Mary College, 1758.

The following is copied from (178) Robert Armistead's family Bible:

Robert Armistead was married to Elisabeth Smith, Jan. 8th, 1789, being in the 23rd year of his age, and his wife, in the 22nd. He was born August 9th, 1766, and she was born Aug. 22nd, 1767, she died Jan. 30th, 1849, 81 years and five months and eight days.

(CHILDREN.)

Westwood Smith Armistead was born June 17th, 1790, on Thursday, at about seven o'clock in the afternoon, at Back Creek, York County, and departed this life Jan. 25th, 1848.

Maria Smith Armistead was born Aug. 18th, 1792, on Saturday, about seven o'clock in the morning, in Norfolk, and died on the 2nd day of July, 1840.

Eliza Armistead was born May 26th, 1794, on Monday about nine o'clock in the morning, in Norfolk.

Louisa Young Armistead was born in Hampton, March 20th, 1796, about seven o'clock Sunday morning, and died in July, , 1832.

Thomas Smith Armistead was born March 30th, 1799, Saturday evening at The Alill in the county of Elizabeth City.

Helen Smith and Emily Smith Armistead (twins) were born at Hampton on Thursday, Jan. 22nd, 1802, in the morning. Helen died March 20th, 1838. Emily Smith died March 1st, 1842, in Hampton, in the fortieth year of her age.

Susan Smith Armistead was born at Hampton, on Sunday, July 22nd, 1804, and died at Back Creek, York Co. Oil Friday 6th day of Sept. 1805, at four o'clock in the afternoon, age 13 months and five days. Her death was supposed to be in consequence of croup, which appeared Wednesday before her death.

Harriet Armistead was born at Hampton, on Tuesday Aug. 26th, about one o'clock in the morning, in the year 1806, and died the 20th day of Oct. 1834.

Robert Augustus Armistead was born at Hampton on Saturday, seventh day of ,May 1808, in the morning."

Robert Armistead departed this life about ten o'clock P. AI. on Sunday 31st of August 1817, age fifty-one years and twenty-two days.

Westwood Smith Armistead, son of Robert A. and Elizabeth Smith, his wife, married Louisa Moore Todd of Smithfield. Isle de Wight Co., Va., on the first day of May, 1813. She was born Nov. 3rd, 1794 (he was twenty-three, and she was nieteen). Issue;

Westwood Todd Armistead, born 26th Jan. 1814, about seven o'clock P. AI. at Smithfield, and departed this life 27th Jan. Oct. 1815.

Robert Smith Armistead was born in Smithfield, 2nd day of April 1815, and departed this life the 5th day of Nov. in the same year.

Nancy Todd Armistead born at Hampton 10th Feb. 1817, between eleven and twelve o'clock P. M.

Elisabeth Smith Armistead, born at Hampton on the 23rd of July 1818, about seven o'clock P. AI.

Louisa Moore Armistead was born about 1819-20. She married, the second time Nov. 24th, 1848, Richard Booker Hope, son of George Hope of Hampton, and his second wife, Patsy Booker, to whom he was married about 1815. Issue, nine children — four died young. The following married and had issue:

Elisabeth Sheild Hope married Charles Page Edwards of Portsmouth. Issue: Louisa, Ruth, Henry, Charles, Alice.

Ruth Vernon Hope married Abel Erastus Kellam of Princess Anne Co. Issue: two children — one died in infancy, the other Hope Kellam born 1882, was educated at Randolph-Macon College, and afterwards at the University of Virigina. Ruth Vernon Hope (the mother) died in 1884.

Nancy Armistead Hope married James Nicholson of Portsmouth. Issue: Nancy, James, Elizabeth.

Samuel Sheild Hope married, first, Eliza Peek of Hampton in 1884. Issue: Samuel Sheild, Hope, Jr., born 1886. He married, second. Mary Barnes of Eagle Point, Va.

Nancy Todd Armistead, dau. of Westwood Smith Armistead, married Rev. James Duval Coulling of the Methodist Church, June 23rd, 1841, son of James Matthias Coulling and Mary Duval, his wife. Issue: James Westwood, who died when he was eight years old.

Louisa Todd Coulling, a woman of high culture and splendid mind, now living (1908) in Tazewell, Va., with her half brother. Judge

Sidney Alatthias Baxter Coulling. Nancy Todd Armistead Coulling died August, 1855, and is buried at Willocks, the Armistead family burying ground. Rev. James D. Coulling married, 1857, second. Mary Selina Baxter, daughter of Hon. Sidney Smith Baxter, for many years Attorney-General of the State. Issue: one son, Sidney Alatthias Baxter Coulling; he was made Judge before he was twenty-four years old; married Lina P. Watts, daughter of Joseph R. Watts and Martha Drake of Norfolk. Issue: S. M. B. Coulling, JR., Louis Roberdeau C., Martha Drake, and Mary Selina C. (twins).

Mary Duval, mother of James Duval Coulling, was the daughter of Benjamin Duval, of Richmond, one of the directors to locate the Public Square upon which to erect the Capitol and Governor's Alansion, when the seat of government was removed from Williamsburg in 1780. As early as 1752 he was vestryman, warden, sheriff, and collector of the parish, and his name is connected with all the principal events of the early city of Richmond. The family are of old Huguenot stock, that came to Virginia in the seventeenth century.

Hon. Sidney Baxter was the son of Dr. George Baxter, founder of Washington College, now Washington and Lee, Lexington, Va.

Elisabeth Smith Armistead, daughter of Westwood S. Armistead, married Dr. Samuel Reade Sheild,'eldest son of Robert Sheild, of York County, and Mary Reade, his wife. Robert Sheild was justice of the peace for York County, Member of the House of Delegates. Robert Sheild was the son of the Rev. Samuel Sheild and Mary Hansford, his wife, married July, 1775. Rev. Samuel Sheild entered William and Mary College 1769; passed through the grammar grade and entered philosophy schools in 1771, and m 1773 received from the Faculty one of the two medals established by Lord Botetourt. Took orders in the Church in 1774: was minister of Drysdale Parish, Caroline County; later became minister of York-Hampton Parish. Issue of Elisabeth Smith Armistead and Samuel Reade Sheild;

1. Mallory Sheild, physician, married Florence W. Garret of Hampton. Issue: two daughters—Mary and Mallory Sheild; the latter married Blair Pegram Wilson, of Smithfield, Va. Mary married Harvey L. Wilson, now of Norfolk. These Wilsons are not related.

2. Mary Sheild died unmarried.

3. Nannie Sheild, married John Milton Willis, of Hampton, son of William Willis and Mrs. Virginia Banks Lattimer (widow). Issue of John AI. Willis and Nannie Sheild: John. W., Royal W., Edmund W., Elsie Willis.

Maria Smith Armistead, daughter of Robert Armistead and Elisabeth Smith, and Thomas Crawford were married at "The Mill," August 28th, 1814; she in twenty-third year of her age, he twenty-five.

The Crawfords were a Scottish family, noted for their commanding presence, great stature, and undaunted bravery; straight forward and honest.

Bishop Meade's *Old Churches and Families:* "There were three churches in Portsmouth Parish—one in the town of Portsmouth in 1762 on a lot in the center of the town, given by William Crawford, Esq., the original proprietor of the land on Which the town is built." In Henning's *Statutes,* we find Act XXIV: "In General Assembly at the college in Williamsburg, Eeb. 1752—in the reign of George II—Gov. Dinwiddie in Virginia ; an act for establishing the town of Portsmouth * * * that William Crawford, Gentleman, has laid out a parcel of land on the south side of Elisabeth River, opposite the town of Norfolk, into one hundred and twenty lots, commodious streets, places for court house—market—public exchanges * * * for a town by the name of Portsmouth."

Maria Smith Armistead and Thomas Crawford, Esq., had one son, William, born May 13th, 1816. "This William Crawford, educated at William and Mary, was a noted teacher of Hampton, Va., in or about 1850; was known far and wide as a mathematician, and was prominently named for a professorship in U. S. Military Academy at West Point, N. Y. This fact was embodied in letters of recommendation which the undersigned found among papers in an old chest in Hampton before the war." (Signed Geo. W. Armistead.)

William Crawford died unmarried in 1855 of yellow fever. Quoting the words of one of the most intelligent citizens of Hampton, "William Crawford was considered the best educated, most cultivated gentleman in this section—in mathematics he had no equal."

After Thomas Crawford's death, his widow, Maria Armistead Crawford, married Col. Christopher Pryor—his estate adjoining the Armistead estates on Back River. Issue by this marriage: Harriet Pryor, Scaife Pryor. After her death, he married again; lived in Alabama. Maria Armistead Pryor's brother, Robert Augustus Armistead, sent for the children, Harriet and Scaife, and raised them with his own children in Hampton. Harriet P. died unmarried after she was grown. Major Edwayd Armistead Semple, of Hampton, whose father, Dr. Semple, married the sister of Col. Pryor, Christiana, said that Scaife Pryor went to Waco, Texas, when he was quite a youth.

NOTE. — Aunt Maria Armistead Crawford Pryor was educated in Norfolk. She had a remarkable talent for music. Hers was the first piano brought to Hampton. In an old outhouse at our home in Hampton was a large black oak chest, filled with what was then called rubbish — now would be treasures. There were piles of her music, printed on colored paper — pink, yellow, blue; also manuscript music composed and written by her — mostly songs.

When she was dying, amidst the hushed stillness of the house was heard the snapping, clanging of metal strings. The family looked wonderingly at each other; then silently accepted this as one of the traditional "death tokens" that generally preceded the death of one of the family. Gruesome tales were told us children of these same "death tokens" — sometimes a light, a falling of a portrait, noise of falling furniture, visions of spirits gliding through the house, silken rustle of a dress down the stairway. Several days after Aunt Maria's death the lid of the piano was lifted, and there lay the strings in a tangled mass — broken and twisted. The older ones of the family have told of seeing this little spindle-legged piano up in the garret, as up there was also a queer shaped string-instrument, called a lute. Another sister, Eliza Armistead, was passionately fond of music. She was petite and merry, even to old age, when she would delight us young folks playing all kinds of old-fashioned tunes on the accordion, which was a new instrument in those days. Our mother often spoke of the beautiful lace and needle work that our father's sisters did. She gave the editor a lace cap made by Aunt Helen for her when a baby, that would do credit to a professional. It was done on the finest net.

Thomas Smith Armistead, son of Robert A. and Elisabeth Smith, married Amanda Dewees, a daughter of Mary Aliles and Andrew Dewees, a merchant of Baltimore, October i, 1830. After her death, he married Mary Getty, daughter of John A. Getty, of Hampton, February, 1848. Issue by first marriage:

Andrew Dewees Armistead married Dora (daughter of John Armistead and Clarissa A. Barnum, of Mathews County), December, 1870. Issue: Ellen, married Mr. George Steele of Rockingham, N, C.; John, Josephine, Edwin, Eva, married Dr, Maxwell Foster of Gloucester County, Va.; Clara, Mary Todd. Andrew Armistead was captain of the Alathews Artillery; served through the whole war, and surrendered at Appomattox, Andrew A. was an A. M. of the University of Virginia and a prominent educator.

2. Amanda Dewees Armistead was educated at Miss Willard's School in Troy, N. Y.; married, July 16, 1863, at Halifax H., Theodoric James Chambliss, son of William Over Chambliss, of Sussex County. Issue; Ann, Mary, William, Dora. Mary and William died young. Anna Armistead Chambliss married, August 27, 1891, Andrew B. Winfield, son of Dr. John A. Winfield, of Sussex County. Issue: one son, Bryant Dewees Winfield. Dora Armistead Chambliss married, June i, 1892, Edwin J. Freeman, son of John Freeman, of Sussex County. Issue: Lewis Armistead F., Edwin Chambliss F., Robert Armistead F. and Mary Dewees.

Alexander Armistead, at the breaking out of the war, enlisted as a private in the Wythe Rifles of Hampton, Thirty-second Virginia Regiment, Corse's Brigade, Pickett's Division. Was killed at the battle of Sharpsburg, September 18, 1863.

Westwood Armistead, though but a youth, served through the whole war in his brother Andrew's company. The following is from a letter of Mrs. Amanda Armistead Chambliss, widow of Theodoric Chambliss

"Mr. Theodoric Chambliss' grandfather served in the Revolutionary War as colonel, I think. He had his old commission, with the State seal of North Carolina on it. During the Civil War, Dr, Abbott, of Massachusetts, a surgeon of the U. S. A., rescued it from the hands of raiders as they were destroying the books and papers at our home. He thinking, from the State seal, that it was an important paper, took it home with him, and after the war returned it to us, thinking we must value such relics of the olden time. It was burned eleven years ago when I lost my house by fire. So I cannot be positive what rank he held or what branch of the service he was in; I think it was colonel."

Issue by the second marriage of Thomas Armistead with Mary Getty: Mary, Thomas, William.

Thomas married Mary Owen, of Halifax County, daughter of James Alunroe Owen and Lucy, his wife, February 20, 1879, at Crystal Hill. Issue: Henrietta, Carrie, Thomas Alexander, Owen, Mary.

William A. married Susan Bridges, of Selma, Alabama, daughter of John A. Bridges. Issue: Lidia Armistead and William Alexander A.

Carrie Armistead married, August 19, 1902, Thomas Edward Hodges, of South Boston, Halifax County. Issue: Elizabeth, born July 13, 1903.

Westwood A. by the first marriage, and Mary A. by last marriage, are unmarried.

Eliza Armistead of Elizabeth City County, daughter of Robert Armistead and Elisabeth Smith, his wife, born March 20, 1790, married, August 31, 1814, John Robinson Todd of Smithfield. Isle de Wight County, Va., at "The Alill," three days after her sister Maria married Thomas Crawford.

NOTE. — The editor heard an old aunt describe "Mr. Todd as a typical gallant of that time; very erect, dressy and proud in his bearing. She recalled him in his knee trousers, shoe-buckles and buff waistcoat, when he would come over to Hampton at the time he was courting Eliza Armistead."

This family of Todds came from Bermuda. Mallory Todd, the first of the family, camie to Virginia about 1760. He married Anne Robinson, daughter of John Robinson and Martha Aloore. Issue: John Robinson T., of Smithfield; Merrit T. and Mallory T., of Norfolk; Mary Moore T., Angelina T., Anne T., and Louisa Moore T., who married Westwood Smith Armistead, of Hampton, brother of Eliza Armistead who married John Robinson Todd.

1. John Robinson Todd married Eliza Armistead.
2. Mary Moore Todd married James B. Southall, of Smithfield.
3. Angelina Todd married William Dickson, of England.
4. Anne Todd married James Tucker, of Bermuda.
5. Merritt and
6. Mallory Todd, of Norfolk.
7. Louisa Moore Todd married Westwood Smith Armistead.

Eliza Armistead and John Todd had ten children — three daughters and seven sons. Four died in infancy — two later — leaving (1) John Moore Todd, (2) Robinson Armistead Todd, (3) Eliza Dickson Todd, (4) Everard Moore Todd.

John Moore Todd, born October 3, 1815, married Sarah B. Ashton, of Maryland, October, 1831. She was of the family of Ashton known in English history, among whom were statesmen and soldiers of Colonial history.

Sarah B. Ashton was the daughter of Col. Henry Ashton and Cecilia Brown Key, who was the" daughter of Hon. Philip Key, of

Charles County, Maryland; member of Congress from St. Mary's County, Maryland. Col. Henry Ashton was first an M. D., later a lawyer; at the time of his death, 1834, Marshal of the District of Columbia and Supreme Court.

John R. Todd studied for the Episcopal ministry at a theological seminary in Ohio, and was the rector of William and Mary Parish, Maryland, for fifty years. Issue of John Todd and Sarah, his wife:

1. John Key Todd, married Mary Stuart.
2. Cecelia Ashton Todd, married Toanni Dent Starke.
3. Ashton Todd, married Katherine Virginia Small.
4. Eliza Armistead Todd, married John Burdette Ashton.
5. Everard Robinson Todd, married Elizabeth McGill Smith.
6. Sarah Virginia Todd.
7. Caroline Ashton Todd.
8. Helen Todd.

Children of John Key Todd and Mary Stuart, his wife: Nellie Todd, Sallie Todd. '

3 Angelina Todd married William Dickson of England, His son, Mallory Dickson married Diana Southall, the parents of Julia Dickson, who married first, George T. Carroll; married second, Everard Moore Todd.

2. Mary Moore Todd married James Southall, son of Col. Turner Southall of Revolutionary fame. He was prominent also in Church and State affairs. In 1759 succeeded to the estate of his father in Henrico County. His father was Darcy Southall, of Ireland, who came to Virginia in 1720 and settled in Henrico County.* Issue of Mary Moore Todd and James Southall: Turier S., Dr. James S., Nannie S., Angelina S., Diana S.

Turner Southall married Eliza Todd. Issue: Dr. William Dickson S. and Turner Harrison S.

Dr. William D. Southall married, first, Harriet Anne Shelton, of Hanover County. Issue, five children; only the last two lived — Harriet B. S. and William D. S.

Dr. James Southall married Louisa Tazewell, of Richmond. Issue: Mary Southall, who married G. Watson James, of Richmond. Va.

Nannie Southall married Everard Moore Todd, son of John R. Todd and Eliza Armistead, his wife: Issue, five daughters and two sons; the latter died young; Mary T., Diana T., Nannie T., Laura T., Helen T. married Tazewell Taylor Spratley, son of Mary Dickson, daughter of Mallory Dickson and Diana Southall,

Mallory Dickson's sister Anne married Tazewell Taylor, cf Norfolk; another sister, Lina, married Bishop Johns.

Mallory Todd built the old Todd homestead in Smithfield. Here Todds, Southalls and Dicksons for several generations were bo:rn. It is now owned and occupied by the children of Everard Moofe Todd and Nannie Southall, his wife. It was added to by the Southalls, and later, again by Everard Todd; a place of unusual interest, stored as it is with treasures in the way of old mahogany, silver, cut-glass and china, each with a history. Besides they have two beautifully painted miniatures of Mallory Todd and James B. Southall, great-grandparents of the present generation. It was a picture, about twenty years ago, to see their old Mammy Gracie, a tall mulatto, with lofty turban and kerchief, seated at the side of the fireplace, cared for and loved by the second generation she had nursed.

2. Robinson Armistead Todd married Nannie Womble, October, 1852. She died in 1865, leaving two sons—John and Armistead Todd, and two daughters—Nannie Tucker T. and Alice T.

John Todd married Eva Carroll, daughter of George Carroll and Fanny Wren, his wife. His children are:

1. George Carroll Todd, born February 1, 1879.
2. John Robinson Todd, born October 11, 1880.
3. Fanny Wren Todd, born November 26, 1881.
4. Hugh Todd, born March, 1883.
5. Thomas Hardy Todd, born August 1, 1890.

1. George Carroll Todd graduated in law at Columbia College, N. Y., when about twenty-one, with highest honor; now a successful young lawyer of New York City. Married, 1905, Pocahontas Smith, of Markham, Fauquier County, Va., daughter of McGill Smith and Mary Me;redith, his wife, of Winchester, Va. Issue: Mary Meredith Todd, born July, 1906.

Armistead Todd, son of R. A. Todd and Nannie Womble, his wife, married Lily Ferrant, of Norfolk. Issue: Ferrant Todd, Armistead Todd, Alicia Todd.

The two daughters are now unmarried and live in Norfolk with their brother, Armistead Todd.

2. Robinson Armistead Todd married second, July, 1866, his cousin, Angelina Dickson Southall. No Children.

3. Eliza Dickson Todd (sister of Robinson, both children of Eliza Armistead and John Todd) married, October, 1870, her cousin, Dr. William Dickson Southall, of Smithfield. He died March, 1872,

leaving a son William and daughter Hattie by a former marriage.

Eliza Todd was a brilliant belle of ante-bellum days. Her wit, gracious manner, and sunny disposition drew around her a charmed corterie of friends wherever she went. At the White Sulphur, where, with her father, she made one of that brilliant assemblage of noted Southern society; at the old Hygeia, Old Point, or dispensing lavish hospitality at her home, "Old Town," near Smithfield; she died in 1895 at the old Todd mansion.

Everard Moore Todd, son of Eliza Armistead and John Robinson Todd, married Nancy Southall, daughter of Mary Moore Todd and James Southall. She died about 1885. In 1887 he married Mrs. Julia Dickson Carroll, widow of George Thomas Carroll, Issue, one daughter, Julia Dickson Todd. Everard Moore Todd died September 25, 1907. His widow and daughter Julia now reside in Norfolk.

Everard Moore Todd was a law graduate of Harvard University, but did not practice his profession. A sketch of his life may be found in Dr. Lyon G. Tyler's "Men of Mark in Virginia."

Julia Dickson, the daughter of Mallory Dickson and Diana Southall, married, first. Mr. George Thomas Carroll. The one child of this marriage, Diana C., died before she reached young womanhood. A lovely young girl, nearly fifteen, a blessing and inspiration for good to all who knew her. Julia Dickson married, second, Everard Moore Todd.

ROBINSON.

Christopher Robinson, born in 1645 Cliesby, Yorkshire, England, was the son of John Robinson, and the brother of John Robinson, Bishop of London. Christopher came to Virginia in 1666; had an estate, "Hewick," on the Rappahannock; was Burgess for Aliddlesex in 1691 ; in the Council same year; Secretary of State 1692. Alarried Agatha, daughter of Bertram Obert; married, second, Catherine, widow of Major Robert Beverley. Of his sons, *John* (1683-1749) was president of the Council and acting Governor, and *Christopher* of Hewlett (1681-1727) was member of House of Burgesses. Christopher married Judith Wormeley.

Mrs. Elizabeth AI. Robinson, of "The Vineyard," Harewood Road, Washington, D. C., gives the following: "John Robinson married Elizabeth . Their son, Anthony R., married Mary Starkey. Issue: (1) John R., married Frances Wade, and (2) Major Anthony, married Diana Starkey. Major Anthony's will proved June 21, 1756. Their sixth child, John Robinson, married Martha Aloore, daughter of Merritt Aloore. They had four children: (1) Everard R., (2) Merritt M. R., (3) Anne R., (4) John R.

"(2) Merritt Moore Robinson married Anne Cooke (widow Nicholas).

"(3) Anne R. married Mallory Todd. Issue: John R. T., Merritt T., Mallory T., Mary Moore T., Angelina T., Anne T., Louisa Moore T."

TODD FAMILY — DICKSON FAMILY.

"The Todds lived for centuries in Yorkshire, England, at Tranby, near Hull. Some of the family in Scotland. Adam Todd of New York State was born in the Highlands and always wore Highland garb. He died in 1765 leaving a widow, Sarah, and four children—Adam, James, Sarah, Alargaret. In *Women of the Revolution* we read of Sarah—her house was 'rebel headquarters.' Washington wrote expressing his thanks and was asked to breakfast with her, and during the meal he arose twice to thank her for her loyalty.' She is buried in old St. Paul's Church, New York. Her daughter Sarah married a Brevort. One of the family owned a large slice of New York City. There was a branch of the family who settled in Kentucky.

"Christopher Todd of Yorkshire was one of the Pilgrim Fathers and settled in New Haven, where he was an important personage almost from the year of its settlement. He was the son of William, who was the son of William, and he, Christopher, with his wife Grace and several children came over to America. What is now a part of the campus of Yale College belonged to Christopher's estate. Many of his descendants now live in New Haven. Christopher bore for Arms the traditional origin of his name—three foxes heads. The Massachusetts branch of the Todd family date back to John, who also came from Yorkshire. He settled in Rowley, Mass., 1637, with his wife Susanna and six children; was a representative in general court for many years. He bore for Arms a fox rampant with a dove for crest. Motto: By cunning not by craft. The Arms borne by Christopher and now by the Connecticut Todds are the same as borne by Todds of Tronby Park, East Riding, Yorkshire. Argent, three foxes heads, coupled gu.—a border vert. Crest—on a chapeau gu. turned ermine a fox sejant ppr. Motto: *Opporlet vivcer.* (It is necessary to live.)

"Mallory Todd the first of the Norfolk or Smithfield branch of

Todds, was the son of John Todd and Angelina Mallory, of Southampton Parish, Bermuda Islands."

The fact that the Arms of the Bermuda or Virginia Todds, and the Yorkshire, England, and Scotch family are the same, identify them as the same family.

DICKSON.

William Dickson, of the Tidewater Virginia family, came from Yorkshire, England. For years he kept in touch with his English tailor, ordering clothes and various other articles from the old country. He married, first, Davis. Issue:
Richard, William, Elizabeth, Mary. Alarried, second, Angelina Todd, daughter of Mallory Todd and Anne Robinson, his wife. Issue: Mallory Todd D., Anne Robinson D., Diana Todd D., Louisa D., Angelina Everard D.

Mallory Todd Dickson married Diana Todd Southall. Issue: Mary Angelina D., Louisa Augusta D., Anna Taylor Dickson, William Mallory D., Julia White D., Tazewell Taylor D., Southall D.

Anne Robinson Dickson married Tazewell Taylor, of Norfolk.

Angelina Eyerard Dickson married, first, Frederick Southgate; second. Bishop Johns of the Episcopal Church.

"The Dickson Arms granted Richard Dickson, Esquire, .of Stockton upon Tees in the county palatine of Durham—Lord of the Manor of Beverley Watertowns in the East Riding of York—to his descendants and other descendants of his late father John Dickson;

"Arms: arg. three mullets gu. within a border engr. az. bezantee, on a chief of the second three palets or.

"Crest on a mount vert—between two branches of palm— a buck lodged in front of a tree all ppr. Motto: *Cubo scd-curo.*"

The Editor inserts the following communication from Mrs, Henry Litcfield West, of Washington, D. C. The Bailey or Baker Armistead has not been traced:

ARMISTEAD.

Ann Armistead, the daughter of Bailey (?) Armistead, married about 1800, George Hope, eldest son of George Hope of Hampton, and his wife, Rebecca (Meredith J Ballard, a young widow. When

Ann Armistead was a girl, her young friends were fond of joking her about not getting married. Her replv was that "there was only one young man in Hampton that she would have, and that was Mr. Hope's son George." George evidently also wanted Mr. Armistead's daughter Ann.

George Hope served in the War of 1812. After a battle which was fought near Hampton, word was brought to Mrs. Hope that her husband had been killed, his head having been blown off by a cannon. The messenger was soon followed by George Hope himself, who told the story of how his gun was struck from his hand, and when he stooped to get it a cannon ball whistled so close to his head his hat was blown off.

George Hope lived on his estate, "Little Bethel," just outside of Hampton, Va, His children by Ann Armistead, who was his first wife, were:

1. Sarah Armistead, born 1801.
2. George, b. 1803; married Evelina Brown of Portsmouth, Va. No children.

Ann (Armistead) Hope died 1814. '

(1) Sarah[3] Armistead Hope (George[2], George[1]) married October 30, 1832, Rev. Vernon Eskridge, U. S. N. Issue:

1. George Burdette, born August 8, 1834; died in infancy.
2. Ann McLin, born December 2, 1835.
3. Richard Washington, born July 28, 1838; died in Portsmouth, Va., 1855 of yellow fever.
4. Sarah Vernon, born January 13, 1841.

(1) Ann[4] McLin Eskridge (Sarah[3], George[2], George[1]) married January 18, 1864, Rev. John Kimball, of Vermont, a Congregational minister, who was chaplain in the United States army during the Civil War. They lived in Washington, D. C., until 1868, when they removed to California. They both died in San Francisco; Mrs. Kimball dying in 1894, and her husband in 1897. Their children were :

1. Mary (Minnie) Hope, born March 3, 1867; died June 16, 1867.
2. John Vernon, born September 23, 1868.

(1) John[5] Vernon Kimball (Ann4, Sarah[3], George[2], George[1]) married Alarion Frances Featherstone, of San Francisco. They have:

1. Hope.
2. John Austin.
3. Earl.
4. Walter Freer.

(1) Sarah[4] Vernon Eskridge (Sarah®, George®, George[1]) married, February 9, 1859, Wm. Henry White, son of John Satter White and Mary Matilda Godwin, daughter of Willis Godwin, of Nansemond County and Portsmouth, and Sarah Crafts, of Portsmouth, Va. W'm. Henry White was lieutenant in the Confederate army, and was killed at the battle of Malvern Hill, July 2, 1862. The children of Sarah Vernon Eskridge and Wm. Henry white:

1. Sarah Eskridge, born March 4, 1860; living, unmarried, in Washington, D. C.

2. Mary Henry Hope, born May 28, 1861. The name of Henry was added after her father's death.

(1) Mary5 Henry Hope White (Sarah4, Sarah3, George[2], George[1]) married, July 25, 1882, Henry Litchfield West, of Washington, D. C., born Staten Island, N. Y., August 20, 1859. Mr. West, who for twenty-five years was connected with the *Washington Post,* was appointed October 16, 1902, as one of the three Commissioners of the District of Columbia. He is also the author of "American Politics" in the *Forum.* The children of Mary Hope West and Henry Litchfield West are:

1. Marion Litchfield, born June 14, 1883.

2. Vernon Eskridge, born July 24, 1886.

3. Mary (Alinnie) Athow, born September 11, 1889.

"The name of the father of Ann Armistead, who married George Hope, is not known positively. My grandmother's half brother. Mr. William B. Hope, who died at the age of eighty-five, told me that he was very sure that the name was Bailey Armistead, but whether Bailey was the first or middle name, he could not say. Uncle William said that Bailey Armistead was a Revolutionary soldier, but his name has not been found among the War Department records. I shall make a search at the Pension Office. The name of Thomas Baker Armistead has been found among the Hampton records connected with the same names as those of my great-grandmother's family.

"My mother remembers hearing of the Seymours. The Jane Seymour spoken of here my mother can remember coming to see my grandmother when mother was a little girl. Ann (Armistead) Hope had a brother William — "Uncle Billy" — who, my mothers thinks, married a Miss Booker; that she was "Betsy" spoken of in the letter, and that his daughter was "Patsy." After Ann (Armistead) Hope's death, George Hope married Patsy Booker, but whether she was the one or not, I do not know.

"The deed in which Thomas Baker Armistead is mentioned, you probably have seen, as it is copied in the *William and Mary*. It is between Thomas Baker Armistead, his wife Ann, Mrs. Mary Seymour of Norfolk, and someone else. 1799 is the date.
Thomas may have been the brother of Mrs. ,Seymour, but not necessarily the father of Ann.
"The commission as chaplain in the Navy for my grandfather, **Vernon Eskridge, is signed by Millard Fillmore as President of the United States, and William Alexander Graham, Secretary of the Navy. It is dated Alarch, 1851.**"

George Hope, of Hampton, Va., was born in Cumberland, England, March 28, 1749; married, 1771, Rebecca Meredith Ballard. Issue, among others, George Hope, married Ann Armistead (daughter Bailey Armistead). Issue: Sarah, George. Alarried, second, Patsy Booker; issue, among others, Richard Hope, married Louisa Armistead.

Wilton Hope, son of George and his wife, Rebecca AI. Ballard, born January 1. 1795, married Jane Barron, daughter of Commodore Barron of the Navy. Issue: Captain James Barron Hope, their only child, Virginia's distinguished poet. James Barron Hope married Annie Whiting, of Hampton. Issue: two daughters, Jane Barron, married Prof. Marr, of Lexington, Va., and Nannie Alallory, married Richard Baker, of Norfolk, Va.

Emily Smith Armistead (twin sister, Helen), the daughter of (178) Robert Armistead and Elizabeth Smith, his wife, married John White Keeling the 30th January, 1828. John W. Keeling was the son of William Langley Keeling and Eliza White, his wife, of Princess Anne County. William L. Keeling was the son of William Keeling who, with Anthony Walke, his friend, came from Cumberland, England, about 1640 and settled in Princess Anne County at Kempville. There is a record that "Thomas Walke and William Keeling were Burgesses in the Assembly 1756-1758. The children of Emily S. Armistead and John White Keeling were: Robert William Parks K., John Edwin K., Thomas Armistead K., Westwood Armistead K., Thomas Armistead K., Melville Cox K., Westwood Armistead K. (Westwood I and 2; Thomas 1 and 2, died.)

Robert W. P. Keeling never married, probably inherited from his father a restless temperament. They were both travelers, seeing many countries. The son spent his life on the seas going from one place to another. His experiences were interesting and marvellous. Finally he became blind and died about 1892.

John Edwin Keeling, of Norfolk, now Asheville, N. C., married Mary Anne, daughter of Elisha Gamage, a prominent merchant and bank president of Norfolk. Issue: Alice[1] K., Mary[3] K., Robert[3] K., Edwin[2] Dewees K., Armistead[4] K.

Alice Grayson Keeling married Herbert C. Allen. Issue; Edwin Allen, Ethan Allen, Raleigh Allen, Margaret Armistead Allen.

Edwin Dewees Keeling married Margaret, daughter of William Benjamin Clayton and Ellen S. Davidson, his wife, of Asheville, N. C. Issue: one daughter, Margareet Dewees Keeling.

Melville Cox Keeling (named for a noted Methodist preacher to whom his father was deeply attached. He was ordained bishop and went as a missionary to Africa. Just as he sailed for Africa the child above mentioned was born), of Berkeley, part of Norfolk, married Sallie, daughter of H. B. C. Walker, of Princess Anne County. Issue: Emily Armistead K. and Harry Walker K.

Emily Armistead Keeling married Ware Wainwright Robertson, formerly of Eastern Shore of Maryland, now of Berkeley. Issue: Miriam R., Alelville Keeling R., Ware Wainwright R., Emily Armistead R., Harry Walker R., and an infant.

Harry Walker Keeling married Lucy Browning Scott, daughter of Richard B. and Susan C. Scott, of Princess Anne County.

John Edwin Keeling joined the Norfolk Light Artillery Blues in 1859; fought with the battery all through the war to Appomattox.

Melville Cox Keeling joined the Norfolk Light Artillery Blues in 1858; was mustered into the Confederate service, and continued in that service until he was released from Point Lookout prison after the war; was badly wounded at the battle of Chancellorsville. He was in a Richmond hospital until he was able to return to his command. Was wounded again at Hatcher's Run; taken prisoner, carried to Point Lookout prison, and remained there until after close of war, when he was released by order of President Andy Johnson. Returned to Norfolk; continued his membership with Norfolk Light Artillery Blues, Battery B, and rose through successive grades until March, 1889, when he was elected captain, which position he held for eighteen years, when he was elected Major of First Battalion of Field Artillery Virginia Volunteers, which rank he now holds (1909). He has been continuously in the service of his State over fifty years. He is also a Mason of high standing, and a zealous member of the

Methodist Church; superintendent of Sunday-school for many years. Though now an old man in years, he is erect, alert and active as a man of forty.

THE WESTWOOD FAMILY. '

From the significance of the various blazons in the Arms described below, the Westwood family was one of distinction in England;

"Arms; sable, a lion rampant; argent, crowned with a mural crown, or; three crosses—crosslet, fitchee, or, Crest, a stork's head ppr. erased gorged with a mural crown or." No motro given.

The lion was usually granted only to those who had served in the King's service, and thus in being crowned with a "mural crown" (being masoned, and the «'top embattled), proved that some of the family had fought in battle. These mural crowns were conferred by the old Romans on the soldier who first scaled the walls of a rampart or besieged town; the cross, too, was a mark or attestation and only confirmed upon "officials." It is said "so superstitiously did those times (William 1st) think of the cross, that they held all things sanctified that bore the signe of it; and therefore it was used religiously in their charters; and this was the origin of persons who could not write their names, to make the sign of a cross instead. The cross as here given is called a cross-crosslet, or one having its limbs also crossed, whicii signifies that they are to extend to the extremities of the Eschtcheon. When the cross is pointed at the base, it is called 'fitche,' or fixed. Crosses of this description are said to have been carried by the early Christians in thei;r prilgrimages, so that they might readily be fixed in the ground whilst performing their devotions. The stork in the crest is emblematic of piety and gratitude. They were held in great veneration by many of the early Kings, and were prohibited by law fyom being disturbed; hence the storks would build their nests on the tops of castles and other high buildings, where they always welcomed and encouraged. The one in the Westwood Arms is 'gorged', or has around its neck also a 'mural' crown, and the whole Escutcheon would read: That the early members of the Westwood family were knights in the King's service, one of whom had been first in the capture of castle or walled town— that some of them had been pilgrims to the Holy Land, or in the wars of the Crusader,; and that they lived in castles, over which flew the sacred stork."

The first of the family in the Colony were Humphrey and Randall Westwood, who settled in York County about 1620. Henning speaks of Humphrey Westwood, as well as William and Worlich Westwood. Humphrey was one of the original company under the charter granted by James I. and dated May 23, 1607.

In 1622 there came to the Colony a William Worlich, age fifteen, in the ship *Bona Nova*. In 1649, 1654, 1659, and perhaps other years, he was a member of the House of Burgesses, and Lieutenant-Colonel of militia for Elizabeth City County.

NOTE.— (Mr. William Westwood, of Hampton, who read eight or ten of the Westwood wills recorded in Clerk's office in Hampton, is authority for the following (among them the will of William We.3twood, who married Elizabeth Worlich) : He went for a second reading of this will and could not find it; therefore could not give date or all the names.)

"William Westwood married Elisabeth Worlich. In his will he mentions 'daughter Elisabeth, who married George Wray, late

This Coat of Arms of the Westwood family was copied from a very old one that has been preserved in the McCreery family for generations. It was done on heavy parchment—an expert copy of the original that was brought from England. Mrs. Indiana Worlich Westwood Williams (now deceased) saw Elizabeth McCreery (several generations back) at work on it. She saw the original, but the present generation do not know what became of it. It is not found in Burke, but Dr. R. A. Brock, genealogist, says he has noted other omissions of Arms in Burke. The McCreerys are descended from the Westwoods.of England.' Another daughter married Thomas Wythe, father of Chancellor Wythe, one of the signers of the Declaration of Independence.

"William W'estwood, son of William W. and Elisabeth Worlich, married Mary Tabb. His will, proved June 23, 1770, mentions the following children: Louisa, married Col. Robert Armistead (of Louisa County) ; Elisabeth, married, first, James Wallace ; second, Thomson Mason; Worlich, married Hannah King; Martha, married Edward Hack Moseley, of Norfolk; Rachel, married Henry King. He also mentions James Westwood, and Merritt Westwood as his grandson; and Sarah, the daughter of James Westwood.

"William Westwood, son of William Westwood and Mary Tabb, married Anne Stith. Will Written in 1780, probated in 1782. "At the writing of the will all of his daughters must have been single;" he speaks of them as "daughters;" "mentions sons William and John Stith, born 1766, died in 1836, May 16th, age seventy-two, when W. T. Westwood, now (1900) town clerk of Hampton, was but two years old." John Stith Westwood was married three times, and W. T. Westwood was child of the last marriage, Elisabeth Stanworth. John Stith Westwood was member of the House of Delegates in 1804-'5, and justice of the peace in 1802."

Indiana Worlich Westwood, daughter of John Stith Westwood, married William H. Williams. Issue: Arthur, Westwood, May.

William James Westwood is another son of John Stith Westwood.

William James Westwood married Kate Owens Williams. Issue: Kate W., Indie W., Mary W., Ida W., Jno. Stith W., Mattie W.

Indie Westwood married James W. Sinton, of Richmond, Va. Issue, two children, James W. Sinton, Jr., Katherine Westwood Sinton.

Kate Westwood married D. C. Lewis. Issue: one son, Beverley C.

Lewis, Jr.

Ida Westwood married W. A. A. Brown, of Brooklyn and Lennox, Mass.

Bishop Meade says that Worlich Westwood was a vestryman in the early church at Hampton, Va., in 1751, as was also Vdlliam Westwood, who seems to have been a promoter in church affairs.

These daughters William Westwood speaks of in his will were called, so says tradition, "the five beautiful Miss Westwoods." They were Mrs. Wyatt and Mrs. Mcghee of Petersburg; Mrs. Ellzy of Leesburg; Mrs. John McCreery (Mary Tabb Westwood) of Richmond; Mrs. William Moseley (Jane W.) of Norfolk.

Martha W., daughter of William Westwood and Mary Tabb, married Edward Hack Aloseley of "Rolston," Princess Anne County, Va. Issue; Burwell Bassett Aloseley, who married Elisabeth Amy Boush of Norfolk. Issue: an only daughter, Catherine Boush, who married Dr. James Cornick, of Princess Anne County, surgeon in the United States Navy, afterwards the Confederate States Navy. Issue: George K. Cornick, Henry C., Byrd C., James Paul Hayne C., Elizabeth Amy Bouch C., Henry C., Catherine C., Philip Barrard C., Prances Henley C., Burwell Bassett Aloseley C.

Frances Henley Cornick married Thomas Hinton Dunn, born in Louisiana (great-grandson of William R. Johnson). Issue: Catherine Aloseley D., Mary Robertson D., Francis Lightfoot D., William Ranson D., Thomas Hinton D., Elizabeth Amy D.

Catherine Aloseley D. married Hamilton Eckenrode, of Fredericksburg. Issue; Frances Cornick E.

Mary Robertson D. married Maurice Norvel Langhorne. Both died within the year of their marriage.

Issue, as far as known, of "the five beautiful Miss Westwoods" :

Mary Tabb Westwood married John AlcCreery, of Petersburg. Issue: Anne Elisabeth, William Westwood, George Magee, Stephen Alexander.

George Magee McCreery married Matilda Werth, daughter of John T. Werth (who was in business with Mr. John Van Lew, and named a son for him.) Issue: William Westwood McCreery, John Van Lew McCreery, George McCreery.

John Van Lew McCreery, born in Norfolk, 1835. Served in the Confederate Army, 1861-1865, in the Richmond Howitzers; married 1865, Nannie Kepler, daughter of Rev. Henry Smith Kepler, for fourteen years rector of old St. John's Church, Richmond, Va, Issue:

George Westwood, died unmarried; Sarah Hanson, Elisabeth Peterkin, Henry Kepler, Matilda Werth died in infancy; Mary Crafton, Nannie Werth, John, Merritt.

Mary Grafton married, 1907, Mr. Duff Green, of Fredericksburg. Issue: Duff Green, Jr., and Arianna Kepler Green. She possesses the miniature of her great-grandmother, Mary Tabb Westwood.

William Westwood McCreery graduated at West Point as second lieutenant of artillery, 1860; resigned to serve in Confederate Army; killed at Gettysburg, July 1, 1863, age twenty-seven, in Pettigrew's Division. "He had often said that should he fall in battle he would like to be color bearer at the time; his wish was granted, as he fell on the breastworks, being the twelfth or thirteenth man killed while bearing our Glorious Banner!"

George Magee McCreery was midshipman 1827, lieutenant in U. S. Navy 1839, lost in the *Grampus** 1843, having taken the place of a brother officer, Bushrod Washington Hunter; sailing with sealed orders. The ship in which he sailed had been condemned. It was never heard of.

Stephen Alexander AlcCreery, brother of George Alagee McCreery and William Westwood AlcCreery, was assistant surgeon in U. S. Navy 1838, surgeon in 1852, lost in the *Albany* September, 1854. All that was ever heard of the ship was a barrel with the name, *Albany*. Stephen Alexander AlcCreery married Mary Starke, whose mother was a sister of William Moseley who married her cousin Jane Westwood.

Rachel Westwood married Henry King, of Norfolk. Issue; Rachel King, John King. Rachel married James Smith, a Scotch merchant of Dumfries, Va. Issue: Mary King Smith, Jane Smith, Robert Smith, Andrew Smith. (The AlcGreerys have a photo of an old painting by this James Smith, with himself, wife, four children; and two miniatures, one contains the likeness ox Mary Tabb and her little daughter Rachel.)

Mary King Smith married Edmund Tyler. Issue: Alice Tyler, married John S. Ewell; issue; Alice Maude Ewell.

Jane Smith married William Gadsby, of Washington. Robert died unmarried. Andrew Smith married Elisabeth Steele.

John King had four daughters; Helen, Jean, Lucy Frances Tinsley, married Mr. Kendrick, of West Virginia, Rachel Westwood K. married John Ellis, of Goochland.

Mrs. Ellzy, of Leesburg, one of the five Westwood sisters, had son

Thomas and daughters, Alice, Lilly, Mary, Alargaret, Ella.

Thomas Louis Ellzy married Helen Mason, daughter of Geo. Mason of "Gunston Hall." Issue: Graham Ellzy, M. D., who married, 8th June, 1870, Mary Cheston Murray, of West River, Maryland. Issue: (1) James Murray Ellzy, M. D., of Philadelphia, who married Sarah Cheston. Issue: James Murray E. and Alice AI. E. (2) Graham Ellzy married Mary Cheston; (3) Mary Ellzy, (4) Fanny Ellzy, (5) Helen unmarried.

Alice Ellzy married Mr. Jordan, of Clifton Forge. Issue: Fanny Westwood J., Ella J., Alice J., Graham J., Helen J.

Helen Eliza Ellzy married Rush Wallace Chancellor, M. D., a descendant of Elisabeth Westwood who married, first, James Wallace; second, Thompson Mason. Issue: Mildred Wallace Chancellor, Samuel Ashby C., William Fitzgerald C., Helen Ellzy C.

Mary Ellzy married Lyman Shepherd, of Canada. Issue: Lyman S., Mary Shepherd married John McCrary. Issue: Anna Murray Shepherd.

Margaret Ellzy, unmarried.

Ella Ellzy, unmarried.

Comparing Mr. William Westwood's statement with Mr. Lyon Tyler's in his *Quarterly,* James Westwood, mentioned in York County records, must have been the brother of William Westwood who married Elizabeth Worlich, who had a son Worlich, a resident of Hampton in 1695, and a son William who married Mary Tabb, as shown by will.

Worlich Westwood married Elisabeth Naylor, a daughter of William Naylor. Worlich Westwood died before 1702, when the widow married Charles Jennings, Jr. Worlich Westwood and Elisabeth, his wife, had three children: Mary W., mentioned in her grandfather, William Naylor's will; Elisabeth Westwood, who married Col. Anthony Armistead,* and William Westwood, who married Mary Wallace, mentioned in a deed in 1728, daughter of Rev. James Wallace and Anne, his wife. Mrs. Anne Wallace in her will proved in 1740, speaks of her grandchildren, Mary Westwood and James Westwood.

NOTE. — Mr. William Wstwood, of Hampton, son of John Stith W., feels sure from conversations he has had with a descendant of the New Jersey branch, that a son of Humphrey Westwood settled in New Jersey, the name Humphrey being still retained in that branch.

William Westwood who married Mary Tabb, and Worlich who

married Elisabeth Naylor, were members of the House of Burgesses; also members of the Convention that formed the State and National Governments, 1744 to 1788. As several wills show that swords and guns were bequeathed to descendants, they must have been in the service of the State. Records show that the Westwoods were prominent in Church Affairs as well. In 1726 William W. was one selected by "His Majestie's Justices" to select a site in the town of Hampton on which to build a Parish Church; and on the spot selected by him in 1727 was erected the present St. John's.

The following letter is copied by Miss Elisabeth Robinson from a manuscript of her aunt, "Miss Cornelia Jefferson Randolph," who died 1872-'73:

STITH FAMILY. .

"Kedar, a Cossac—or Arab (Tartar) of Maurienneburg, somewhere in the Caucassian Mountains, came in the fifteenth century, before the battle of Agincourt, to Western Europe—probably, France: he carried on the smith's trade, and was the inventor of horse-shoeing. Horses were first used in the battle cf Agincourt. Kedar,—the name was after called Kidder. (In England, when sir-names were first adopted, the name designated the trade, occupation, civil or military station, or service) "stithy, a smith's shop; he called himself Stith. The Stiths seem to have had a disposition to literature; one of them in Queen Elisabeth's time, or before, wrote a romance, called 'Lost Island,' from which Shakespeare took his story of 'The Tempest.' This fact is mentioned in notes in the first editions of Shakespeare. The author married Rebecca Bohlen. This information about the literary turn of the Stiths and about 'Lost Island,' came from an old lady, Miss Jeanette Douglass, of New York, one of the Stiths, who owned about thirty of the works of Stith, the author of 'Lost Island.' "

It is said that John Rolfe's mother was a Stith. Rev. William Stith, an Episcopal clergyman, who came over to this country, wrote on Architecture and Engineering (see Wo;rcester's *Ancient His.*). Anne Stith, who married William Westwood was a direct descendant of Pocahontas. Thomas Rolfe, son of Pocahontas, married a Miss Poythress; their daughter Jane Rolfe, married Col. Robert Bolling, issue, John Bolling, married Miss Kennon, issue, a daughter, who married Richard Randolph, issue, Mary Randolph, who married

William Stith, whose daughter married William Stith the historian, his son John married Elisabeth Anderson; their daughter Anne married W. Westwood.

ROMANCE OF THE BEAUTIFUL ELISABETH WESTWOOD.

This is told in *William and Mary Quarterly*, Vol. XIII., No. 3, by Miss Emily Macrae, of Orangefield, Stafford County, in her account of the Wallace family. Mr. Tyler says in *William and Mary*, Vol. IX., No. 2;

"Rev. James Wallace was born in Errol, Perthshire, Scotland, 1667, and died in Elisabeth City County, Va., at his home, Erroll, on Back River, Nov. 3rd, 1712. His tombstone bearing his coat of arms, is still to be seen there. He served for twenty-one years as minister of Elisabeth City, and practiced physic also. He married Anne widow of Thomas Wythe — grandfather of George Wythe, July nth, 1695. Issue: (1) Euphan; (2) Anne Wallace, who married Col. Robert Armistead (son of William, son of Anthony, son of William the Emigrant), (2) a daughter, who married Ballard, (4) Mary, who married William Westwood. (5) John, (6) James. This last married Martha , and her will was proved in 1768, according to which they had (1) Robert, student at William and Mary in 1753. who had James and Wilson. (2) Alartha, married Thomas Tabb; (3) Elisabeth married John Seldon; (4) Mary married Richard Ball of Lancaster; (5) Euphan married Judge William Roscoe Wilson Curie; (6) Anne married George Wray, (7) James Wallace, student Wm. and Mary in 1758, burgess for Elizabeth City Co. in 1769 & 1772, justice of the county and member of the county Committee of Safety 1775. He married Elisabeth Westwood, daughter of William Westwood, and had issue: (1) Robert Wallace, student William and Mary in 1775. James, (3) William, (4) Alartha, (5) Euphan,-(6) Elisabeth who married John McCrea, (7) Mary.

"*Elisabeth* Westwood Wallace, widow of James Wallace, married second, Hon. Thomson Alason, of Stafford Co., and appears to have had two sons, Westwood Thomson Alason and William Temple Tompson Alason. He had by previous marriage Stevens and John Thomson Alason. In his will proved Sep. 26th 1784 he ordered 'that neither of his two younger sons shall reside on the south side of James River or below Williamsburg before they respectfully attain the age of twenty one, lest they should imbibe more exalted notions of their own than I should wish any child of mine to possess.' "

Miss Emily Alacrae says: "James Wallace fled from Scotland in the rebellion of '45. He was born at Erroll in Scotland; his birth attested by three lairds. He settled on Back River, in Elizabeth City Co. He brought with him an immense table service of plate, on which was engraved the Wallace Arms, he being a collateral descendant of Sir William Wallace. The dinner set of silver consisted of two tureens and ladles, a full set of covered dishes, pickle and butter dishes, knives and forks and every appurtenance that belongs to a dinner and breakfast set of table silver, all the most massive silver. He, James Wallace married Elizabeth Westwood of Hampton Va (my great-grandmother). She was remarkable for her great beauty, accomplishments, strength of intellect and piety. Their children were eleven — six cf whom attained the age of maturity — Robert, James, Euphon, Mary, Alartha, Eliza. Mary died single, all were beautiful, though she was probably the most lovely. Euphon married Bailey Washington (my grandfather). Martha married Mr. James; Eliza married John Macrae, of Orangefield, Prince William Co., Va. Robert by the laws of primogeniture, inherited the princely fortune of his father. He married Miss Mallory near Hampton, Va., and left one son who died Unmarried leaving his property to his mother's relations. The family seat of the Wallaces on Back River was called 'Erroll' after the seat of the Wallaces in Scotland. Elizabeth Westwood's mother was a Miss Howard, of the house of Norfolk, England. She was a near relative of one of the Colonial Governors of Virginia of that name, Francis Howard, Baron of Effingham, born in England 1630, died there 1694; son of Sir Charles Howard, Governor of Virginia 1684 to 1688." (Appleton's *Cyclopedia Am. Biog.*, Vol. , page 207.)

"I will hereafter narrate a romantic incident which caused Elizabeth Westwood,* who was the Widow Wallace, to move to Chappawansic, Prince William Co., Va. Elizabeth Westwood's mother or grandmother was a first cousin of Anne Boleyn. One of Elizabeth Westwood's sisters, Louisa, married Col. Robert Armistead of Louisa Co., Va. Their daughter, Polly Armistead, was a celebrated belle and beauty. She married Stevens Thomson Alason of 'Raspberry Plains,' Loudoun Co., Va.

"One of Elizabeth Westwood's sisters married Mr. King, of Norfolk. After his death she married Dr. McClurg, of Hampton. Dr. McClurg's son married Miss Seldon of Buck Roe near Hampton, Va. Their only daughter married Mir. Wickham, of Richmond, a distinguished lawyer.

"Elizabeth Westwood had two brothers, Worlick and William.

"Now comes the romance. When Elizabeth Westwood was about sixteen years of age she made a visit to her cousins, the daughters of Governor Digges, one of the Colonial Governors who was living at Denby, near Williamsburg, Va. Whilst there, there was a great deal of talk of an Assembly ball which was to come off at Williamsburg, and as Elizabeth W. did not leave home with the expectation of attending the Assembly, she was not prepared, having her party costumes in Hampton, where she lived. Her cousins, the Digges family, insisted on her remaining to attend the Assembly, saying they would lend her a dress. Yielding to their importunities she decided to remain and wear her own simple white dress. Soon after the guests assembled at the ball Air. Thomson Alason was introduced. He had just returned from England, where he had been educated. His eyes rested on the beautiful Elizabeth Westwood, and he had neither eyes nor ears for any other being in the room. She was equally pleased with him. Miss Digges was a cousin of Mr. Alason, and it appears she was bent on captivating him herself. Consequently she told Mr. Alason that Elizabeth was engaged to be married and she told Elizabeth that Thomson Alason was trifling with her. Consequently when he called to see her the day after the ball, she declined to make her appearance. Thus were two young beings separated to meet in maturer years. About six months after this date Elizabeth Westwood married the wealthy James Wallace of 'Erroll,' and several years after, Thomson Alason married. He lived at Chappawamsic near Dumfries. He frequently attended court at Williamsburg and was often asked by James Wallace to visit him, which he as often promised to do. On one occasion. Mr. Wallace said to Mr. Alason, 'My oft repeated invitations have been so frequently slighted, with a promise of fulfilment, that I will not extend them again.' Mr. Alason then told Mr. Wallace that he had entertained peculiar sentiments of regard to his wife, when she was young, and he would prefer not seeing her again.

"Years swept on. Mrs. Wallace became a widow; Mr. Mason a widower. Mrs. Wallace was noted for her benevolence. Two Revolutionary soldiers from Stafford Co., who were wounded were cared for by the widow Wallace, she dressing the wounds. When they recovered sufficiently to leave Hampton they returned to therr home, which was near Mr. Mason. They mentioned the circumstance to him, remarking on the beauty of the widow Wallace. She had been a widow several years, but there was at that period very little communication between the upper and lower counties of the State and this was the first intimation Mr. Mason had of the fact. The next day he ordered his coach and four and went from Chappawansic to 'Erroll' a distance of several hundred miles. He was received graciously by the widow, but had to make several visits before she would consent to be betrothed.

"After his marriage with Elizabeth Westwood he had two sons. Temple Westwood, and William. Temple Westwood married Miss Noland; no issue. William married Miss Anne Carroll of Baltimore, an heiress. They had sixteen children. They lived at Temple Hall near Leesburg. Their oldest daughter married Dr. McGill of Winchester. When Mr. Thomson Alason was in England, he sojourned with Sir William Temple, his first cousin. He called his son after him. Dean Swift was a great deal in the family of Sir William Temple at the time Thomson Alason was there, and he had many humorous anecdotes and incidents to narrate in connection with the Dean. William Wirt says of Mr. Mason that he was the most distinguished lawyer that Virginia had produced up to this time. He was a brother of the statesman, George Alason of 'Gunston Hall.'

"Miss Digges on her death bed sent to her cousins Thomson Mason and Elizabeth Westwood to beg forgiveness for the false parts she had played.

"The first James Wallace's daughter, who married Mr. Seiden of Buck Roe, fell heir to most of his elegant plate."

Mary Tabb, who married William Westwood, was the daughter of Thomas Tabb and Elisabeth Moss, widow of Henry Howard, who died in 1711. Issue, besides Mary, John Tabb married Mary Sclater, Thomas married Mary Armistead, Henry, Diana T. married John Robinson, Rachel T., Martha T. married Thos. Kirby (second wife), Edward Tabb.

"Briarfield," the home of the Westwoods for generations, was four miles from Hampton.

187. Robert Augustus Armistead was the youngest of eleven children of 178. Robert A. and Elizabeth Smith, his wife His father 178. Robert inherited the bulk of the property of his great-grandfather Anthony, who married Elizabeth Westwood. The children of Anthony and Elizabeth Westwood were: Westwood, Anthony, Hannah; the latter married but had no children. Westwood

and Anthony inherited their father's wealth. Anthony was the progenitor of the North Carolina branch. Westwood A. and Mary Tabb had only one son, 172. Westwood, and two daughters, Elizabeth and Mary, who both married men of wealth—Elizabeth, Thomas Smith of York; Mary, Dr. Pope, an Englishman. Mary had no children. 172. Westwood's son Robert and Elizabeth's daughter Elizabeth married—two streams of wealth flowing together to 178. Robert A., the father of 187. Robert Augustus Armistead. 178. Robert's only brother, Westwood, died. They were the only children of 172. Westwood A. and Mary Jenkins, his wife.

178. Robert Armistead was what was called a high liver— hunting, feasting, entertaining in a lavish manner, like an English gentleman of ye olden time. He married when twenty-three Elizabeth Smith, his cousin, who was tall and handsome, with the dignity of a queen, and as a queen she ruled in her social circle and home. Born "to the purple" she maintained Macertain stately bearing and living; till her death at the age of 81. "She carried herself as erect and proudly as in her first womanhood." This statement is from a contemporary. A grandson whom she raised after his mother, her daughter, died, writes of her and the old home as follows:

"The old home occupied a large square of land in Hampton— the house near the corner where King and Queen Streets cross. Her eldest son, Westwood, later built his home on the far corner. The choice residential section of Hampton was owned by Westwood Armistead and his descendants.

"My memory of Grandmother Armistead's appearance is that she was a large, majestic looking woman with clear, full grey eyes, iron grey hair, and fine erect carriage. She was remarkably active and energetic, looking after business and domestic duties in person. She ruled her household as one accustomed to authority, and was a grand specimen of the old colonial age. She continued active and vigorous till a short time before her death at eighty-one years. *Was* a devout member of Old St. John's P. E. Church, and fully believed that no other church was to be mentioned with her's. As to the servants, they were too numerous to name. I will simply name a few: Aunt Lizzy (or mammy) as we all called her, was chief, and carried the keys. Every morning after breakfast she appeared before her mistress and would say, 'Miss Elizabeth, what are your commands for the day madam?' After receiving those commands, Miss Elizabeth was to have no anxiety about those commands being fully attended to. Aunt

Lizzie was a tall, fine looking mulatto, with all the ladylike airs and graces of her pattern (Miss Elizabeth) and was said to be one of the most accomplished and best housekeepers in all that section. She was not only loved and trusted by her mistress, but also loved by the entire household. Her husband (Uncle Charles) was to a large extent a gentleman of leisure, his only business (in the shape of work) to keep the wood pile high for house and kitchen. These two were the bosses of the army of younger ones composing the colorry or household. In addition to these, there were twelve or fifteen grown men who were hired to the United States Government to work on the Rip Raps, now Eort Wool, just across from Old Point. Grandmother's family consisted of eight girls and three boys; each girl had a maid and each boy a man. Grandmother usually appeared in black silk dress, lace collar and cap. On State occasions she was more elaborately dressed in brocade with all additional frills. She was a fine looking, handsome woman.

"'Willocks,' with the house and mill (to which you refer), were originally one plantation, and was owned by Grandfather Armistead, but in my early days it had passed out of the ownership of grandmother, with the exception of an acre which was the family burial plot, and where some of her children and grandchildren are buried. From what I learned as a boy, Grandfather Armistead was an English gentleman with habits pertaining thereto, and at his death grandmother administered on the estate, which was a large one, but much encumbered. By her energy and business tact she succeeded in paying off large debts and retained the larger part of the estate. During my childhood she lived at the old homestead in Hampton, where General Washington and other celebrated Revolutionary men were entertained.

NOTE. — The older children of Robert Augustine Armistead will recall that Carlos was his body servant, and William Davis his brother Westwood's. The latter was elected to the Senate when *Virginia* was placed by the Yankees after the war among "Districts,' and called District No. One. He was one of the most conservative and sensible men in that body. Later was appointed keeper of the Light House at Old Point. About 1873 in the summer when the wife and daughter of R. A. Armistead were at the old Hygiea, Old Point, they went over to the Light House to see William; they found him and family at dinner. They arose instantly and remained standing while "miss marthy" talked about "old times."

Mary Ann, the maid of Robert A. A.'s eldest daughter, Harriet, taught school after the war in Boston. She told the family when on a visit to them, that the school authorities would not believe that her young mistress had taught her arithmetic and geography as well as reading and writing.

THE LINE OF 187. ROBERT AUGUSTINE ARMISTEAD.

I. Anthony Armistead, of Kirk Deighton, Yorkshire, England, married Frances Thomson. Issue: (2) William Armistead the emigrant, who with his wife Anne came to Virginia in 1635. Issue: (3) William[3] A., (4) John[3] A., (5) Anthony[3] A., (5) Frances[3] A.

(5) Anthony[3] A. married Hannah Elliason: Issue, among others, 83. Anthony (lieutenant-colonel of militia), who married Elizabeth Westwood. Issue, among others, 169. Westwood A. married Mary Tabb. Issue: 172. Westwood A, 173. Elizabeth A., 174. Mary A.

172. Westwood A. married Mary Jenkins. Issue: 178. Robert Armistead, 179. Westwood, d. s. p. 172. Westwood A.'s will, made January 18, 1782, proved June 22, 1786, names wife Mary Jenkins and only two children Robert, and Westwood who died.

178. Robert Armistead, born August 9th, 1766; died August 31st, 1817, married his cousin, Elizabeth Smith, born August 22, 1767. Their youngest child, 187. Robert Augustine Armistead, married Martha Anne Savage. The children of this marriage were:

(1) Elizabeth Smith A., (2) Martha Anne A., (3) Westwood Wadsworth A. (these died young), (4) Robert Armistead, (5) Geoirge Wesley A., (6) Harriet Savage A., (7) Thomas Smith A., (8) Mary Louisa A., (9) Wilbur Teackle A., (10) Virginia Savage A., (11) Emily Smith A., (12) Westwood Smith A.

No. I. baptized by Rev. Christopher Thomas. No. 2. by Rev. Wm. S. Peyton. No. 3. by Rev. Geo. A. Bain. No. 4. by Rev. Vernon Eskridge. No. 5. by Rev. Vernon Eskridge. No. 6. by Rev. V. Eskridge. No. 7. by Rev. James D. Coulling. No. 8. by Rev. Isaac Willis. No. 9. by Rev. R. A. Armistead. No. 10. by Rev. John Bailey (an Englishman). No. 11. by Rev. R. A. Armistead. No. 12. by Rev. R. A. Armistead. All baptized at eight days old, except George—he at nine days old—delayed by the extreme illness of his mother. At this baptismal service, which was performed in the bed chamber of the mother, the family partook of cake and wine.

Robert Augustus Armistead, even as a youth, possessed strong as well as magnetic characteristics of mind and manner, which made for independence in thinking and acting. This was shown in his deciding, when only eighteen, to leave the Church of his mother—of his forefathers—and to join the Methodist Church. A very devout Methodist clergyman came to Hampton preaching and exhorting all to a life of purety and consecration. Emily Armistead, Robert's sister went to hear him, taking with her as escort at night her brother Robert; he lying out on the grass with other companions till the service was over. One night she asked him to go in with her, which he did. From that time he became very much interested and decided to join the Methodist Church, and at once told his mother of his desire and determination. He was met with strong opposition and distress, for she was a staunch Church woman. Finally she threatened to disinherit him. He took it all calmly, but never flinched from his determination. There had been a woeful declension in the spirituality and morals of both clergy and laity of the Episcopal Church in Virginia.

Among his private papers, after death, was found the following:

'I, Robert Armistead was converted the 26th of Oct. 1826 (when eighteen).

'I obtained license to preach from the Quarterly Conference Oct. 16th 1835 (lay preacher).

'I was ordained Deacon by Bishop Beverly Waugh Feb. 23rd 1840 at Farmville Va.

'I was ordained at Elder in 1840 in Centenary Church, Richmond Va.

'In the year 1829 I drew up a statement in writing setting forth my entire consecration to Father—Son—and Holy Spirit; after engaging in prayer and while upon my knees I placed mv signature to it—since that time, the most solemn in my life—I have ever felt that I, in a peculiar sense belonged to God."

Looking into the holy of holies of this man of God seems like desecration; but it is for the godly admonition of his descendants that it appears here; besides it is the key that unlocks every part of . his nature, and peering in we see the controlling power of his whole life.

February 28, 1828, when just past twenty, he married the daughter of Teackle Taylor Savage and Martha Jane Wade, his wife—she seventeen and two months. Her birthday verse in Prov. 31st chapter somewhat expresses her life, "Her children rise up and call her blessed; her husband also, and he praiseth her." A woman of gentle dignity, firm but loving, devoting her life to the bringing up of her children. She was the mother of twelve.

Robert and his young wife made their home with his mother at the old Armistead place in Hampton. For a description and picture of her home, see Savage excursus. Their three first children died very young—Martha and Westwood a year old; Elizabeth Smith, the eldest, about three. Robert considered their death due to ignorance of the physician, so he commenced to study medicine—the botanic system, as set forth by Dr. Samuel Thompson, of Boston, in various books published about that time. Of the nine other children all attained maturity. As a result of the study of the Thompsonian theory he made three valuable medicines—a cure for cholera, for neuraliga, for dyspepsia. During the cholera in and around Hampton in the forties, he was sent for day and night, and never lost a case—both time and medicine he gladly gave. The other two remedies are equally valuable, and are treasured and used by the family. He was a great sufferer from indigestion and cured himself. He was a many-sided man; his mechanical turn would have, if cultivated, placed him in the front rank of mechanics. From his youth he was a student and to the end of his life. A friend wrote of him;

"He was a remarkable man. Though modest and retiring, he was the embodiment of energy and conscientiousness, which made him a felt power for good; a scholar reading the Greek and Latin tongue readily, and was thoroughly conversant with the most advanced philosophical thought of the day; and from pure love of learning, continued his studious habits to the very close of his long life."

His ordination as local preacher did not interfere with his mercantile business and farming. He owned a fine farm, "Oakland," just across the creek or river. On the water side there were abundant oyster beds. "Oakland" is now a part of Hampton, in full view from electric cars that run from Old Point to Hampton. Besides, he owned and operated a castor-bean press. Every Sunday his favorite horse, Kitty, would be hitched to a low-swinging phaeton buggy and off he would go to Eox Hill, Poquoson, and other places on mission work intent.

In 1845 he built a very large new brick house on the same site as the old home, in the old-time style of four large rooms on a floor, wide hall running from front to back door. About this time his mother gave up the reins of household government into his and his wife's hands. His mother died January —, 1849, after a sudden, sharp illness.

This new home, like the old, was famous for its lavish hospitality. The preachers' room was always ready for the man of God of whatever name, but mostly the Methodist.

When the war broke out the family refugeed first to Williamsburg, then Petersburg, Richmond, North Carolina, and back to Richmond just before the evacuation. After which all lived in the country for a year; then returned to Richmond.

Soon after the close of the war Robert A. Armistead went into the active work of the ministry of the Alethodist Church.

Early Sunday morning, June 1, 1879, Martha Anne Savage Armistead, his faithful wife, passed from earth to heaven, after a painful illness of ten days, surrounded by her loving children, several of whom came from distant States.

Not long after the death of his wife, Robert A. Armistead retired from the work of the ministry, overcome by age and feeble health, and lived quietly at the home of his son Robert unmarried, and of his youngest daughter Emily, also unmarried. Here he continued his study and reading, keeping up with the scientific and religious questions of the day — writing thesis after thesis reconciling science with religion. He died in 1891. and is buried by the side of his wife in beautiful Hollywood.

Robert Armistead, fourth child of Robert A. Armistead and Martha Anne Savage, his wife, was born may 7, 1834, in Hampton, Va.; was educated at Randolph-Macon College. Enlisted in the First Company of Richmond Howitzers, April 21, 1861; appointed third corporal at organization of the Company, at Richmond College may 11, 1861; promoted to first corporal October I, 1861 ; elected second lieutenant November 17, 1861; resigned in the fall of 1862; was transferred to torpedo service, winter of 1863.

In 1884, on the death of his brother, Thomas Smith Armistead, April 14th, and of his wife Lucy Anne Grant, July 15th, Robert Armistead adopted his brother's five children — Thomas, Mary Beverley, John, Lucy, and Emily. He took them to live with him and his sister, Emily Armistead, in Richmond, where they were raised as their own children. He died in Richmond, *Va.*, April 20, 1894, unmarried.

Harriet Savage Armistead, sixth child, and eldest daughter of Robert A. Armistead and Martha Anne Savage, was born in Hampton, December 17, 1837, about 12 o'clock A. M.; died in

Richmond, Va., January 27, 1865, age twenty-seven; interred in Hollywood. The first of the family not buried at "Willocks," the family graveyard in Elizabeth City County. Beautiful in character as well as person, she was the leading spirit in her home in Hampton, which was famed for lavish hospitality.

Emily Smith Armistead, eleventh child of Robert A. Armistead and Martha Anne Savage, was born in Hampton, Va.; is now living in Richmond, Va. She was educated at D. Lee Powell's school in Richmond, Va. Possessed of high moral qualities, combined with intellectual culture and strong self-reliance, she has wonderfully guided and influenced the family committed to her care.

Virginia Savage Armistead, tenth child of Robert A. Armistead and Martha Anne Savage his wife, was born in Hampton. Alarried Asher Waterman Garber, November 30, 1870, in Richmond, Va., where they now live. No children. She was educated at Petersburg College, taking a full diploma July 4, 1866.

Thomas Smith Armistead, seventh child of Robert A. Armistead and Martha Anne Savage his wife, was born in Hampton, December 4, 1839, about 12 A. AI. Was studying medicine when the war broke out; was a member of the "original Howitzer Company on duty at Harper's Ferry and Charlestown, Va., during the John Brown war, November and December, 1859. Reenlisted in First Company of Howitzers, April 21, 1861 ; appointed commissary sergeant, September 1, 1861. Served until the close of the war at Appomattox, Va., April 9, 1865. Was separated from the Company there, and surrendered with Colonel Hardaway's Battalion of Artillery.

He was married to Lucy Anne Grant (born January 15, 1847) of Columbia, Fluvanna County, Va., on the 14th of April, 1868, at noon, by the Rev. John D. Powell of the Episcopal Church. Lucy Anne Grant was the daughter of Beverly Grant, of Richmond, Va., and Mary Jane Ligon, of Pittsylvania County. Mary Jane Ligon, born June 28, 1819, daughter of Benjamin Ligon, son of Joseph Ligon, born January 23, 1786, and Ketura Jackson, born December 23, 1794, daughter of James and Mary Jackson. Beverly Grant, born September 13, 1811, twin brother of Richard, was the son of John Samuel Grant, of Chesterfield County, and Mary Stuart, of King and Queen County. The Grant burying ground is in Chesterfield County, surrounded by a brick wall.

John Samuel Grant and Mary Stuart were married in 1805 or 6; she sixteen years old; died when she was forty. Issue of this marriage fifteen children — two sets of twins! Issue, among others, James Henry Grant, second son, born October 16, 1807, and Beverly Grant.

Two Grant brothers came to America from Scotland. One settled in Virginia, on James River; one went South. The children of John Samuel Grant and Mary Stuart his wife, were: AVilliam Henry, (2) James Henry, (3) Beverley and Richard, twins, (4) Richard died in California, (5) John Samuel, Frances Elinor, (7) Martha Ann, (8) George W., (9) Leroy Jefferson, (10) Alexander, and five who died in childhood or infancy.

(5) John Samuel and (8) George W. went to Georgia.

(6) Frances Elinor Grant married Thos. Edward Cox, of Henrico County. He was the son of Edward Cox and Adeline Elizabeth Harris. F. Elinor Grant and T. E. Cox had one daughter, Martha Ellen Cox, who married Robert Bosher, of Richmond. Issue: (Dr.) Robert, Percy, Elinor (married George Brewster, of New York City; issue, a son), Elizabeth (married Thomas Purcell; issue, two daughters and a son), Lewis married Roberta Smith, of Richmond.

(7) Martha Ann Grant married Thomas Worsham (an adopted child).

(9) Leroy Grant married Mary Minor. Issue: three sons and three daughters.

(10) Alexander died young.

Mrs. Robert Bosher has portraits of her grandfather and mother Cox, and her great-grandmother.

Issue of Thomas Smith Armistead and Lucy Anne Grant his wife: Beverly Grant, born October 30, 1869: died July 3, 1870.

1. Thomas Savage Armistead, born May 19, 1871 ; baptized June 26, 1871 by his grandfather. Rev. Robert A. Armistead; married his cousin, Anne Elisabeth Grant, at "Grantland," Henrico County, Va., November 11, 1902. Issue: Thomas Savage Armistead, Jr., born January 9, 1906, and Robert Beverly Armistead, born August 19, 1910.

Anne Elizabeth Grant is the daughter of Walter E. Grant and Elisabeth Augustine, married October 17, 1877.

Walter E. Grant is the son of James Henry Grant and Anne Elisabeth Crenshaw, who was the daughter of Spotswood Dabney Crenshaw and Winifred Graves his wife. Elisabeth Augustine was the daughter of Joseph Augustine, a native of Corsica, (born March 9, 1833, died September 15, 1864) and Lucinda Elisabeth Vaughan, of Caroline County, Va., his wife. The mother of Joseph Augustine was

Mary Madeline Maranichi, of Corsica, France. Lucinda E. Vaughan was the daughter of Reverdy Vaughan and Martha Elizabeth Chiles. There was a Col. Walter Chiles of James City County who was a Councillor and Speaker of House of Burgesses, 1651-1653.

2. Mary Beverly Armistead, daughter of Thomas Smith Armistead and Lucy Anne Grant, married William Edward Leake, November , 1895. Issue: Beverly Armistead, Ethel Wilbur, Robert Armistead, William Edward, Jr. They are living in Birmingham, Ala.

William E. Leake, born 21st of December, 1864, is the son of Thaddeus Constantine Leake, born August 17, 1829, and Nannie Coles Shelton, born November 25, 1830, of Louisa County, Va.; married November 23, 1853 Hanover County. Issue: T.Leake, Jr., William Edward Leake, Evelyn Archer (Mrs. Binford), and Kate Shelton Leake (Mrs. G. W. Jones). T. C. Leake, Sr., was the son of Walter Leake and Mahalah Johnson his wife, of Henrico County.

The line of Nannie Coles Shelton, mother of William Edward Leake, runs thus:

Colonel William Randolph, of Turkey Island, born in England 1651, emigrated to Virginia about 1669. Speaker of House of Burgesses; member of King's Council. Alarried Mary Isham, of Bermuda Hundred. Issue, among others. Col. William Randolph, born at Turkey Island November, 1681; a member of the Council; Treasurer of Virginia; married Elizabeth, daughter of Peter Beverly and Eliza Peyton, of Gloucester, June 22, 1709. Issue, among others, Mary Randolph, married John Price from Wales. Issue, among others. Captain Thomas Price, born 29th August, 1754, of "Cool Water," Hanover County, Va., an officer in American Revolution; married Barbara Winston, of Hanover County. Issue, among others. Mary Randolph Price, born at "Cool Water," Hanover County, October 6, 1776; married December 27, 1792, Isaac Coles, of Coles Hill, Hanover County. Issue, among others, Maria Coles; married William Shelton. Issue, among others, Nannie Coles Shelton; married Thaddeus Leake.

Barbara Winston was the daughter of James Winston and Anne Parrel, his wife. James Winston inherited from his mother, Barbara Overton (daughter of Col. William Overton, of England and Virginia), 1443 acres of land on the south side of North Anna River, Hanover County, Va. James Winston's father was John Winston (sometimes called James) from Wales; emigrated to America about 1702 and settled in Hanover County.

Captain Thomas Price, who married Barbara Winston, had a sister Elizabeth Price who married Captain George Dabney of "The Grove," Hanover County. He was captain in Revolutionary Army, in the Legion of his brother Col. Charles Dabney.

NOTE.—The above Shelton-Price data is taken from *The Price Family*, compiled by Theodore H. Price and Charlotte Price.

The Leake family is of English descent. The founder of the family came to Virginia in 1785 and settled in Goochland County.

3.   John Grant Armistead, son of Thomas Smith Armistead and Lucy Anne Grant, his wife, married November 11, 1909, at St. Paul's Church, Richmond, Va., Rosalie, daughter of Thomas Catesby Jones and Rosalie Fontaine, his wife, daughter of Col. Edmund Fontaine of Beaver Dam, Hanover County, Va. Thos. Catesby Jones is the son of William Roy Jones and Isabella Tailiaferro, his wife, of Marlfield, Gloucester County, Va. Thos. C. Jones is a lineal descendant of Capt. Roger Jones who came to Virginia in 1680. Arms, "Field sable, a fess or—bet. 3 children's heads, proper (quartered with the Hoskins Arms, his mother being sole heiress) in a field party per pale—azure-gules—a chevron engraled or bet, 3 lions argent—rampant. Crest—a helmet a child's head proper."

The Catesbys are from Northamptonshire, England.

Rosalie Fontaine, wife of Thos. Catesby Jones, is descended from the noble family of de la Fontaine of France.

Rosalie Fontaine is the twelfth child of Col. Edmund Fontaine of Beaver Dam, and Maria Louise Shackleford, his wife, of Hanover County.

Col. Edmond Fontaine was the son of William Fontaine and Ann Morris, his wife. William Fontaine was colonel of a regiment in the Revolutionary War, and was present with his regiment at Yorktown when Lord Cornwallis surrendered.

Maria Louise Shackleford was the daughter of Lynn Shackleford and Elizabeth Dabney, his wife.

4.   Lucie Grant Armistead, daughter of Thomas S. Armistead and Lucie Grant, his wife.

5.   Emily Armistead, youngest child of Thomas Smith Armistead and Lucy Grant, his wife, married Robert Eden Peyton, Jr., November 11, 1910, at home. R. E. Peyton, Jr., is the son of Robert Eden Peyton and Corrie Foster, his wife; both of Fauquier County, Va. R. E. Peyton was the son of Dr. R. E. Peyton, of Fauquier, and

Nannette Lee Jones, who was the daughter of General Walter Jones and Anne Lucinda Lee, the daughter of Charles Lee and Anne Lee, his wife and cousin, married at Chantilly, Westmoreland County, Va., nth February, 1789; she was born December 1, 1770; died 1804; buried at "Shooter's Hill," the home of her brother, Ludwell Lee. Anne Lee was the daughter of Richard Henry Lee, who was the son of Thomas Lee and Hannah Ludwell, his wife. All of Thomas Lee's sons were born at "Stratford Hall." Charles Lee was the brother of Light Horse Harry Lee.

"The Peyton family of Cambridgeshire, England, as well as that of their descendants, the Peytons of Westmoreland, Stafford, and Gloucester Counties, Virginia, is one of great antiquity and distinction. According to historians, the founder of the family was one of the great barons who accompanied William the Conqueror to England and obtained from him many valuable manors and lordships as a recompense for their gallant deeds and military service."

Robert Eden Peyton, Jr.'s family reside at "Edenburn," Fauquier County, a part of that grand old estate of "Gordonsdale," granted by Lord Fairfax to one of the family.

Corrie Gover Foster, the wife of Robert E. Peyton, is the daughter of Thomas Redmond Foster and Mary Ann Smith, his wife, of Loudoun County. Thomas R. Foster, the son of Isaac Foster and Priscilla Hunton, his wife, of Fauquier County. Mary Ann Smith, the daughter of Lewis Marshall Smith and Catherine Hutchison, his wife, of Loudoun. Lewis M. Smith, son of Lewis Smith and Mary Nelson, his wife; he the son of John Smith who came to Virginia from England in 1700. He settled in Westmoreland County, Va., and married Elizabeth Alarshall, aunt of Chief Justice Alarshall. ,

Robert E. Peyton, Jr., and Emily Armistead, his wife, had given them when married two heirlooms — a round silver try, on feet, with the Lee Arms in the center, descended through Anne Lee from her father, Richard Henry Lee, and a silver cream pitcher, in the shape of a cow, about four and a half inches long by two and a half high. The cow's tail, tossed in a curve to brush off a fly in the middle of her back, is the handle; by the fly the hd is lifted to pour in the cream. The cow's neck is extended, mouth open in a moo-moo, the cream pouring from open mouth. The hall marks indicate that the Lee tray was made in London by Richard Rugg in 1773-'4. The cow made in London by Thomas Issod in 1764-'5.

The Arms of the Peyton family of Westmoreland and Stafford Counties: Sable—a cross engrailed or—in second quarter a mullet argent—all within a bordure ermine.

Asher Waterman Garber, who married V. S. Armistead, is descended on his great-grandmother's side from the sturdy Scotch-Irish clan of Cunningham; on the grandfather's side from German stock; both of which settled in Augusta County early in the eighteenth century. His mother, Frances Hancock, of Princess Anne County, was a descendant of one of two brothers—Nathaniel Hancock settled in Massachusetts, from whom came Governor John Hancock; the other, Simon, settled in Princess Anne County, Va., from whom came Frances H., daughter of Simon Hancock and Susan Singleton, his wife. He was born at "Lebanon," September 15, 1834, an estate near Staunton that descended to his family through his grandmother, Margareet Smith, a daughter of Capt. Thomas Smith, of the Revolutionary War.

He was educated at the Staunton Academy and was engaged in the foundry business with his father, who owned a foundry near Staunton which was destroyed by the Yankees. He belonged to the Staunton Artillery before the war broke out. The day that Virginia seceded he left Staunton for Harper's Ferry as second lieutenant of Staunton Artillery, and from that day to the surrender at Appomattox, was at the front. John Imboden was captain; afterwards made general of cavalry. The Staunton Artillery was organized and equipped several months previous to the war. A. W. Garber was captain in 1862. Quoting the words of Senator John W. Daniel; "This famous battery which made its mark from Manassas to Appomattox on many of the greatest fields of the Civil War—First and Second Manassas, Sharpsburg, Chancellorsville, Gettysburg, The Wilderness, at Bloody Angle, Spotsylvania, Cold Harbor. In the Valley, at Cedar Creek, it joined in holding the enemy at bay when the lines were broken. It fought as infantry from Petersburg to Appomattox, and there, with its gallant and battle-smeared commander, closed a career full of honorable service and distinction." He was wounded at First Manassas while fighting on Jackson's line; in the same battle a younger brother, Edward Valentine Garber, was killed while leading a charge—he was captain of Company A, Fifty-second Virginia Regiment. In the battle of Berryville A. W. Garber was shot through his thigh, his horse had been shot under him about half hour before.

At Second Manassas he received an order in person from General Stonewall Jackson. At Spotsylvania, May loth, he received an order in person from General Lee. For full account of the Staunton Artillery record, see Vol. XXXIII., *Southern Historieal Papers.*

He had two other brothers in the war, Michael Garber, a lieutenant in Staunton Artillery, and Thomas Michie Garber, who was killed at Upperville just as he mounted a stone wall with the colors in his hand. The following is from the pen of Governor O'Ferrell;

"For some time prior to the battle of Upperville the color-bearer of the Twelfth Cavalry was Tom Garber, a member of my company. It did not take me long to determine of what metal he was made. In a fight he was in his element, and the hotter it was the better he liked it. He was only seventeen years of age, yet he was over six feet in height, splendidly built, and much more mature every way than most boys of his age. He had been raised in the saddle and was a superb rider. A vacancy occurred in the color sergeancy of the regiment—how it occurred I do not now remember—and Tom applied for the position, and it was given him, and never in any war, on any field, were the colors of an army more grandly and heroically borne.

"He entered the charge at Upperville in the van, with his colors streaming in the breeze above his head as he charged down the field to the stone fence. There under the rain of lead he stood waving the stars and bars until just as I was shot, when he reeled in his saddle, and still clinging to his, flag staff he fell to the ground dead. He was a brother of Major A. W. Garber, of Richmond, whose record as the commander of Garber's Battery is too well known to require any enconiums from me. Of all the brave and intrepid boys whom it was my pleasure and privilege to observe during the four years of strife, I never saw one who was the superior of Tom Garber; and as brave and dashing as our cavalrymen were generally. I do not detract from them when I declare that I recall comparatively few who were his equals, taking them all in all. He rests in Thornrose Cemetery at Staunton beneath the sod of old Augusta, and while she can boast of many gallant sons, she has none more gallant than the young color-bearer of the Twelfth Cavalry, who yielded up his life at Upperville."

Shortly after the war A. W. Garber established the Richmond Transfer business and a Railroad and Steamship Ticket Office, which he built up to great success, being, after some years, the owner and proprietor. Later it was made into a joint stock company, and finally passed out of his hands. Now, in old ago, he is as game, as brave, as heroic as when on the battlefield. He is a devout member of Grace Episcopal Church.

DESCENDANTS OF GEORGE W. ARMISTEAD.

George W. Armistead, son of (178) Robert A. Armistead and Martha Savage, his wife, was born in Hampton, Va., October 4, 1835. He, as well as his older brother, Robert, was educated at Randolph-Macon College, where he took his A. AI. and graduated about 1857. He studied law under the Hon. James Lyons in Richmond, and received his license to practice law in 1859. June 13, 1860, in Petersburg, Va., he married Anne Maria Harrison, a belle of ante-bellum days of rare attractiveness, born July 16, 1835, in Charles City County, daughter of William Southall Harrison* and Lucenia Anderson, who was the daughter of Nathan and Marianna Anderson, of Chesterfield County. Marianna was the daughter of John Mayo, of Richmond, and Mary Tabb, of Gloucester. Mrs. George W. Armistead has in her possession portraits of her Alayo family.

George W Armistead was a young man of unusual brilliancy and mental force, as shown by his college record and later as an editor and writer for various periodicals. In the fall of 1860 he took charge of the Ashland Female Seminary. When the war opened the town was cavalry headquarters for the Army at Northern Virginia; the excitement incident thereto made it needful to close the school. He went into service first in Captain J. Hankins Field Artillery Battery. J. D. Hankins, of Bacon Castle, Surry County, Va., was a "splendid fellow and warm personal friend." After being with his battery about a year, to his great surprise he was transferred to the Navy—James River Squadron, Training School *Patrick Henry*, as professor, with rank of lieutenant. He remained there until the evacuation, when the cadets and professors were ordered as an escort to treasure train from Richmond to the South ; first to Augusta, Ga., then back to Thomasville, N. C., where it and the whole command were captured. He tramped back to Charlotte, N. C., where he was parolled; then on to Richmond, where his wife and two little boys were, to find that they had been burned out at the evacuation. He practiced law in Richmond, and later on moved to Tennessee. He made his home in Nashville, Tenn., where he lived for years, the editor and founder of a live temperance paper. *The Issue,* established in 1885. He and his wife are now living in Hopkinsville, Ky., where their daughter, Mrs. Harry Cate, resides.

The children of George Armistead and Anne Harrison, his wife, are as follows: George Harrison, William Southall Harrison, Annie Harrison, Robert Augustus, Wirt Mayo, and Mary Lucenia.

(1) George Harrison Armistead, born August 21, 1861, at Ashland, Va., graduated at the High School in Richmond when fifteen, taking first honor — a gold star — in a large class. When his father moved from Virginia he sent him to the University of Mississippi, where he soon took his degree, making the highest scholarship marks taken up to that time in the University. He then went to Vanderbilt University, where he took his law degree. In Nashville and elsewhere in the South he earned the reputation of being a brilliant speaker. March 14, 1889, he married Jessie Parkes, eldest daughter of Joseph L. Parkes, cashier of the National Pank of Franklin, Tenn.

Joseph L. Parkes is an Englishman by birth ; a relative of Sir Arthur Parkes, the eminent Australian statesman and jurist. The mother of Jessie Parkes Armistead is Louise Everly, daughter of General Silas Walker, one of Tennessee's most distinguished lawyers.

George Harrison Armistead resides with his family in Franklin, Tenn., where he is editor of a live, influential newspaper. Their children are: George Harrison A., Joseph Parkes A., Leonard Kearn A., Annie A., Jessie Parkes A., Louise Mayo A., Edward Carmack A., James Hamner A.

(2) William Southall Harrison Armistead, born in Richmond, Va., August II, 1864, attended the Vanderbilt University; settled in South Pittsburg, Tenn., where he married, October 20, 1888, Katherine Houston, of South Pittsburg, Tenn., daughter of William Houston, who was the nephew of Governor Sam Houston. On maternal side she was the great-niece of "Bonnie Kate Sevier" of Indian fame, wife of Governor Sevier, and niece of Col. Arthur S. Colyar, of Nashville, Tenn., member of Confederate Congress, who at eighty-seven years of age wrote the *Life of Andrew Jackson.* Issue: William Houston, Katherine Sevier, Robert P., Houston, Elbert Ina Virginia, and Harrison.

(3) Annie Harrison Armistead, born October 3, 1869, in Richmond, Va.; educated at Price's College, Nashville, Tenn.: married James H. Cate, of Rumsey, McLean County, Ky., November 8, 1887,

in Nashville. Tenn., and died in Rumsey, Ky., March 13, 1896, leaving issue: Annie ArmisteadV., James H. C., John Mayo C., Robert William C., George Harrison C.

(4) Robert Augustus Armistead, born in Brunswick County, Va., January 9, 1867. Unmarried; resides in Nashville, Tenn.

(5) Wirt Alayo Armistead, born in Richmond, Va., September 8, 1872, married Sarah Cate (of Hartford, Ky.), March 30, 1901, at Henderson, Ky.

Sarah Cate, wife of Wirt Alayo Armistead, and *James Henry Cate*, her brother, who married *first*, Annie Harrison Armistead; *second*, her sister Mary Lucenia Armistead, are both the children cf James and Mary Cate of Owensboro, Kentucky. Their maternal grandmother, Sarah Nichols, married Phipps; their maternal great-grandmother was Margaret Randolph of Virginia, who married Nichols.

The children of Wirt AL Armistead and Sarah Cate, his wife, are: Wirt Alayo A., Jr., James Cate A. and Frances Allina A.

(6) Mary Lucenia Armistead, born in Richmond, Va., married James H. Cate in Nashville, Tenn., September 20, 1899. Issue: Wirt Armistead C., Mary Lou C., Elizabeth Alayo C., Margareet Randolph C., Robert Armistead C. (died in infancy), and Dorothy Harrison C. They reside in Hopkinsville, Ky.

Annie Armistead Cate, eldest child of James H. Cate and Anne H. Armistead his first wife, married, March 8, 1909, Frank R. King, of Leighton, Ala.

F. R. Kings maternal grandmother was Fanny Louise Boggs, cf Philadelphia, whose mother, Margaret Dent, was sister of Mrs. U. S. Grant's mother. His great-grandmother was Steptoe Pickett, who married Sarah Felicia Chilton, of Fauquier County. It is said that the Picketts were Huguenots. Of the three brothers who came to the colonies, one settled in New England, one in Carolina, and one in Virginia. William Pickett, son of the Virginia emigrant, married Elizabeth, daughter of Hon. Alordecai Cooke and Elizabeth Buckner, his wife, of Gloucester County.

The following paper was read before the Tennessee Woman's Historical Association:

CATHERINE SHERRILL SEVIER.

"The settlers who planted civilization west of the Alleghenic.s were mostly North Carolinians and Virginians; the culled wheat of that Old Dominion who possessed those good qualities which made the name Virginian a badge of honor throughout the colonies. Among those extraordinary people were two families which are connected with my subject, and who were considered 'well-to-do' people of the pioneer days; one from Virginia, the family of John Sevier, and the other from North Carolina, which was the family of Samuel Sherrill. The latter consisted of several sons and two daughters, Susan, who married Col. Taylor, a gentleman of distinction, and Catherine Sherrill, the subject of my paper, who was destined to be a queen of society.

"Catherine first opened her blue eyes into this world at her father's home on the banks of the Yadkin in North Carolina. She comes to notice in history for the first time when about the age of twenty: a strikingly attractive young lady, tall and willowy, quite erect in carriage; possessing a wealth of brown hair which agreed wondrously well with her clear complexion; a roman nose and a square chin, combining beauty with strength and force of character and endowed with a lovely disposition, this beautiful girl thoroughly enjoyed the life of a pioneer, and was not only one of the handsomest but *the bravest and best* girls of the settlement who faced the dangers of frontier life.

"It was in 1776 when the bravery and presence of mind and *flectness*, the last for which this child of the wilderness was famed, were put to the test, making a romantic incident in her life which has come down in history. It was at Fort Watauga, in the summer time, that the pioneers were warned of the approach of the Cherokees, and most of the settlers had gathered in the fort. Not fearing an immediate attack, early in the morning, July 31st, several women ventured outside the fort, among them Catherine Sherrill. They had been out only a short while when they were startled by a war whoop. Screaming, they made a rush for the gate—all reaching it save one, Catherine Sherrill, who had wandered farther than the others. She darted with the fleetness of the wind when she saw the Indians between her and the fort. Among those inside who saw her peril was Capt. John Sevier, who, with several other men rushed out of the gate hoping to rescue her. But Capt. James Robertson, realizing how futile were their efforts against three hundred Indians, called them in and began firing upon the enemy with their rifles. Catherine, realizing the situation turned and made a dash for the other side of the fort, the walls of which were eight feet high. It was now a race for life, but with the agility of a deer she reached the wall. She was aided by some one within, but his foot slipped and they each fell on opposite sides of the wall.The Indians were close upon her; their bullets and arrows around her like hail. It was now leap the wall or die, for she could not live a captive. With one mighty spring she gained the top. Captain Sevier was there and caught her in his arms as she leaped inside, greeting her with 'Bonnie Kate, a brave girl for a foot race.'

"Captain Sevier was at this time a married man, having married at the age of seventeen in Virginia, Sarah Hawkins, who had remained with her younger children in Virginia until Captain Sevier and the oldest sons had located and improved a home in the wilderness of the Watauga Valley. She died in Virginia in 1779, leaving ten children. In 1780, within four years after Catherine Sherrill's thrilling and romantic escape from the Indians, she was married to Captain John Sevier. The women of those days were taught all the arts of domestic life, and Catherine Sherrill Sevier, now the mistress of the Sevier estate. 'Plum Grove, assumed the duties of the household quite gracefully and with much devotion to her husband for a period of forty years.

*   *   *   *

"To the prudent and judicious actions of Mrs. Catherine Sevier was due much of her husband's popularity and success. When the establishment of the State of Frankland was effected by those settlers who were dissatisfied with the state of affairs under North Carolina's control. John Sevier was chosen the first, as well as the last. Governor of the new State. This gave some offense, and Governor Sevier was entrapped and lured by the enemies into North Carolina. Again did Mrs. Sevier show her unusual qualities of daring and promptly arranged and urged his friends to rescue him. After these times were over and the new State became Tennessee. Governor Sevier, the idol of his people, was again chosen as their Governor, and was re-elected again and again, and vet again, serving twelve years, the limited term of eligibility to the office. During this period the Governor's mansion, known as 'The Hospitable Mansion, was a home of culture and refinement and graceful hospitality, where levees and brilliant receptions were held, graced by the beauty and gallantry of Tennessee, and over which this superb woman. Mrs. Catherine Sherrill Sevier reigned as queen, and whose wit and brilliancy not only brightened the life of her adoring husband, but those with whom she came in contract."

Mary Louisa Armistead, daughter of Robert Augustus Armistead and Martha Ann Savage, his wife, was born in Hampton, va., where her girlhood was spent. She was educated at Col. John B. Cary's school—Hampton Academy.

During the war she. with the rest of the family, refugeed from place to place—always near the front. The longest stay was in Petersburg, till a shell came crashing through the next house, another burying itself under the porch of her home, which necessitated another move—one of nine—till the family settled permanently in Richmond in 1866. After the break-up from Hampton, her father determined to keep near the fighting line so as to be in touch with his sons.

Mary Lou Armistead was a veritable war-time belle, her vivacity, music and singing charming away for the time all thought of hardship and danger which encompassed those brave men, some of whom met death a few hours after their voices and hers mingled in those dear old songs that come echoing through that glorious past like "bells at evening pealing." It was in Richmond that she met William C. Nelson, whom she married in 1867.

She was one of the pioneers in establishing a Southern Chautauqua at Monteagle, Tenn., spending her first summer there in a tent. The family have spent their summers there for the past thirty years—perhaps more—she holding various offices in the management. For years she has been chairman of the committee to choose books for the library. The cultured atmosphere of this Chautauqua has been, and still is, thoroughly congenial to her and her family. Nashville, Tenn., is their winter home.

NELSON EXCURSUS.

Edward Nelson, son of James Nelson, of Essex County, England, was born A. D. 1690. He had one sister, Elizabeth, older than himself, their parents dying when they were very young. They resided with an uncle who lived in a small village near London. Edward Nelson in boyhood was of an erratic disposition and in consequence of the harshness of his uncle and guardian became tired of school. Making the acquaintance of the captain of an English merchantman, he became quite fond of him, and the captain returned this affection. On one occasion, when the vessel lay in port, and whilst young Edward was allowed a vacation from studies, the captain, by glowing accounts of the pleasures of a sailor's life, so fired the imagination of his youthful friend that Edward determined to accompany him on his next voyage. Having preconcerted an arrangement with the captain, he, one Sunday morning, feigned sickness in order to remain at home whilst his uncle and family attended church. In their absence he made up a small bundle of clothing, and avoiding the observation of the servants, succeeded in getting on board the vessel which sailed a few hours afterwards. At that period he was only fourteen years of age. After an adventurous life of fourteen years upon the ocean, during which he visited almost every port of the then known world, he landed in Virginia and settled on Little River, in the county of Hanover, then called New Kent. During his voyage he had the misfortune to lose one of his eyes. The year after landing in Virginia he married Mary Garland, the second daughter of Edward and Jane Garland, who had settled in that county many years prior to that time. Issue, among others, James Nelson, who married in 1750 Keziah Harris. Issue, among others, Peter Carr Nelson, who married, December 4, 1789, Nancy Lawrence, Issue, among others, James Henry Nelson, who moved to Holly Springs, Miss., and married, November 26, 1840, Maria Courtney Goodrich (James). Issue, among others, William Cowper Nelson, who married, March 26, 1867, at Centenary Churcn, Richmond, Va. Mary Louisa Armistead, Daughter of Robert A. Armistead and Martha Anne Savage, of Hampton, Va. Issue: Martha Armistead Nelson; Maria Courtney Nelson, died June 17, 1871, Richmond, Va.; James Henry Nelson, died September 4, 1872, Nashville, Tenn.; William Clarence Nelson, died May 14, 1876, Nashville, Tenn.; Mary Louise Nelson; Robert Armistead Nelson; Virginia Garber Nelson; Kinlock Falconer Nelson, died July 9, 1885, Nashville, Tenn.; Wilbur Armistead Nelson,

Rev. Peter Carr Nelson, born 1757, was rector of St. Mattins Parish, Hanover County, Va., in 1789. According to Bishop Meade's *Old Families of Virginia* he was still rector of the parish in 1799, and was pastor of the Old Fork Church in 1808 or 1809 according to Dr. Jeter's *Baptist Ministers of Virginia*. He was baptized by immersion, together with his wife, and connected himself with the Baptist Church. He died February 15, 1827, and was buried at the Old Fork Church by the side of his wife, Nancy Lawrence, who died in May,

1814, in the fortyfifth year of her age.

Rev. Peter Carr Nelson was educated by Mr. Anderson Beil, a Scotchman, who also educated the children of the Berkeleys and Pages. He entered William and Mary College (the University not then being endowed) ; graduated with great distinction. Soon after went to Philadelphia, took orders, and preached twenty years in the Old Fork Church (Episcopal), Hanover. He married Anne Lawrence, daughter of Mr. Edward Lawrence and Fannie Taylor, who was sister of Mr. Thomas Taylor, a prominent citizen of Richmond, Va., and first cousin to the Gaits, Ellises, Harrisons.

Peter Nelson was esteemed the most learned man of his age. He left five sons and three daughters, remarkable for literary culture and high order of mind. The eldest of his three daughters married Rev. Thomas N. Fox of the English family—his father being nephew of Lord Holland and cousin of the celebrated statesman. Their daughter Elizabeth was considered by the learned men of that time to possess "more mental and moral energy" than any other woman they had ever known. Mary Nelson, the youngest, was alike celebrated for great persona) beauty and lovely character. Fanny Nelson was an intelligent and useful woman. The eldest sons of these three ladies were remarkable for their high order of intellect. Wallace Day, son of Frances, attained great distinction as a lawyer. Mary Nelson Schooler's son, although he died young, wrote some works which became text-books in England.

WILLIAM COWPER NELSON'S WAR RECORD.

"William Cowper Nelson entered Barksdale's Brigade (we think it was the Thirteenth Alississippi Infantry) Army of Northern Virginia, in spring of 1861 as a private, and wintered in Pensacola. Served in this brigade until the latter part of 1862 or early part of 1863, when he was transferred and commissioned lieutenant of ordinance for Harris' Mississippi Brigade, Mahone's Division, Hill's Corps, A. N. Va., and with this command served until the surrender at Appomattox. In spring of 1865 was commissioned captain, but army surrendered before this commission went into effect. Was commended in *Army Bulletin* for bravery in carrying dispatches under fire at Fredericksburg, where his brigade was the last to fall back. Was in the battles around Richmond, Second Manassas, Sharpsburg, Fredericksburg, etc."

Extract from the Kentucky and Tennessee Board of Underwriters:

"As secretary of the Board, Colonel Nelson brought to the service of the associated companies the fruits of a long, active and valuable experience in underwriting. Possessing a mind of great breadth and intelligence, highly trained in scholarship, and by application to the problems of underwriting in the field and in the office, he rendered services of great value to the interests committed to his care. Strong in his convictions, firm in his business purposes, he was animated solely by the desire to do justice under all circumstances.

"Colonel Nelson's personal qualities greatly endeared him to all the members of this Association. His wide and varied scholarship, his genial humor and great kindness of heart and generosity of nature, made him, under all circumstances, a delightful friend and companion."

W. C. Nelson was born in Holly Springs, Miss., September 7, 1841 ; died in Louisville, Ky., July 2, 1904.

Martha Armistead Nelson, eldest daughter of William C. Nelson and Mary Lou Armistead, married Claude Waller, of Nashville, Tenn., December, 1895, in New Orleans, La.

Judge Claude Waller, of Nashville, Tenn., general counsel for N. C. & St. L. R. R., is the son of William Waller, of Henderson County, Kentucky, and Elizabeth Muir, his wife, of Nelson County, Kentucky, married November 10, 1836, near Bardstown. Nelson County. See *Old King Wilharn Homes and Families* for English line of the Waller family of Notinghamshire from the twelfth century.

William Waller (father of Claude) was the son of Aaren Waller, who was the son of John Waller. This John was the son of John who went from Virginia to Maryland, thence to Kentucky, to what is now known as Washington County. There is a tradition that he was taken prisoner by the Indians on his journey and carried to Ohio, where he was kept for more than a year, escaping and rejoining his family in Kentucky. His son John settled in what is now Union County, in 1806-'7, as shown by deed registered in County Court of Henderson (which then included Union County) "conveying to John Waller of Washington Co. about two thousand acres of land lying a few miles from the present county seat of Union Co."

(1) John Waller, of England, born 1617, married Mary Key; settled in New Kent County, Va., 1635. He brought with him a seal with the Waller Arms, which is now in the possession of cue of his descendants. He had a son (2) John (Col. John W.). of Enfield, King

William County, afterwards moved to New port, Spotsylvania County, born 1673; died 1754. Alarried probably about 1700 Dorothy King. He was sheriff of King William County, 1702; burgess 1710; first clerk of Spotsylvania County 1722-1742. Issue: Mary, married Zackery Lewis; Edmund, (3) John, Thomas, Benjamin, William. (3) John Waller was born about 1706-7, and was probably the John who emigrated to Kentucky.

Elizabeth Muir (wife of William Waller, of Kentucky), daughter of (3) William L. Muir, who was the son of (2) William Aluir, an AI. D. of the Edinburgh University; his father, William Aluir, was also an AI. D. of Ayr, Scotland. (2) William Aluir, eldest son, came to this country just prior to the Revolutionary War, intending to return to Scotland, but he married an English lady, Loch, and settled in Mary land, close to the Potomac, until 1806, when he settled in Nelson County, Kentucky, about two and a half miles from Bardstown. where he practiced his profession until he was eighty-four; died when eighty-six. The above statement was written by him. and is in the possession of the family.

Issue of Claude Waller and Martha Armistead Nelson, his wife: William, James Muir, Robert Armistead and Martha Nelson.

"Deep in the recesses of a lonely group of pnes in the edge of a wood" in Spotsylvania County is the tomb of William Waller (third clerk of Spotsylvania), who died January lo, 1760, 45 years and 7 months.

Among the libraries of Colonial Virginia was that Colonel John Waller of New Port, first clerk of Spotsylvania, inventory recorded in Spotsylvania County, February 5, 1755. His daughter Mary, who married Zachery Lewis, had a descendant, Lewis Littlepage, who accompanied Mr. Jay, the United States Minister at Madrid, to that city. He volunteered in an expedition against Minorca in 1781, and was with the Count Nassau at the seige of Gibralter. He afterwards went to Warsaw, where he "enjoyed the esteem and confidence of Stanislaus, King of Poland." Littlepage held, under that monarch, the office of Ambassador to Russia. Lewis Littlepage died in Fredericksburg, Va., in 1802, being in the fortieth year of his age. John, son of above Col. John, is supposed to be the John who went from Virginia to Kentucky as before stated, from whom is descended Judge Claude Waller, now living in Nashville, Tenn.

"Enfield," the original home of the Waller family in King William County, Va., is situated on the bank of the Mattapony River; the land is part of the original grant to John Waller b; King Charles. The patent is still in existence. The house is more than one hundred and fifty years old, and has been occupied by a long line of Wallers. It was from here that Benjamin Waller, who married Miss Travis, started to Alabama in 1820.

The following by Mr. Stanard, Secretary Virginia Historical Society, that most accurate of genealogists:

"Waller, one of the most ancient and distinguished among the English gentry, was founded by Alured de Waller, a Norman who settled in County of Kent and died in 1183. From him descended the Wallers of that and other countries. Richard Waller distinguished himself at the battle of Agincourt, where he took prisoner the French prince, Duke of Orleans. Henry fifth, in honor of his services added, to the ancient Arms of the family (which were "sable, three walnut leaves or. between two bendlets az) the crest, a walnut tree proper, or the sinister side an escutcheon pendant, charged with the Arms of France (three fleur de lis) with a label of three points and the motto: 'Haec fructus virtutis.' The first of the Virginia branch, John W. (AI. D.), either a descendant or near relative of the poet Edmund Waller, a prominent citizen of New Port, Paganel, Buckinghamshire, England, was living in 1688. Married Mary Issue: Leonard, William, John, Mary, Thomas, Stephen, Benjamin, Edmund (AI. D.), James, Jemima.

"Dr. Edmund Waller was a senior fellow of St. John's College, Cambridge, where he died in 1745.

"The third son, John Waller, came to Virginia in latter part of seventeenth century, and settled in King and Queen County, afterward King William on Mattapony. He was sheriff 1702, justice 1705, burgess 1719. When the county of Spotsylvania was formed, 1721, he was the first clerk, which he held till 1742: died in 1754. Possessed a silver seal, with same crest, arms, and motto described above. He, John Waller, married Dorothea King. The Rev. W. E. Waller, born 1750, minister more than fifty years, removed to Kentucky 1781, but died in his native county July, 1830. He had five sons — two of them ministers in Kentucky. A third, William Smith Waller, born 1785, died 1855, a prominent banker in Kentucky; married Catherine Breckenridge. Issue: four sons and three daughters."

Wilbur Teackle Armistead, fifth son and ninth child of Robert Augustine Armistead and Martha Ann Savage, his wife, was only seventeen when the war broke out. Joined Company K, First

Regiment of Engineers, A. N. *Va.*, Col. T. AI. R. Talcott commander; surrendered and was parolled at Appomattox C. H,, Va., April 9, 1865. He had several hair-breadth escapes and interesting experiences. Was the recipient of a pass from General R. E. Lee worded, "Pass W. T. Armistead, private, anywhere within the lines." In 1867 he went to Boliva, Tenn., 10 live; there married, October 26, 1869, Lucie Bills, daughter of John Houston Bills and Lucy Ann Duke—sister of Col. R. T. W. Duke, a prominent and distinguished family of Albemarle County, Va. Lucy Ann Duke was the widow of David Wood of that county. John Houston Bills was a direct descendant of John Bills and Dorothy, his wife, who came to this country, Massachusetts, prior to 1635, and owned a large part of the land on which the City of Boston now stands. Lucie, wife of W. T. Armistead, died at "Sunnyside." Albemarle County, Va., the home of her uncle. Col. Duke, March 9, 1893; buried in Hollywood, Richmond. Va. No children by this marriage.

After this, W. T. Armistead moved back to Richmond, and June 20, 1895, married in Memphis, Tenn., Emma LeMaster, daughter of Nathaniel Eield LeMaster and Olivia Ann Rawlings, his wife. Issue by this marriage: Nathaniel LeMaster Armistead, born August 8, 1896, in Richmond, Va.; Emma Olivia Armistead, born in Memphis, March 20, 1904; Wilbur Teackle Armistead (a daughter), born in Corinth, Miss., December 16, 1905, where they now reside (1908).

Wilbur T. Armistead possesses many of the characteri.stics of his father—notably, his independence in thought and action.

LeMaster.

John LeAlaster, the grandfather of James Sturgis LeAlaster, came to Virginia in 1700 and obtained grants of land in Amherst County, which was then a wild region. The Floyds also settled here, coming from Wales. William Floyd married Abidiali Davis, daughter of Robert Davis, who owned large tracts of the richest lands in Amherst. In 1751, at the age of 18, married Miss Burfoot; she died a year later. Col. John Floyd moved to Botetourt County. In 1774 Col. Floyd went to Kentucky together with his two brothers-in-law John LeAlaster, who married Jemima Floyd, and Peter Sturgus, who married Abidiah Floyd. Col. Floyd owned a fine estate on Beargrass Creek, six miles from Louisville. He built a fort and stockade. •

John LeMaster emigrated at an early date to Virginia, and

married Jemima Floyd. Issue, among others, John Floyd LeMaster.

Sturgus was also an early settler in Virginia, and married Abidiah Floyd. Issue, among others, Peter Sturgus, who married Anne Tyler and had one child, a daughter, Margaret.

Peter Sturgus and John LeAlaster were both killed in the same fight with the Indians in the fort near Louisville. The same day Anne Tyler Sturgus with her infant, Alargaret, was on her way to the fort to see her husband, when she was captured by the Indians and marched to Montreal, where she remained a prisoner nearly a year. Was exchanged by the British who had taken charge of all prisoners when they reached Alontreal. She returned to Louisville a year from the day of her capture.

John Floyd LeAlaster, son of Jane Floyd and John LeAlaster, married Margareet Sturgus the infant captive. Issue: two sons, Charles and James Sturgus LeAlaster, the former killed in the first duel ever fought in Kentucky. James Sturgus LeAlaster married Penelope Pope Field. James Sturgus, brother of Peter Sturgus, married Jamima Floyd LeAlaster, widow of John LeAlaster, killed by the Indians. Their daughter, Cynthia Sturgus, married William Pope, son of Col. William Pope, of Jefferson County, Ky.; their daughter Jane married Maj. Abner Field.

The Floyd notes were copied from *Floyd Family*, written by Mrs. Letitia P. Floyd, wife of Governor John Floyd, of Virginia.

Olivia Ann Rawlings, wife of Nathaniel Field LeAlaster, was the daughter of J. J. Rawlings and Olivia Anne Sedgwick, of Calvert County, Md. The mother of Olivia Ann Sedgwick was a Miss Alexander, of Lancaster County, Va.

Mr. J. J. Rawlings was of an old and prominent family of Calvert County, Md.; his mother was a Miss Claire of same county. Mr. J. J. Rawlings was one of the earliest settlers of Memphis, when it was known as Chickasaw Bluffs.

William Pope, of Jefferson County, Ky., son of William Pope, of Fauquier County, Va., and Miss Notherton emigrated to Kentucky in 1779 with his wife Penelope Edwards, daughter of Hayden Edwards. Issue, among others, Jane Pope, who married Maj. Abner Field, an early settler of Kentucky, and one of the first representatives in the Virginia House of Burgesses. Issue, among others, Penelope Pope Field, who married. May 5, 1824, James Sturgus LeMaster. Soon after their marriage they moved near Athens, Ala. In 1833 they went down the Tennessee River in flat boats to Memphis, and settled near

Raleigh, the county seat of Shelby. In 1837 they moved to "Greenwood," the LeMaster home estate, nine miles southeast of Memphis, where they lived until their death, James Sturgus dying in 1874, aged 74 years, and Penelope dying in 1880, aged 79 years.

They had ten children, among them Nathaniel Field LeMaster, born February 13, 1836; married Olivia A. Rawlings October, 1857. Issue, among others, Emma LeMaster, who married Wilbur Teackle Armistead, of Richmond, Va., June 20, 1895, in Memphis; James Sturgus LeMaster, and William Pope LeMaster, who married, 1906, Sadie Railey, of Denver, Colorado, in which State they now reside. Issue: Nathaniel F. LeMatser, Jr.

The Popes were pioneers of the State of Kentucky and prominent in State and military affairs; intermarried with the Prestons, Brookes, Sturgus, Bullocks, Oidhoms, Fields, Tontonies.

Westwood Smith, twelfth child and sixth son of Robert Augustine Armistead and Martha Ann Savage, his wife, was born 17th day of May, 1854; died in Chicago suddenly when thirty-five years old; buried in Hollywood, Richmond, Va. He was educated at private schools in Richmond, Va., and Ranolph-Macon College. In 1883, October 10th, he married Mary Adele Talbott, of Richmond, Va. Issue, Caroline Talbott Armistead.

Mary Adele Talbott, daughter of Charles Talbott and Caroline Moore Benson, his wife, was born in Richmond, Va.

Charles Talbott, of English ancestry, was born in Anne Arundel County (now Howard County), Maryland, September 15, 1813. Was the son of John Lawrence and Mary (Porter) Talbott, who was the son of Richard and Ruth Dorsey (widow Todd) Talbott, and who descended from Richard Talbott, who received in 1649 a patent from the Proprietary Government cf the Province for a tract of land called "Timber Neck," located on the south side of West River in Anne Arundel County, Maryland. He also acquired large bodies of land, afterwards his home, known as "Poplar Knoll," which remained in possession of the family until 1755.

In 1655 Richard1 Talbott married Elizabeth Ewen, daughter of Major Richard Ewen, a prominent man in the Province Richard Talbott came to Maryland by invitation of Governor Stone in 1649, settling there at the same period with Sir William Talbott, Col. George Talbott, who were all relatives of Lord Baltimore.

Clipped from the *Trade Journal:*

"The mechanical world will be interested in knowing that the late Charles Talbott, of the house of Talbott & Sons, of Richmond, Va., was the inventor and builder of the first portable steam engine ever constructed. This occurred in 1840. Mr. Talbott possessed a rare mechanical genius which was illustrated in the extensive and prosperous business he founded in Richmond. He was, moreover, a man of great moral worth, and his sudden death, which occurred but a little more than a year ago, at the age of sixty-eight years, was deeply lamented by all who knew him. His genius, and his life, which was marked for honorable deeds, are a monument more enduring than stone."

Charles Talbott married, May 31. 1836, Caroline Moore Benson, who was born in Princess Anne, Somerset County, Maryland, October 17. 1813. She was the daughter of George and Jane (Anderson) Benson, and granddaughter of Adam and Amelia (Benson) Anderson, and settled in Richmond, Va., in 1837.

During the Civil War, Shockoe Machine Works, owned by the Talbotts, were turned over to the Confederate Government for the manufacture of machinery, etc. He then retired to his country seat, "Midlothian," in Gloucester County, Va., remaining there until the close of the war, returning to Richmond to continue his business, which grew to be one of the largest in the South before his death, December 17, 1881.

April 24, 1910, the following appeared in the *Times-Dispatch*, twenty-eight years after Mr. Talbott's death:

"On April 24, 1882, the chimes of Centenary Church first rang out as a memorial to the founder of the Talbott family in Richmond, a man who was most closely allied with the business life, the social life, and the religious life of this city in his day, and who went to his grave full of years and rich in the esteem and respect of his fellow townsmen."

Ruth Dorsey, the grandmother of Charles Talbott, came of a distinguished family of Maryland. The Dorsey or D'Arcy, originally French, trace back to the days of the Crusaders. They followed William the Norman to England; later settled in Ireland, where they were powerful in the councils of the nation.

The Arms of the Irish branch are now borne by the Maryland family.

Edward Dorsey came to Maryland in 1642. His son (Hon.) John Dorsey was member of House of Burgesses, 1692-1700, 1703-1710,

156

when he became member of the Council; was also at that time commissioned colonel of militia. (*Maryland Archives,* Vols. XIII., XXVI-XXIX., and *Colonial Dames Register* 1908, by Dr. C. C. Johnson.) The line runs thus: Honorable John Dorsey married Pleasants Ely; their son Edward Dorsey married Ruth Gillis; their son Captain John Dorsey married Elizabeth Hill; their *daughter* Ruth Dorsey married Richard Talbott; their son John Lawrence Talbott married, second, Mary Porter; their son Charles Talbott married Caroline Benson, *all* of Maryland.

The family Bible of Robert Armistead and Elizabeth Smith, his wife, being unusual in size, illustrations, and type, and the date torn out, the editor wrote to Rev. John Wright, a Bible expert, sendng a section of a torn illustration and of title page, to learn what she could of the Bible—which is seventeen inches long, ten and a half wide, four thick; bound in calf, covered with black bombazine. Mr. Wright replied promptly and courteously in the following letters: It is gratifying to know that this Bible will be listed among those in Mr. Wright's second edition of *Historic Bibles.*

"St. Paul, January 4, 1907.

"Dear Mrs. Garber:

"An American reprint of your Bible appeared in New Yoik in 1801. It was edited by Rev. Paul Wright, D. D., Vicar of Oakley. I have written to England to the present Vicar of Oakley to ask if he can give me the date of the English edition. I have returned the title page and portion of the engraving.

"If I can have a biography of the original owner of this Bible, I can use it for the second edition of *Historic Bibles.* Was ne patriot or orator?

"Sincerely yours,

"John Wright."

"St. Paul, February 8, 1908.

"My Dear Mrs. Garber:

"I thank you for your splendid family history so complete in every respect. I shall consult it freely in making up my manuscript. I have written to the librarian of the British Museum in regard to the date of your Bible. Will let you know as soon as I hear from him.

"Sincerely yours,

"JOHN WRIGHT."

ST. Paul, *March* 3, 1908.

"My Dear Mrs. Garber:

"I have just heard from the librarian of the British Aluseum. Fortunately they have a duplicate of your Bible in that institution, and the date is 1782.

"I trust this will be of great satisfaction to you.

"Sincerely yours,

"JOHN WRIGHT."

SMITHS.

This summer (1907), while in Hampton examining Armistead wills in the Clerk's office, we happened to mention to mr. William Westwood, who was kindly assisting us, that we were still uncertain about our grandmother, Elizabeth Smith's line. The older members of the family were all gone who could have have taken delight in it, but during his life time we never thought of such things, and cared less. Our grandmother, Elizabeth Smith, we had always heard from our father, was of superb appearance, dressed always in accord with her dignity and position—a clever woman of fine executive ability. She thought much of her Smith lineage, giving her name to more than half of her children. Our only clew was that OUT father frequently spoke of a cousin, Lawrence Smith, who was a cotemporary, and lived in Hampton. As soon as we mentioned this fact to Mr. Westwood, he told us that a daughter of that Mr. Lawrence Smith, Mrs. Cumming, lived in Hampton, and could no doubt put us in the way of finding out all that we desired. We were soon at Mrs. Cumming's residence on Armistead Avenue, and to our great delight she told us that Elizabeth Smith's father, Thomas Smith, and her father's grandfather, Lawrence Smith, of Yorktown, were twin brothers. She had heard her father say this repeatedly. She referred us to Mr. Tyler's Temple Farm records.

Returning to Richmond, we found the Lawrence Smith records, but decided to go to Yorktown to examine a deed referred to by Mr. Tyler; as well as wills.

That day in Yorktown will ever be remembered as one of the most interesting of our life. We had a delightful trip from West Point on the York River steamer, which landed us there after dark. "Mine host of the Swan Tavern" (built on the site of the old Swan Tavern) piloted us over a sandy, rough-and-tumble road; no sidewalks, no light but the stars. We soon retired, sleeping in a high te.ster bedstead; arose early the next morning, and strolled, before breakfast, through the old town.

SAIITH OF TOTNESS, DEVONSHIRE, ENGLAND.

Taken from the Arms on the tomb of Mildred Smith (sister of
Thomas Smith), who married David Jamison, Lieutenant
Governor of Virginia. The tomb is at Temple
Farm, impaled with the Jamison Arms.

that seems to have gone into a trance that has lasted for a century and a half.

Just across, on a side road, is the Episcopal Church, built in 1700, of cemented marl or oyster shells, its simple structural lines and solidity speaking proudly of the taste and craftsmanship of our forefathers. Further on, the first Custom Flouse in America recalls what a busy mart of trade this town once was, the river alive with ships coming from and going to the old world. Near by is a rambling, old brick house, with its sloping roof and dormer windows, looking like a frowzy-browed, weather-beaten old man. When we came to the Nelson House we felt all the reverence that is its due, as it stands there, majestic and grave in its desolation. Visions came of us of our mother and Aunt Margaret tripping up those steps in high-heeled slippers and white satin gowns ; their youth, beauty, and bright anticipations of the brilliant ball to Lafayette. How we children loved to hear her tell of the exciting preparations, going to Norfolk for the buying and making of the gowns — mother's was white satin — she was sixteen; aunt Margaret older; their long white kid gloves had stamped on them miniature pictures of Lafayette. We remember seeing the beautiful thread lace worn in those days.

Across the road from the Nelson House is an old, high-pointed, dormer window house, where the Nelsons lived before the new house was built. Just behind this, another old brick house, and further on another, all saying as "plain as whisper in the air, the place is haunted" — haunted with visions of dainty maids and stately dames, doughty esquires and lordly planters. We could hear the clarion voice of the Revolution echoing from Middle Plantation around the circle of the colonies, back to this hallowed ground, where our Washington forced the haughty English nobleman to surrender to American independence.

We retraced our steps as in a dream. After breakfast we again drifted back to the colonial past in going ever old deeds and wills in the Clerk's office. After reading our great-great-grand-father, Edmund Smith's will, and learning that "Temple Farm" was the Smith homestead, as well as "Bay Tree Plantation," we were more than anxious to go over the ground. We were simply amazed, as we drove along, at the grand water view, where the York sweeps out boldly to the bay. Never saw a finer location — the river makes a bend, sweeping around the bluff that slopes gradually inland. The house is in a fair state of preservation; the huge beams in the cellar look as if they were there for another century. Its existence as a plantation goes back to 1633; it was once owned by Governor Harvey. Here, one of those traveling courts, which met by rotation in certain gentlemen's houses in the early seventeenth century, was probably held. Fierce circumstances have occurred on this historic spot. Governor Harvey mortgaged the land to George Menefie, and George Ludlow was the next owner. It touched the land of Nicholas Martian, on which Yorktown stands. George Ludlow left this land to his nephew, Lieutenant-Colonel Thomas Ludlow. Mary, widow of this Thomas, married Reverend Peter Temple; and it is most probable that Temple farm thus got one of its names. Major Lawrence Smith, of Gloucester, was its next owner. The old tale of Mr. Temple and Governor Spotswood's bodies resting within this land is pretty well exploded. Major Smith bought Temple farm in 1686, and in 1691 he laid Benjamin Reade's land out into the present town. The lots were half-acres.

Major Lawrence Smith's first wife was Mildred Chisman, grandmother of Thomas Smith of York. Lawrence Smith's second wife was Alildred, daughter of John Reade and great-granddaughter of the first owner of Yorktown. She was sister of Mrs. Thomas Nelson, and for her sake probably Lawrence Smith bought land in the locality of her birth and early association. Robert Smith sold it in 1769 to Augustine Aloore, who had married his sister, Lucy Smith. Augustine Moore died in 1788, and left Temple farm, now called (quite as often) the "Moore house," to his "ever worthy friend. General Thomas Nelson," at the death of his wife. He had no children. The articles of surrender were signed in the old house, pictorially so familiar to everybody — which was in 1781 the property of Augustine Aloore.

It was built by the Ludlows and sold to Lawrence Smith in 1686. It was occupied by his descendants at the time that Washington stayed there and Lord Cornwallis surrendered. The place seemed so desolate the empty rooms and echoing hall, melancholy at heart, with the sorrows and joys that seem to hallow every nook and cranny. As we stood in and passed through the silent rooms, we felt like stepping softly and speaking low in reverence for the history, the romance, the joys and sadness that float around the old mansion from the misty past.

As we drove to Lee Hall in the evening, we felt as if awakening from a dream.

The following is Mrs. Diana Whiting Cumming's affidavit: 'I, Diana Whiting Gumming, of Hampton, Virginia, 1907, do hereby affirm that my father, Charles Lawrence Smith, repeatedly said to me that Thomas Smith of York County, who married Elisabeth Armistead, whose daughter, Elisabeth Smith, married Robert

Armistead of Elizabeth City County (1789), was the twin brother of Lawrence Smith, father of John Tabb Smith, who was the father of Charles Lawrence Smith, my father. August 30, 1907."

This Thomas Smith and Lawrence Smith were the sons of Edmund Smith, whose will is given.

Smith of Totness, Devonshire, England, settled in Abingdon Parish, Gloucester County, Va.

The first Major Lawrence Smith was a man of great influence and estate. He bore the coat-of-arms of the Smiths of Totness, County of Devon, England. He married Mary , and his will was dated August 8th, 1700, but no copy thereof has been preserved. The following children are mentioned in the records of York and Essex Counties:

2. *John*, Esq., member of the Council, eldest son. 3. *Lawrence*, who settled in York County, and whose descendants are given in *Quarterly*, II., pages 10 *ct seq.* 4. *Willam.* There is, about 1734, mention in Spotsylvania records of Thomas Ballard Smith, son of William Smith, who may have been this William. 5. *Augustinc.* 6. *Charles.* 7. *Elisabeth,* who married Captain John Battaile, of St. Mary's Parish, Essex County. In Essex records Lawrence Smith makes a deed to his "son-in-law" Capt. John Battaile, 16 June, 1700. Also recorded in February, 1708-'9, guardian's bond of Augustine Smith, in behalf of "Lawrence Battaile, grandson of Major Lawrence Smith." The will of Captain John Battaile, dated 20th January, 1708 and proved 10th February, 1709, names Elizabeth, sons John Lawrence, Hay and Nicholas Battaile, after various devises, gives residue to be equally divided between his wife and son John, when his wife marries or son comes of age; witnessed by Captain John Catlett, Mr. Francis Taliaferro and Mr. James Harrison; mentions also "Brother Charles Taliaferro," and Mr. William Thornton. 8. *Sarah*, married John Taliaferro, son of the emigrant, Robert Taliaferro, and had issue Lawrence, John, Charles, Robert, Zachariah, Richard, William, Mary, Elizabeth, Sarah and Catharine.

2. John[2] Smith (Lawrence Ist Smith) was councillor, etc., resided in Abingdon Parish, and died there about 1719-'20. He married Elizabeth Cox, daughter and heiress of Henry Cox whose will was proved in Rappahannock County. The wife •of Henry Cox was Arabella Strachey, daughter of Mr. William Strachey, of Gloucester County, grandson of William Strachey, secretary to Lord Delaware in 1610. In the Strachey pedigree Henry Cox's name is erroneously given as John Cox. Issue of John Smith and Elizabeth Cox: 9. John,

died October 12, 1701; 10. Mary, born April 14, 1691, died March 15, 1724, married John Cooke,* of Ware Parish, Gloucester County; 11. Lawrence; 12. Mildred, born April, 1699; 13. John, born March 22, 1702'3.

11. Lawrence[3] Smith (John[2], Lawrence[1] married Mary, and appears to have had, 14. Elizabeth, baptized June
24, 1721; 15. John, born February 24, 1722, but must have died without issue; 16. Lawrence, son and heir, born August 30, 1727. Mrs. Mary Smith, wife of Mr. Lawrence Smith, died July 10, 1728.

16. Lawrence4 (Lawrence[3], John[2], Major Lawrence[1] Smith) exchanged in 1753 two tracts of land in Gloucester, descended from Major Lawrence Smith, for 4,000 acres owned by Warner Lewis in Spotsylvania County. Hening's *Statutes-at-Large*, V., 407-412.)

13. John[3] Smith (John[2], Lawrence[1]) married Mary , and had issue, 17. Mary, born 1735; 18. Mildred, born 1736; and 19. Robert, born January 29, 1736-'7. Mrs. Mary Smith, relict of Mr. John Smith, deceased, departed this life November 29. 1737

5. Augustine[2] Smith* (Major Lawrence[1]) lived in the Parish of St. Mary's, Essex County. In 1722 he qualified as one of the first bench of justices for Spotsylvania County. His will was proved in Orange County, July 20, 1736, and names issue, 20, Thomas, of Prince William County, 21. Mary, wife of Robert Slaughter.

6. Charles[3] Smith (Major Lawrence* Smith). There is a deed in Essex dated April 8, 1704, from John Smith, eldest son of Lawrence Smith, to "brother Charles Smith." He lived in that part of Essex afterwards Caroline, and died about 1710, when his widow, Dorothy Smith, Augustine Smith and R. Buckner gave bond in Essex court as his administrators. He left issue, eldest son, 22. Robert, who was the founder of Port Royal, in Caroline county. He died before 1740, leaving issue four children; 23. Lawrence, 24. Charles, 25. Sarah, who married Charles Venable, and 27 Dorothy.

From the Smiths of "Temple Farm," near Yorktown, is descended Elizabeth Smith who married (178) Robert Armistead.

Major Lawrence Smith o£ Abington Parish, Gloucester, was a man of great influence and estate. He married Mary , and his will was dated August 8, 1700, but no copy thereof has been preserved. In 1686 "Temple Farm," Yorktown, was sold to Major Lawrence Smith. He was surveyor for the Crown for the counties of York and Gloucester. In 1691 he laid out the town of Yorktown on the land of Benjamin Reade, and received fifty acres for the same.

NoTE.— (The original drawing the editor saw this summer in Clerk's office at Yorktown.)

Issue of Major (1) Lawrence Smith and Mary, his wife: (2) *John*[2] (3) *Lawrence*[2], (4) *William*[2], (5) *Augustine*[2], (6) *Charles*[2], (7) *Elisabeth*[2], (8) *Sarah*[2].

In 1674 Major Lawrence Smith appears in "historic annals." "At a grand Assembly held in James Cittie between the 30th of Sep. 1674 and 17th March 1675 in which war was declared against the Indians: among other provisions for carrying it on, was ordered out one hundred and eleven men out of Gloucester to be garrisoned at one fort near the falls of the Rappahannock, under the command of Major Lawrence Smith. In 1679, major Lawrence Smith was empowered to have in readiness, at beat of drum, fifty able bodied men well armed, etc., and two hundred more within space of a mile back prepared always to march twenty miles in every direction ; he to execute martial discipline among said soldiers, both in peace and war, the said Lawrence Smith, with two others to hear and determine all cases, civil and criminal, that may arise within said limits, as a county court might do, and make by-laws for the same."

Col. Lawrence Smith received immense grants of land from the Crown in the Rappahannock region three miles wide and five miles long in one tract.

The author of *Ingram's Proceedings* forcibly describes maj. Smith as a "gentleman that in his time had hued out many a knotty piece of work and soe the better knew how to handle such rugged fellows as the Baconians were found to be."

Major Lawrence Smith patented certain land in Gloucester which he named "Seven Hall" in 1662, where he lived. Robert Talliaferro, of Cornwall England, emigrant, patented lands in Gloucester 1655-1662 on a swamp running into Poropotank Creek. He, with Lawrence Smith, patented 6,300 acres on Rappahannock. His son, Col. John Talliaferro, married Sarah Smith, daughter of Lawrence Smith. Issue; Lawrence Talliaferro, married Sarah Thornton, and was the father of William Thornton of King and Queen, grandfather of Philip Talliaferro of "Hockley."

In 1699 the Governor recommended Lawrence Smith among the "gentlemen of estate and standing" suitable for appointment to the Council. He died in 1700, and the honor of which the father was deemed worthy fell upon his oldest son John. (Councillors were appointed by the Crown from among the men of highest social standing and greatest estates.)

(2) John[2] Smith was councillor and county lieutenant; resided in Abington Parish and died 1719-20. He married Elizabeth Cox. Issue of John Smith and Elizabeth Cox, his wife: Mary, Lawrence, Mildred, John.

A deed June 24, 1703, in York County Court from John Smith of Abington Parish to brother Lawrence Smith reciting a clause of their father's will "Lawrence Smith late of Glouchester the testator gave 1300 acres in Abington parish to John Smith and his lands in York parish and County to his son Lawrence Smith and remainder to his grandson, who died Oct. 12th 1701."

Another son of Maj. (1) Lawrence Smith, called Col. (2) Lawrence, became the owner of the plantation at Wormeley's Creek (a large tract in York) ; we have the title set out in (York records) 1716 as follows: "The law decided for Col. Lawrence Smith." He was colonel, justice, and sheriff of York, married first, Mildred Chisman, daughter of Capt. Thomas Chisman; second, Mildred, daughter of John Reade. Edmund Smith was the son by first marriage with Mildred Chisman. Lawrence Smith's will proved 18th day , 1715, mentions son Lawrence.

John Chisman, born 1597, came to York County, Va., 1621; was justice in 1635; burgess 1642-'3; appointed to the Council 1652 with rank of colonel. He married Margaret Edmund Chisman was his brother, a justice in 1652; married Mary ; will proved in 1673. Two children of George Reade and Elizabeth Martain. his wife, married Chismans— Elizabeth R. married Captain Thomas Chisman, Francis R. married Jane Chisman.

Edmund Smith married Agnes, daughter of Richard Sclater of York County. Issue: Lawrence and.Thomas (twins), Mildred, Mary.

The will of Edmund Smith, dated December 13th, 1750, proved March 18th, 1750, bequeaths to his son Lawrence—to his son Thomas—to his daughter Mildred—to his daughter Mary and to his wife, his land in Spotsylvania Co. directed to be sold.

Thomas Smith, twin brother of Lawrence Smith, sons of Edmund Smith, married Elizabeth Armistead. Thomas Smith's daughter, Elizabeth, who married 178. Robert Armistead, had twins.

"Abington Parish regrister: 1725, Sarah and Mary Smith, twins, daughters of Lawrence Smith; born June 1oth; baptised July 4th."

Following the Smith line down:

Thomas Smith married, about 1766, 173 Elizabeth Armistead,

daughter of 169. Westwood Armistead and Mary Tabb, his wife, who was daughter of Colonel John Tabb, of Elizabeth City County, and Mary, his wife, daughter of the Rev. James Sclater, of Charles Parish, York County, who died November 19th, 1723.

Children of Thomas Smith and Elizabeth Armistead:

Elizabeth, born August 22, 1767. Mary, who married Mr. Young, of Scotland; they resided alternately in Spotsylvania and Elizabeth County.

Elizabeth Smith married her cousin, 178. Robert Armistead, of Elizabeth City County.

Thomas Smith's deed, referred to by Mr. Tyler, *William and Mary Quarterly,* Vol. VII., p. 20, reads as follows:

"This indenture, made this, the eighth day of Nov., in the year one thousand and seven hundred and ninety eight, Between Thomas Smith of the County of York of the one part, and Robert Armistead of the. County of Elizabeth City of the other part, Witnesseth that for, or in consideration of, the sum of three hundred pounds, current money of Virginia, to him the said Thomas Smith in hand paid at or before the sealing and delivery of these presents, by him, the said Robert Armistead, one certain tract or parcel of Land lying in the Co. of York containing 313 acres more or less commonly called and known of the name of Bay Tree plantation bounded by the lands of John A. Rogers and Thos. Chismon.

"(Signed)   THOS. SMITH (L S)

"Signed sealed and delivered in the presence of
"PETER COODWIN JR
"MORTON COODWIN
"PETER COODWIN SR
          "Teste   ROBERT HUGH-WALLER
                                        * "C. Y. C.
                              "(Clerke, York County)"

An indenture 1789 bet Thos Smith of York Co. (executor of Lawrence Smith) and one Davedson of a certain tract of land purchased by him, Lawrence Smith from Cen. Thos. Nelson— sealed and delivered in the presence of Alatthew Pope, William Cary, John Tabb Smith—deeds no. 6, page 407—York Co. records.

The above Lawrence Smith's will is dated July, 1789-

Lawrence Smith's will, nth day of , 1736, mentions

son Lawrence, beloved wife Alildred; and then, to son Robert and his heirs forever: to son *Edmund,* all the remaining part of the land within the same patent formerly known as the Ludlow patent — to him and his heir forever — to Lawrence a Yorktown lot.

The Mliil property to my three sons and my wife, etc. To my son *Edmund,* all the negroes stock and goods, household stuff and all other personal estate, that I have formerly possessed him with. I give and bequeath to my loving wife and to my five children which I had by her, viz.:

Margaret, Catherine, *Robert,** Lucy and Lawrence, and all the remaining part of my estate of what kind or nature so ever within his Majestie's Dominions to be equally divided among them.

That my loving wife should have the management of the whole estate during her widowhood without giving any security for the same * * * but if y wife should marry * * *

I constitute and appoint my beloved friend William Nelson, son to Mr. Thomas Nelson of York-town, and my son *Edmund Smith* to be trustees of this my last will and testament * *

LAWRENCE SMITH.

Sealed signed published and delivered in the presence of
JOHN BUCKNER
JOHN BALLARD
WILLIAM NELSON
ISHMAEL MOODY
Lawrence Smith's will, 1734.

A. Gabriel Ludlow, emigrant from Denton, England, patented lands in Gloucester County. Married and had Sarah Ludlow, who married Col. John Carter, and was the mother of "King" Carter.

The widow of Thos. Ludlow married Rev. Peter Temple. They occupied Temple Farm, as it is now called, at the time of the sale to Lawrence Smith. Mildred Smith (Edmund[3], Lawrence[2], Lawrence[1]), sister of Thomas Smith, married David Jamison, Lieutenant-Governor of Virginia. Her tomb is at Temple Farm, ornamented with Jamison Arms impaled with Smith. She was granddaughter of Major Lawrence Smith. Another granddaughter married Augustine Moore, of York.

This clipping from *Times-Dispatch* by Mrs. Sallie Nelson Robins, seems to belong right here:

"VIRGINIAN DESCENT FROM ROYALTY.

"To most of us Americans this has a spurious ring, and the desire for royal descent in the heart of a citizen of the United States seems somewhat of an anacronism. But no stranger is it than the pleasure which a denizen of the region north of Mason and Dixon's line experiences in the fact that he comes from a Southern planter who was also a slaveholder. This is a distinction that even the fiercest abolitionist covets. No one who frequents the Virginia Historical Society and sees the genealogical fanatics can doubt this fact. The 'searcher' may belong to the Grand Army of the Republic or live in Kansas or Ohio—but if he has a Southern forbear he rejoices, and if this forbear held slaves the better pleased is he.

"There are only twelve royal personages from whom the 'people' may derive descent. They are known as 'the twelve royal leakages'; from some of them American citizens come.

"So one child of John, one of Plenry III, five of Edward I., four of Edward III, and one of Henry VII. form the twelve 'leakages' of the royal blood.

"It is mostly through a succession of female lines that descent from royalty can be traced.

"Lately there seems to be a revival of interest in the 'Daughters of the Crown,' an American organization, and these notes may be useful to some who aspire to this honor. There are, of course, many attractive features of this society, but perhaps the visible sign of membership—the insignia, or badge—is most compelling. It is so beautiful that one can hardly restrain one's self from addressing the happy owner as 'Your Royal Highness" or 'Your Crace!' These non-essentials have their place and power, and make one of the many recreations of life."

Lor those of the Lawrence Smith line who care to trace back to titled lineage, I give the following;

King Edward Third of England married and had among others, *Lionel, Duke of Clarence,* whose only daughter, *Lady Phillipa Plantagenet,* married Ldward Mortimer, Lari of March. Their daughter, *Lady Elisabeth Mortimer,* married Sir Henry Percy (Hotspur). His son, *Henry Percy,* married Lady Lleanor Neville. Issue: *Henry Percy,* third Earl of Northumberland. who married Lady Lleanor Poynings; their daughter. *Lady Margaret Percy,* married Sir

William Cascoigne. Their daughter. *Lady Elisabeth Gascoigne* married Sir Ceorge Telboise, a Norman knight, follower of William the Conqueror. Their daughter. *Lady Anna Telboise,* married Sir Ldmund Dymoke,* Alaster of Schrivelsby Court. His daughter, *Frances Dymoke,* married, August 20, 1566, Sir Thomas Windebank, Clerk of the Signet to "good Queen Bess." Their daughter, *Mildred Windebank,* married Robert Reade, Esquire, of Yorkshire. Their son. *Honorable George Reade,* came to Virginia in 1637, married Elizabeth Martian. Issue, among others, *Elisabeth Reade,* who married Thomas Chismon. Issue, among others, *Mildred Chismon,* who married Col. Lawrence Smith of York, whose son *Edmund Smith* married Agnes Sclater and had, among others, *Thomas Smith,* who married Elizabeth Armistead, daughter of (169) Westwood Armistead and Mary Tabb. *Elisabeth Smith,* daughter of Thomas Smith and Elizabeth Armistead, married her cousin (178) Robert Armistead. Issue: *Westzvood Smith Armistead, Maria Smith Armistead, Elisa Armistead, Louisa Armistead, Thomas Smith Arniistead, Helen Smith* and *Emily* (twins), *Susan Smith Armistead, Harriet Armistead,* and *Robert Augustine Armistead,* who married Martha Savage.

Scrivelsby Court, † England, Sir John Dymoke's estate, is still kept in repair and a show place of interest. The chapel, a quaint structure, has some parts five centuries old. Among the tombs is that of Sir Robert Dymoke. It has a plate of brass, on which is a figure of a knight in full armour, inscription and arms.

Mrs. Sallie Nelson Robins, the versatile writer, editor of those charming genealogical bits in the Sunday *Times-Dispatch,* in speaking of descent from -royal blood, says: "The burden of such extended obligation fairly takes one's breath away — one seems to elongate like a modern sky rocket and then go out in a 'fiz.' "

In addition to above, the following clipping from *Times-Dispateh* is inserted:

"George Reade, who settled at Yorktown in the seventeentli century, was the son of Robert Reade, of Link'enholt, and Lady Mildred Windebank, and through her his descendants have for a progenitor Louis VII. of Lrance. These descendants are so numerous that to give the surnames only is impossible, but among them are the Washingtons, Nelslons, Pages, Seldens, Marshalls, Taliaferros, etc. Old George Reade is a joke among genealogists. ,

"He bobs up serene and unperturbed on the majority of the papers of those who aspire to membership in patriotic societies.

Charlemagne, Lmperor of the West and King of Lrance, is represented in Virginia by the Burwells, Bassetts, Amblers, Colstons, Harrisons, Armisteads, Baylors, Mayos, and these names derive this distinction from Abigail Smith, whose mother was a Bacon. This family dominated in Virginia by the intrepid rebel, has a most interesting line, embracing such fascinating personalities as the Lody Poppa, daughter of Pepin de Seniis, Count Berengarins, of Bayen and Valois. Who would not be proud of such stately cadence, if nothing else.

"Pepin de Seniis was grandson of Bernard, King of Lombardy, and he was grandson of Charlemagne of the West. This is no fairy tale, but scientifically demonstrated; chapter and verse can easily be given."

When Chiskiack, on York River, was open for settlement in 1630. Nicholas NiCrtine (Martian), from Belgium, obtained land at Yorktown. In 1645 Nicholas Martian married Jane Isabella Beach. His oldest daughter Elizabeth, by his first wife, who crossed the ocean with him, married Colonel Ceo'rge Reade, whose daughter Mildred R. married Colonel Augustine Warner, of Cloucester County. Hon. Ceorge Reade came to Virginia in 1637, settled in York County. "Col. Ceorge Reade, Deputy Sec. 1640-1642, nephew of Sir Francis Windebrook, Sec. cf State to Charles 1st and his brother Robert was clerk to the same. He was descended from an ancient family in Southampton Co. England, who traced to Alfred the Creat." His granddaughter, Elizabeth Reade, daughter of Col. Ceorge Reade and Elizabeth Martian, married Captain Thomas Chismon, brother of Col. John Chismon, of King's Council, both the sons of Maj. Edmund Chismon.

Issue of Thomas Chismon and Elizabeth Reade: Thomas, Edmund, John, Mildred, Elizabeth.

Mildred Chismon married Lawrence Smith, of York. Issue; Edmund S., married Agnes Sclater; died 1750. Issue (1) Mildred S., married David Jamison, of Yorktown, Lieutenant-Covernor of Virginia; (2) Mary S., (3-4) Thomas Smith and Lawrence.

After Mildred Chismon's death, Col. Lawrence Smith married Mildred Reade, widow of Ceorge Reade. Issue: (1) Margaret S., (2) Catherine S., (3) Robert S., born 1733; died 1777; married Mary Calthorpe, and had eight children; married second, Rachel Kirby — one daughter Mary S.; (4) Lawrence S., (5) Lucy S., married Augustine Moore; died 1797.

The articles of Cornwallis' surrender were signed in 1781 'in the old Smith mansion then occupied by Augustine Moore.

MALLORY — KING — SMITH.

Lawrence Smith, twin brother of Thomas Smith, both sons of Edmund Smith and Mildred Chisman, his wife (Edmund Smith's will proved March 18, 1750), married Tabb, of Gloucester County. Issue, among others, Mildred Smith and John Tabb Smith, who married first, Miss Corbin, of Gloucester County. Issue: Maria Smith, who married Dr. George Hope, of Hampton. Mildred Smith married Captain Wills.

John Tabb Smith married second, about 1812, the widow of Jacob Wray, who was Diana Alallory, daughter of Col. Francis Alallory. Issue by second marriage: Oiarles Lawrence Smith, who married *Susannah Whiting Latimer.* Issue: Diana Whiting Smith, Charles Lawrence Smith (died young), Mary Eliza Smith, who married Robert Turnbul. Diana Whiting Smith married first, John Sinclair Armistead, son of John A., of Elizabeth City County. Issue: Charles Lawrence A. (died young), married Samuel Gumming, of Hampton. Issue: Hugh Smith Gumming, Samuel Gordon Gumming.

Susannah Whiting Latimer was the daughter of Thomas Latimer and Whiting Jennings.

Charles Lawrence Smith married Diana Alallory, daughter of Col. Francis Mallory and Mary King, his wife. Mary King was the daughter *of Charles King. Her sister Hannah King married Worlich Westwood.

Charles King married Elizabeth Tabb. Issue five children. Mary married Col. F. Alallory. Issue; Elizabeth King M., Mary King M., Charles King M, Diana M., Aliles AI. Hannah (born April 4, 1751, married Worlich Westwood).

John Tabb Smith took Lawrence, his son, eleven years old, with him when he was invited to dine at the Nelson House, Yorktown, with LaFayette in 1824.

William King, son it is believed of Alichael King, of Nansemond County, married Mary, daughter of Joshua Curie, of Elizabeth City County, and Rosea, his wife, afterwards Tucker. Mary survived her husband. Issue, among others, Charles King, who married Elizabeth Tabb, daughter of Thomas Tabb and Mary Armistead, his wife. Mary Armistead Tabb married three times — first, Thomas Tabb; second,

171

Alatthew Wills ; third. Col. Robert Armistead (his second wife). In her will she mentions two sons, John Tabb, Jr., and Thomas Tabb; two daughters, Elizabeth King and Rachel King. "Gives the silver spoons marked T. T. to her son Thos. Tabb, and the silver poringer to her daughter Elizabeth King marked A. A. E." (Anthony Armistead and Elizabeth Armistead).

Charles King and Elizabeth Tabb, his wife, had five'children. Mary King married Col. Francis Mallory She mentions in her will, 1789, (1) Elizabeth Mallory, (2) Mary King Mallory, (3) Charles King Mallory, (4) Diana Mallory, married first, Jacob Wray; second, John Tabb Smith.

(3) Charles King Mallory was born about 1781. Soon after graduating at William and Mary he was appointed by Virginia Council a member of the Legislature. Was Lieutenant-Governor of Virginia during War of 1812. He married Frances Lowry Stephenson, daughter of William Stephenson, officer in the Revolutionary War. Issue: Francis Mallory, William Stephenson Alallory, Charles King Mallory, Catherine Beverley Mallory and Mary King Mallory.

Hannah King, daughter of Charles King and Elizabeth Tabb, his wife, married Worlich Westwood, of Elizabeth City County. Charles King, her father, who was very wealthy, "built an elegant mansion on King Street in Hampton for his daughter Hannah Westwood." They were living there during the War of 1812, when Admiral Cockburn made it his headquarters. "The beautiful Hannah was a prisoner in several of the upper rooms, but attended by her maid, and served handsomely with her own silver, glass and china." A willing prisoner, no doubt, for protection. The lawlessness of that time in and around Hampton is a black page of English history.

See an account in *Harper's Monthly*, 1863, Vol. XXVIII., State Librairy, December, 1863, to May, 1864, from which the following extract is taken:

"Beckwith and Cockburn the marauder made their headquarters at the fine brick mansion of Mrs. Westwood on the street leading to the mansion; in the garden the remains of the brave Williams (lieutenant-colonel) were buried with solemn funeral rites the same day."

This "fine brick mansion" was bought and occupied about 1814-15 by Teackle Taylor Savage. It was the girlhood home of Martha Ann his daughter, who married 187. Robert Armistead. She was born in 1810. From here she was married February 28, 1828. Her sister

Margaret, a month previous, January 31st, married her father's ward, George Gilbert Parker.

SAVAGE FAMILY.

In King's Chapel Burial Ground, in Boston, is found the tombstone of Major Thomas Savage, the emigrant of the name, who died 1681. It bears the Arms above, as do several seals used by immediate descendants. These Arms are the ancient armorial devices of the Savages of Rock Savage and Clifton, in the County of Chester, England. Earl Rivers bore the same Arms.

Mr. Tyler says the Savage family may be styled the oldest in the State, as Thomas Savage is probably the earliest imigrant, from whom descent has been traced. * * Thomas Savage of the Eastern Shore of Virginia, started his plantation. Savage's Neck, and owned the whole — the present site of Eastville. On Cherry Stone farm are two old graveyards, near the present Cherry House residence. Margareet Savage, wife of Littleton Savage, daughter of William Burton, Gent., who departed this life the 6th day of Dec., 1772, in the thirty-fiftn year of her age. "Here lies the body of Col. Littleton Savage. * * * Here lies the body of Leah Savage, second wife of Coll. Littleton Savage, and daughter of Thomas Teagle, who departed this life 5th day of June 1795-"

At a meeting of the Phi Beta Kappa Society, April 19th, 1779, "Mr. Thomas Littleton Savage being recommended as a worthy member of this Society, was ballotted for, and initiated in due form. Mr. Bowdoin being about to depart for Europe, requested the company of the Society at the Raleigh tavern, where he gave them a 'very elegant Entertainment.' ir. Savage and Mr. Berkeley delivered compositions, pro. and Con. on the question whether a wise State hath any Interest nearer at hand than the Education of Youth."

The Howards of Virginia have always claimed descent in direct line from Lord Thomas Howard (son of fourth Duke of Norfolk), his mother being Margaret, daughter and heir of Thomas, Lord Audley of Walden, K. G. The Chidley Wade family claim descent from one of the brothers of Effingham, Lord Francis Howard. The following is from York County records:

John Howard patented lands in James City County, September 20, 1637, near Richneck. i. John Howard, member of the House of Burgesses, 1654. His will mentions wife Margaret. Issue: Henry,

William, Frances, Elisabeth. Henry Howard, the eldest, married Elisabeth Wade. He died without issue. She married Thomas Tabb.

Col. Frances Howard (Heyward), brother of Henry, was born May 15, 1700. He was justice, burgess, and was the first to spell his name Howard, though it had been so pronounced. He married Martha , and had three daughters and one son, Henry, who married Frances Colthorpe. The York County records show that Col. Henry Howard and Frances Colthorpe had issue, John Howard, who married Anne Shield, whose daughter, Alargaret, married William Kirby, of York County. Issue; Anne Kirby, born in 1760, August 31st, married Chidley Wade. (See 187 Robert Armistead line.)

There were three members of the Howard family in the "Virginia Company" — John, Rev. John, or John, clerk, and Sir John Howard, knight.

Thomas Colthorpe Howard, clerk of the Hustings Court of Richmond, died 1834, age forty-nine, married Catherine, daughter of Nathaniel Pope, of Chilton, Hanover County. Issue: Nathaniel, William, Dr. Marion, Ellen, and Conway Robinson.

HOWARD, KIRBY, WADE, SAVAGE, TEACKLE NOTES.

The following is copied from the *Baltimore Sun* under the head of "Virginia Heraldry";

"In the Virginia records it stated that Sir Francis Howard, Lord Howard, of Effingham, England, Governor of Virginia,

SAVAGE.
A Te Pro Te.

was the father of Lady Margareet Howard who married Major Kirby of the British Army. Their daughter, Ann Kirby, married Chidley Wade, and their daughter, Martha Jones Wade, married Teackle Taylor Savage, of Pungoteague, Accomac Co., Virginia."

Margaret Taylor Savage, oldest daughter of Teackle Savage and Martha, his wife, married Ceorge Gilbert Parker, a descendant of one of the oldest and best families in Lngland. The Eari of Alorley was a Parker, also the Laris of Macclesfield the Lnglish navy has had more Admirals of that name than any other.

Two Parkers, brothers, took up land in Virginia in 1650; one in Isle of Wight County, the other in Accomac County. The Isle of Wight Parker called his seat "Macclesfield," which still bears that name. The Accomac Parker was named George. Judge George Parker was his descendant, as was also Robert Parker, of Watts Island, whose son George, born July 26, 1770, married for his second wife Peggy Floyd, of Norfolk, February 24, 1803. To whom was born a son, George Gilbert Parker, October 6, 1806, who married, January 28, 1828, Margareet Savage, great-granddaughter of Major Kirby, of England, and Margareet Howard. Issue: William Henry Parker, of Hampton, who married Ann Rebecca Clarke, of Charles City County, September 27, 1865. Issue: William Henry, now a physician in Richmond, Va.; Gilbert, Alargaret, Annie, John; the two last died unmarried; the rest are living in Richmond.

Dr. William Henry Parker married Alma Jennings, of Richmond. Issue: Willard Newton Parker, and twin girls, Annie and Camilla.

William H. Parker married Anne Rebecca Clarke, of Charles City County, daughter of John Joseph Clarke, of Colesville (allied to the Roane, Royall and Eppes families), and Margareet Archer, daughter of John and Elizabeth Chamberlayne Batte Archer, of Bermuda Hundred. The family of Archer lived continuously for two hundred years at Bermuda Hundred, the original home, "Archer Hall," destroyed during the Revoluti in by Arnold's troops and rebuilt, was the birthplace of Mrs. Parker (1835). One of her grandsires, Henry Randolph, the head of the oldest branch of Virginia Randolphs, and uncle of William Randolph, of Turkey Island, was clerk of Henrico 1656, and clerk of the House of Burgesses from 1656 to his death, 1673. His second wife was Judith Soane (married December, 1661), daughter of Henry Soane, Speaker of the House of Burgesses (1660-1666), and according to Bruce's *Social Life of Virginia in the Seventeenth Century,* "*a* lady of the highest social position." Their son. Captain Henry Randolph, married Sarah, daughter of Col. Thomas Swann, a distinguished councillor and burgess, and had issue. Captain Henry Randolph, who married (1714) Elizabeth Eppes (daughter of Col. Francis Eppes, justice, sheriff, burgess 1691, grandson of Lieut.-Col. Erancis Eppes, councillor 1635, and Anne Isham, sister of Mrs. William Randolph, of Turkey Island). Their daughter, Sarah, born 1715, married, 1733, John Archer of Bermuda Hundred (justice 1737, and first sheriff of Chesterfield, 1749), grandson of Judith (Soane) Randolph by her second husband, Major Peter Feild.

Mrs. Henry Randolph (widow) and Major Peter Feild (justice, sheriff, burgess 1688), were married October 21, 1678, and had two daughters. Mary and Martha Feild, co-heiresses. Mary married Thomas Jefferson, grandfather of Thomas Jefferson, the President of the United States. Martha married John Archer, whose son, John Archer, married Sarah Randolph, thus uniting the grandson of Judith Soane by her second husband, Major Peter Feild, with her great-granddaughter by her first husband, Henry Randolph. John and Sarah (Randolph) Archer had issue another John, member of the County Committee of Safety of Chesterfield (1774-'76), married to Eliza Trent, who had issue John, the last Archer of Bermuda Hundred. His wife was Elizabeth Chamberlayne Batte, of Prince George County. These Archers are descended from the ancient Umberslade Archers, Warwickshire, England. According to tradition the motto is the same as Sir Humphrey Gilbert's, who married John Archer, daughter of John Archer of Otterden, and maid of honor to Queen Elizabeth, 1577 – *"Maliern Mori quain Mutare !*

Wm. H. Parker, of Hampton, and Anne, his wife, both deceased, had issue John Archer and Anne Willcox, deceased, Gilbert Floyd, Dr. William Henry, Jr., and Margaret Waring, who married in 1900 Dr. Oliver Francis Blankingship, nephew of the late Judge Francis Rives, of Petersburg, and General Wm. B. Shands, of Southampton.

See *The Critie,* September 3, 1888, May 5, 19, 1889, and *William and Mary Quarterly,* Vol. IV., p. 125. Bible records.

The following record was found among some old papers of a descendant of Margaret Howard and Major Kirby:

"Copied from the Wade family Bible in James City Co., Virginia

"Martha Jones Wade, daughter of Chidley Wade, and Ann, his wife. Born Oct. 20, 1778.

"Thomas Wade, son of Chidley Wade and Ann, his wife. Bo;rn January 9, 1781.

"James Wade, son of Chidley Wade and Ann his wife, boin

February 9, 1783.

"Elizabeth Howard Wade, daughter of Chidley Wade and Ann, his wife. Born April 5, 1785.

"Chidley Wade, son of Chidley Wade and Ann his wife. Born July 20, 1787.

"Second marriage of Ann Wade. •

"Ann Childs Mackendree, daughter of John Mackendree and Ann, his wife. Born March 5, 1791.

"Sally Alackendree, daughter of John Mackendree and Ann, his wife, born May 2nd, 1793.

"Sir Henry Howard cf York Co., Va., was the father cf Lady Margaret Howard. Lady Margaret Howard married Alaj. Kirby of the British Army. Her daughter, Ann Kirby, married Chidley Wade.

"Elizabeth Howard married John Stores. One child, William K. Stores.

"Second marriage. .

"Job Byard Mills by whom Hannah M. Mills, Sept. 13, 1808.

"Job Byard Mlills. •

"George Wade Mlills.

"James Wade Mills.

"lartha Ann Wade Mills, born Dec. 15, 1822.

"Alfred Wade Mills, born April 15, 1825.

"John Dix Alills, born April 5, 1828." '

TEACKLE.

Rev. Thomas Teackle, first minister of Hungers Parish, Accomac County, Virginia, born 1624 in Gloucestershire, England. His father was slain in battle fighting under the banner of Charles 1st. Being persecuted by Cromwell, he came to America in 1656, and settled at Craddock, an estate in Accomac County, where he performed the functions of his sacred calling until his death, January 26th, 1695. He married twice—first, Isabella, the widow of Lieut.-Col. Edward Douglass; no issue. His second wife was Alargaret, daughter of Robert and Mary Temple Nelson, of London, England, of the same family as Admiral Nelson. Through the Temples, her ancestry is traced back to 1427, to Godiva, the heroine of Tennyson's poem. Issue: John, Catherine, and Elizabeth left descendants.

1.   John Teackle, of Craddock, son of Rev. (1) Thomas T., born September 2, 1673; died December 3, 1721, at Yorktown, Va.; married,

November 2, 1710, Susannah, daughter of Arthur and Sarah Brown Upshur. Issue: 3. Thomas T., born November II, 1711; died July 20, 1769; married Elisabeth Custis, daughter of John Custis of East Shore, Virginia. Issue: (4) Thomas Teackle, and others.

(4) Thomas Teackle, of Craddock, son of (3) Thomas Teackle, married Elisabeth, daughter of Abel and Rachel Revel Upshur, and died April 15, 1784. She died January 14, 1782. Issue, among others, Margareet Teackle, born 1771, who married Thomas Savage. The family Bible in our possession records that Teackle Taylor Savage (from Pungoteague, Accomac County, Va.,) married, July 14, 1804, Martha Jones Wade (widow of Rev. Edmund Ellis), of James City. The children of this marriage, Margaret, George, Martha, Edmund, Virginia, Comfort.

The following is copied from the Land Office in Richmond, Va.:

"Patent no. 251, on Savage Creek Accomac Co. Va.

"Mrs. Thomas Savage relict of Ensign Thomas Savage, a parcel of land called Savage's Choice, formerly granted her deceased husband from the Indian King of the Eastern Shore. Issued in 1635.

"To Thomas Savage, by Sir William Berkeley, by consent and good will of Council of State, 500 acres of land in Northhampton Co. Va."

"To Captain George Savage, under George Washington, served through the French and Indian war, receiving in 1770, his allotment of lands under proclamation of Gov. Dinwiddie."

Martha Ann Savage, daughter of Teackle Taylor Savage and Martha Jones Wade married (187) Robert Armistead, son of Robert Armistead and Elisabeth Smith, daughter of Thomas Smith, who was the son of Edmund Smith, son of Lawrence Smith, of Abington Parish, Gloucester Co., Va. For issue sec 187. Robert Armistead.

KIRBY NOTES.

William and Mary Quarterly, Vol. XIII., No. 3.

"Thomas Kirby, in Charles Parish, York Co., in 1645, married Mary ; personal estate considerable; married second, Catherine Tompkins; issue by the two marriages, sixteen children. John 4. Kirby (Thos.[3], Robert[2], Thos.[1]) married Mary Shield, daughter of Robert Shield; died 1753, issue Thos., John, Sarah, Frances, Mary, Robert, Rachel, born September 24, 1754, married first, Robert Smith, son of

Lawrence, distinguished in early Virginia history; issue, one daughter, Mary Smith. Bennet[3] (Thos.[3] Robert[1]), will proved October, 1782, married Prances Parsons, daughter of James Parsons (will proved May 19, 1735) and Dorothy Wade, daughter of Armiger Wade. A burgess for York County 1655, 1656. Issue: Bennet, Frances, Mary, William, born July 16, 1736. William Kirby (Bennet[3], Robert[2], Thos.[1]) married Margareet Howard (daugnter of John Howard and Anne Shield), born August 27, 1714. Anne Shield, daughter of Robert Shield, his will proved in York County 1785. Issue: Anne Kirby, born August 31, 1760, married Chidley Wade in 1778 (marriage bond)." Issue, among others, Martha Jones Wade, born in 1778, married July 14, 1804, Captain Teackle Savage. Issue: Margaret, George, Alartha, Edmund, Virginia, Comfort; the latter died in childhood; Virginia, unmarried, died in Richmond, Va., January 24, 1902. She spent her youth in Hampton, Va., amid the luxurious surroundings of ante-bellum days in the handsomest colonial mansion of that section, bought by her father, Teackle Savage, from Worlich Westwood. Six or eight half-circle stone steps led up to the double-door front entrance, graduating from a large base to a smaller platform; the entrance had a massive brass knocker, hinges, lock, and knob, as had all the doors. A very wide hall through the middle of four large rooms on the first floor, the same on the second, besides garret and basement, with massive foundation and heavy beams. The floors were highly polished, the windows deeply seated, with inside blinds, the window seats paneled beneath. The garden, with its memorable fig bushes, sloped down to the creek, or river, flowing into Elisabeth River.

In the War of 1861, when Hampton was burned, the walls stood like grim sentinels, in the midst of utter desolation. The United States authorities had them pulled down and the bricks removed to Old Point. The stone steps were taken to New Jersey.

Teackle Savage owned vessels that carried the United States mail, produce and freight of all kinds between Hampton, Norfolk and Baltimore. Hampton in those days was quite a naval station. Teackle Savage owned seven or eight houses in Hampton, besides large tracts of land in the West—in Illinois and Missouri. The papers and deeds were mislaid or destroyed. He sent his sons to Hallowell School in Alexandria.

WADE.

E. Armiger Wade—Armigall Wade, Esq., of Bellsize Park, Hampstead, England, was the father of Sir William Wade, prominent at the time of Elizabeth and James 1st. Park's history of the family contains an account of the family. Armiger Wade is said to have been descendant of Sir Armigall Wade of Bellsize, near Hampstead, England. (See Hayden, 571, and *Wiilliam and Mary Quarterly,* Vol. II., p. 161.) The will of Armiger Wade was proved August 13, 1708.

The following was sent by a descendant who wrote she copied it from some James City Records before the war of 1861. — THE EDITOR.

"Sir Henry Howard of York Co., Va., the father of Lady Ma;rgaret Howard, who married Maj. Kirby of the Brittish Army. Her daughter, Anne Kirby, married Chidley Wade; issue: Chidley, Elisabeth Howard, Martha Jones. Elisabeth H. Wade married first, John Stores; second. Job Mills; issue: John Bayard M., Hannah, Francis, Marion, Job Bayard, George Wade, Martha Ann Wade, Alfred Wade, John Dix. Alfred W. Alills was the father of Dr. William A. Alills, now living in Baltimore."

Martha Jones Wade married, in 1804, Teackle Taylor Saage, from Pungoteague, Accomac County. Issue: Margaret Teackle S., *Martha Anne S.,* George W. S., Edmund Ellis S., Virginia Wade S.

George Wade Savage married first, Harriet Armistead, daughter of 178. Robert Armistead and Elisabeth Smith; 110 issue. Married second, Frances Dunn, of Warwick County. Issue, one daughter, Georgietta Savage, married in Richmond, Va., September 23, 1862, Dr. David L. McLaughlin, surgeon in the Confederate Army. Issue: Mary Virginia, William Russell, George Savage, and Linnetta Milton; all living in New York City except George S., who died at the age of thirty-three — a man of talent and energy.

The name McLaughlin was originally Mac Lachlan, Scotch. The first of the name in America was David McLaughlin who; with his wife, ———— Holmes, settled in West Winfield, New York State. The old homestead is still owned by a descendant, Mrs. V. E. Eggleston. William McL., son of above, was born at West Winfield, September 30, 1805 ; died 1890. His wife was Lucinda Smith, born 1806; died 1889. They had three children, one of whom was (Dr.) David Linneus McL., born May 28, 1832. He moved to Louisiana before the war between the States.

CALTHROPE.

Calthrope. — In Bloomfield's *History of Norfolk Le Neve's Pedigree of Knights*, the Calthrope family is traced through many generations. "Sir James Calthrope of Stirston, England, Ao. 30th Elizabeth and 9th James first." married Barbara, daughtqr of John Bacon, Esq., of Hesset, Norfolk, England. She was buried in Cockthorp Church. Issue: (a) Sir Henry Calthrope third son from whom those of Ampton, Suffolk Co., are descended. His son. Sir James Calthorpe, was knighted by Cromwell in 1650. He married Dorothy, daughter of Sir James Reynolds, one of Cromwell's Admirals.

(b) Philip.

(c) Christopher, Esq., who married Maud, daughter and coheir of John Thurston, Esq., of Brome, Norfolk. Issue: James, Christopher, Edward, Oliver, and two daughters.

This Christopher came to Virginia in 1662. Was a relative of President Nathaniel Bacon of the Virginia Council. *William and Mary,* Vol. II.: "In 1622 a youth by name Christopher Calthorpe came with Lieut. Purfray to Virginia in the ship *Furtherance.*" On the 23rd of March 1623, George Sandys writes to Samuel Wrote a long letter from "James Cittie," in which, among other things, he says: "I used Mr. Calthorpe at his landing with all the courtesie I could and brought him acquainted with the Governor. I profered him the Entertainment of my home and my own Chamber to lodge in etc. * * * " In 1635 Christopher Calthorpe, then called captain, obtained two patents of land.

In 1658 "Colonel Christopher Calthorpe with five others held court for York Co."

In 1659 "Col. Christopher Calthorpe was member of House of Burgesses from York Co."

James Calthorpe (son of Col. Christopher) and Anne, his wife, had issue: James who married Elizabeth , and had twins Elemelech and Ruth. Elemelech married Mary Robinson. Issue: Mary and Frances Calthrope, who married Col. Henry Howard, of York County. They resided on Back River Elizabeth City County. Issue, among others, (1) Prisilla Howard, born 1768, who married Robert Armistead; (2) Margareet Howard, who married Maj. Kirby, of the British Army. Their daughter, Anne Kirby, married Chidley Wade. Issue, among others, Martha Jones Wade, who married Teackle Taylor Savage in 1804.

"Frances Calthrope and sister Mary, children of Elimelech Calthrope, were schooled by the Rev. Theodosius Staige, cf Charles Parish."

"In 1746 'Calthrope Neck' was divided between his two daughters Frances and Mary."

The grandmother of Christopher Calthrope who came to Virginia in 1622, was Barbara, before mentioned daughter of John Bacon, of Hesset, England. Nathaniel Bacon the rebel married Elizabeth, daughter of Sir Edward Duke of Benhall and Elizabeth Calthrope, his wife. (*William and Mary Quarterly*, Vol.n.)

In a Heraldic exhibition at the Society of Antiquarians in 1863 there was seen a roll of vellum beautifully illuminated with the Calthrope Arms and Crest. The former quartering Bacon and Wythe. The descent of the Calthropes was given from Sir William Calthrope 1461, to Sir Philip Calthrope who married Anne, daughter of Sir William Boleyn. The relation of the family to Anne Boleyn is shown.

In a collection of drawings of portraits by Holbein, cotemporary of Henry VIII., are, among others, those of Sir Thomas Mloore, Sir Thomas Wyatt, and Elizabeth, daughter of Sir Philip Calthrope.

"Thorpland," where the Sinclair family of York County now reside, formerly the home of Calthrope Howard, hands down the name of the ancient habitation of the Calthrope in England.

NOTE. — Mary Louisa Armistead Nelson relates the goulish story of the "Calthrope Light." How it followed the family from England appearing in a most mysterious way on the ship *Furtherance* that brought over the youth Christopher Calthrope. On landing it disappeared from the ship, but was seen again and again in the dwelling of the Calthropes, particularly before a death. This ghost story has been handed down from generation to generation for nearly three hundred years. — EDITOR V. A. C.

ANTHONY ARMISTEAD.

(87) Anthony5, (William4, Anthony[3], William[2], Anthony) married Margaret Starkey; resided in Warwick County, and in 1737 received a deed from his step-mother, Rebecca King (Rebecca Moss[1] Armistead King[2]) one-half the plantation and orchard in Elizabeth City County, "where she now lives," as the same given him by his late father, Major William Armistead. His will, dated December 29, 1737, proved February 13, 1737~'38, names sons (96) John6, (97) Anthony6.

(96) John[3] Armistead, son of (87) Anthony[3] Armistead, had issue, (100) Starkey7 A., eldest son, to whom in 1769 he gave 160 acres in Elizabeth City County, being the land which (82) William A. Armistead, by his will dated January 5, 1714, gave his son Hinde A, and in default of heirs of his body, then to the next surviving male heir, and which upon his death descended to (96) John6 A., Sr. John A.'s will was proved in 1791; names (Starkey being dead), (101) John*, to whom he gave 1000acres in North Carolina, (102) Robert, to whom he gave negroes that he is now in possession of in

Northampton County, N. C., (103) Elizabeth Armistead married Thomas Smith. (96) John³ A. married first, Anne, mentioned in deed; second, Elizabeth , named in will.

(100)   Starkey A. married Mary Tabb, of Alathews County, in 1773; his will proved 1775 mentions no children; names "brother Robert, father John, wife Mary, niece Mary Smith, mother Elizabeth A., friends Thomas Smith and Robert Armistead of Mathews Co."

(101) John Armistead married Elizabeth Royster.

"(102) Robert7 . A., son of (96) John, was perhaps 'Robert Armistead, Sen.,' whose will, January 24, 1793, names children (104)   William under age to whom he devises all lands in Elizabeth City and York County, and (105) Elizabeth, for whose support he required all his stock of every kind and money due in North Carolina to be devoted."

(87)William (William4, Anthony³, William², Anthony¹) made his will Eebruary 15, 1724; names wife Judith and six children.

(88)John5 Armistead (William4, Anthony³, William®, Anthony¹) removed to New Kent and was vestryman of Blissland Parish in 1722. Col. Wilson Miles, Cary writes; "In 1868 I derived from Miss Susan Cary, of Gloucester, born 1791, then seventy-seven years old, of a most retentive memory, and a remarkably clear head for genealogy, the following account of her Armistead ancestry, and as she was the granddaughter of Colonel Gill Armistead, who died in 1762, she would be presumed to know the facts from her mother, Susanna Armistead, who died at the age of eighty-one in 1834, which would place her birth in 1753. According to Miss Cary her immediate ancestor, William A., of Elizabeth City, was a relative of "Harry Armistead of Hesse," in Alathews County. William A. had at least three children, William, (2) John, who went from Elizabeth City County to New Kent County and married Miss Gill, an heiress, and (3) Hannah A., who married Miles Cary, of Warwick. Col. John Armistead, of New Kent, had four children — William, father of Mrs. Dandridge; John, father of William, Agnes and Susan (Mrs. Russel) ; and Gill, who married Betty Allen, of James City, and she married second, John Lewis, of Williamsburg. Gill6 Armistead's children were, (1) William7, who ran away at sixteen and served eight years in the Revolution; he married Elizabeth Armistead, daughter of Booth A., of Elizabeth City County, and had Booth, Gill, Fanny, Contolas (named for a French officer in the American Revolutionary War), Elizabeth, Virginia (a chancery suit in Williamsburg shows that

Virginia A. (daughter of William and Elizabeth A.) married T. B. Allen, of Elizabeth City County; the suit regarding a mill which her "great-grandfather, Robert Armistead of York Co.," father of Booth Armistead, built in 1739. She came of age 1820. The mill was four miles from Hampton, one mile from James River), and Catherine.

Elizabeth7 Armistead, daughter of Gill6 Armistead, married Miles Seiden, of "Tree Hill," and had eleven children.

Susanna7 married hercousin. Colonel John Cary, son of Miles Cary and Hannah Armistead, of Back River, Elizabeth City County.

Miles Seiden (Aliles³, Joseph², Samuel¹) was reared in the old general court office which was the school in which all the county clerks were educated; clerk of Henrico; a man of good education, well acquainted with business generally, represented Henrico in General Assembly for many years. Member of Council in 1785. He married, March 27, 1774, Elizabeth Armistead, born March 9, 1752, daughter of Gill Armistead, at the hbme of her stepfather, John Lewis, in Williamsburg.

Susanna Armistead (daughter of Col. John6 Armistead, of New Kent County, and Miss Gill, his wife,) married William Russell, who, from dates and other facts, is supposed to be the William Russell mentioned in Congressional Records as colonel in the Revolutionary War, commissioned December 19, 1776.

Armistead Russell, son of Susanna Armistead and William Russell, married Elvira Clayton in 1776. She was the daughter of William Clayton, Clerk of New Kent County, and Elvira, his wife. Children of Armistead Russell and Elvira Clayton were Elizabeth Armistead R., Elvira Clayton R., and Armistead Russell, Jr. The latter married Sallie Ann Meredith, of New Kent, and had four daughters — (1) Elizabeth Meredith Russell,
(2) Elivra Clayton Russell, (3) Emma Armistead Russell, (4) Sarah Clopton Russell.

(1) Elizabeth Meredith Russell married Col. Thomas Bibb Bigger, of Richmond, and had Thomas R. B., died young; William James B., *John Bell BA*, Sallie Russell B., Elvira Clayton B., Margaret Smith B., Elizabeth Tate B., Lucy B., Charles Purcell B., Mary Erances B., Charlotte Myers B.

(2) Elvira Clayton Russell married James Cowles.

(3) Emma Armistead Russell married John Caskie.

(4) Sarah Clopton Russell married Nathaniel August, for years a banker of Richmond. Children of this marriage; (Col.) James, A.,

Catherine Pearson A., Emma Josephine A., who married Rev.. G. C. Abbitt, now of Hopkinsville, Ky., formerly rector of St. Mark's, Richmond, Va.

(1) Anthony[1] married Erances Thomson. Issue (2) William[2].

(2) William[3] married Anne. Issue; (3) William[3] A., (4) John[3] A., (5) Anthony[3] A., (6) Erances[3].

(5) Anthony[3] married Hannah Elliason. Issue; (82) William4, (83) Anthony4, (84) Robert4, (85) Judith4, (86) Hannah*.

(82) William4 married several times. Eirst, Hannah Hinde; second, Rebecca Moss. Issue; (87) Anthony5, (88) William5, (89) John5, (90) Hinde5, (91) Robert5, (92) AIoss[3] (93) Edward®, (94) Hannah[5], (95) Judith[3] A.

(89)(Col.) John A., of New Kent County, married Miss Gill. Issue; (1) Gill6, (2) William6, (3) John6, (4) Gill Armistead6 married, May 23, 1751, Betty Allen. Issue;

(I) Betty Armistead[7], born March 9, 1752; died April, 1833. Married, March 27, 1774, at Mr. John Lewis', in Williamsburg, Aliles Seiden. (2) Susanna A., born 1753; died 1834. Alarried Col. John Cary. (3) Mary Armistead married Thacker Burwell, whose son William A. B. was private secretary to Jefferson.

(4) Frances Armistead (daughter Gill Armistead and Bettie Allen, his wife, of New Kent County) married Col. John Ambler, of Jamestown, Va., 1782. She died 1789. Issue: Edward Ambler and Mary Cary Ambler. Edward Ambler married first, Sarah Holcombe, of Amelia County; married second, Tazewell. Issue Mary Ambler, married Caskie, and resides in Richmond, Va. Mary Cary Ambler married J. H. Smith, of King and Queen County, Va. Issue, among others. Mary Eliza Smith, married Dr. J. J. Gravatt, born 1817. Issue, among others, Rev. John James Gravatt, married Indie W. Jones, of Hampton, Va., and Bishop William Loyall Gravatt, married Sidney S. Peyton. (5) Martha A., married Colonel Green. (6) William7 A., married Elizabeth Armistead, daughter of Booth Armistead, cf Elizabeth City County.

(2) William6 A., son of John5 A., of New Kent, was major in 1772-1775; vestryman of Blissland Parish. Alarried Mary, widow of Baker, the niece of James Nicholas who left her, Mary, £500, in the event of death Abraham Nicholas, also a special legacy of £1,000. Issue of (2) William6 A. and Mary: Susanna A., who married first, William5 Dandridge (Dandridge[1], of London, Col. William[2] D., Bartholomew[3] D., John4 D.) son of Bartholomew D., brother of Mrs.

Washington. Issue, among others, Sianna Dandridge, who married John Williams, father of John L. Williams, of Richmond, Va.

Susanna Armistead Dandridge married second, about 1805, David Dorrington. Major William6 A. died before 1784.

Col. John6 A., son of John5 A., of New Kent, was a resident of St. Peter's Parish, New Kent. Colonel of militia and first State Senator from Charles City County and New Kent. "Col. Armistead departed this life May 2, 1779." — St. Peter's Register. Married Agnes. Issue: (1) William7 A., born June 5, 1754; (2) Agnes; (3) Susan. Issue by second wife. Mary Burbage (whose mother is said to have been a Dandridge) : (4) Robert* B. Armistead, administrator of his mother, who died 1792; (5) Lucy B., who married Aylett Waller. December 4, 1801, and moved to Tennessee.

(90) Robert5 A. (son of Maj. William4 A., Anthony3, William2, Anthony1) married Anne, daughter of Rev. James Wallace, who came from Erroll in Perthshire, Scotland. 'Tn 1737 the trustees of Eaton's Free School rented him a portion of the land for the natural lives of his sons Robert, William, James, conditioned on his building two tobacco houses 30 ft. by 20 ft. and two dwellings each 26 ft. by 16 ft. to be well framed of good white oak or poplar; on his planting an orchard of two hundred winter apple trees and keeping them well fenced and trimmed, and on his paying to the trustees the annual rent of six pounds current money. Robert Armistead was a prominent man in Elizabeth City County, being for many years church warden of the Parish and Colonel of the Militia." His will is dated July 28, 1771, and was proved November 24, 1774, and it names (123) William6 A., (124) James6 A., (125) Robert6 A., (126) Mary6 A., married Joseph Seiden.

WILL OF COL. ROBERT ARMISTEAD.

In the name of God Amen, I, Robert Armistead, the elder of Elizabeth City Co. Va. being sick of body but sound mind do make this my last Will and Testament in Manner following: Imprimis, I recommend my soul to God its Maker. I give and bequeath unto my son William Armistead all the Lands I possess at Sawyers Swamp, to him and his heirs forever.

Item — I give the Plantation whereon I formerly lived to Son James Armistead, provide he shall live during the Term mentioned in a Lease granted to me for the same by the Trustees of Eaton's Free

School, it being part of said Land. And in case :f his Death before the expiration of the said Lease then I give the same unto my Son William Armistead.

Item—I give all the slaves now in my Son-in-law, Joseph Selden's Posson and their increase to him and his heirs, which have been delivered to me some time.

Item—I give and bequeath to my Son William Armistead and his Heirs my slaves Wallace and Bess, In trust neverless upon this Condition and for no other. To hold in Trust for the Use of my Son James Armistead during his natural life subject in any James's debts and after his Death in Trust and the children of him, the sd. James and their heirs.

Item—I give to my Son Thomas Armistead and his Heirs, my Negro Boy named Cato.

Item—I give to my Son Moss Wallace Armistead my Negro Boy Toney to whom and his Heirs which together with what Money and other things I have given him will make him equal with my other children and is all I intend to do for him.

Item—I give unto my Son Robert Armistead and his Heirs my Negroes Boatswane, Phoebe, Charles, Juba, Rose and Dinah.

Item—I give my Negro Girl Nanny to my Grandaughter Euphon Armistead, daughter of my son William, to her and her heirs.

Item—I give all the Residue of my Shares and personal Estate to my two Sons William and Thomas Armistead to them and their Heirs equally to be divided between them. What provision I've here made for my Son James together with what Money I have before given him and have been obliged to pay for him is all I intend to do for him. ,

Item—I herein release all my children from all Debts they may owe me at the Time of my Death.

Lastly, I constitute and appoint my Son William Armistead and my Eriend Richard Cary, Executors of this my last Will and Testament hereby revoking all other Wills heretofore by me made. And I order that my Estate be not appraised or my Executors held to Security. In witness whereof I have hereto set my Hand and Seal this 28th Day of July Anno. Dorn. 1771.

Signed, Sealed published and declared by the Testator to be his last Will and Testament in Presence of us.

RICHARD CARY.

....

....

R. ARMISTEAD [Seal.]

Son William Armistead above married Mary Latham Curie, sister of Judge William Roscoe W. Curie.

Euphon above married Joseph Seiden.

(123) William6 Armistead married twice. Issue by first marriage: (1) Euphon Armistead, married William A. Graves; (2) Sarah Armistead; (3) Mary Armistead; (4) Anne Armisteail, married Starkey Robinson, of Richmond, and had Anthony, Polly, William Armistead, Fanny, Eliza, and Robert Robinson; Robert Armistead.

(123) William Armistead married second. Mary Latham Curie, daughter of Wilson Curie and Priscilla Aleade, and widow of Robert Wallace. Issue: (6) William Armistead; (7) Moss Armistead, and (8) Rebecca Armistead.

(6) William Armistead married first, Martha (Patsy) Booker. Issue: (1) Mary Booker Armistead. He married second, Elizabeth Armistead, of North Carolina, and had (2) William Aloss Armistead, married Rebecca Phillips; (3) Catherine Armistead, married Walker Watts; (4) Robert Armistead, married , of New Orleans.

(7) Aloss Armistead married first, Mary Booker, and had Alartha, who married John Whiting; married second, Mildred Sclater and had William Armistead. Aloss Armistead died in 1813.

(8) Rebecca Armistead married first, John Sheppard. Issue: (1) John; (2) Mary Curie, who married J. Phillips; (3) Eliza Curie. Rebecca Armistead married second, Elijah Phillips, and had (1) Rebecca, who married William Aloss Armistead above; (2) Sarah, who married Edward King; (3) Lavinia, married William Holt; (4) Jefferson Curie Phillips, who married Caroline Phillips.

Another record has William Armistead married Mary Latham Curie, sister of Judge Wm. Roscoe Wilson Curie, and had James, Robert (clerk of Blandford Church), Thomas, who married in 1777 Margareet Farom (widow) and had a daughter Anna Currie Armistead. Moss Wallace A. married Catherine.

Robert Armistead was clerk of Blandford Church, in Petersburg, from 1771 to 1787. Thomas Armistead was living in the same place in 1780. Probably one of the two was father of Theodorick Armistead, Esq., navy agent of the United States, at Norfolk, in 1812. This gentleman was born in Petersburg in 1777, and became one of the leading citizens of Norfolk, being foremost in every scheme of industry or charity. He died in his thirty-sixth year, on November 20, 1812. His will was proved in Norfolk city. The will of his step-mother, Juliana Armistead, was proved February 26, 1832. He had issue, Martha Juliana Armistead and Elizabeth Tucker Armistead. He appears to have had two brothers: (1) Thomas Armistead, who married Mary Allison, and had son James Allison Armistead; and (2) William A. Armistead, executor of Juliana Armistead. He married Hannah, daughter of "the late Thomas Newton," on March 13, 1808. Mrs. Juliana Armistead mentions also in her will "nieces Fanny Long, formerly Fanny Quenlin, and Lucy Segar, now Lucy Page, daughter of John Segar, and Lucy Anderson, his wife, nephew Edward Fisher, friend Polly Armistead."

(123) William6 A., son of Col. Robert5 A., married His will proved September 26, 1799, names (127) Robert7, (128) Euphon, married William Graves, (129) Anne, married Starkey Robinson, (130) Sarah, (131) Mary, (132) William, (133) Moss, who died 1813, leaving wife Mildred and children Martha and William (134) Rebecca, who married Elijah Phillips,

(127) Robert* A., son of William6 A., married Hannah Patrick, born April 27, 1765, daughter of John and Hannah Patrick, of New Poquoson Parish, York County; married second, Pricilla Tabb, daughter of Alaj. Henry Tabb. Issue by first marriage: (135) William, born March 14, 1785, settled in Ohio; (136) Patrick, major of militia at battle of Hampton, 1812, born April 7, 1787; (137) Mary Manson, born November 6, 1789, married Francis Mennis Armistead; (138) Anne, d. s. p., 1815, Issue by second marriage: (139) Maria Tabb, married first, Mr. George; second, William M. Peyton; by first marriage, Enoch George; by second marriage, William Yelverton Peyton, d. s. p.

(140)   Robert8, who married Julia Samuel Travis, daughter of Captain Samuel Travis and Elizabeth Bright, daughter of Samuel Bright.

(141)   Robert Travis Armistead, attorney-at-law, residing in Williamsburg, who married Mary Frances Armistead, daughter of Frank AL Armistead and Mary Armistead, his wife, daughter of (127) Robert A.; (142) William C. A.; Wm. Champion A. d. s. p., in Confederate Army 1865; (143) Susan P. A. D., infant; (144) Samuel P. d., infant; (145) Henry Tabb A., married Rebecca Holt; (146) Cary Peyton A., married Dora Jones, daughter of Rowland Jones; (147) Julia A. (single); (148) Mary A., married Wrginius T. Holt, of Hampton; issue, Lavinia, Lady May, Julia, Robert.

(105)   William6 A. (William5, William4, Anthony3, William2, Anthony1) married Elizabeth Aloseley, daughter of Captain William

Aloseley, of Princess Anne County before 1734. Issue: (no) Hannah, (111 William, (112) Anthony, (113) Moseley.

(111 William7 A., son of William6 A., may have been the "William Armistead, Jr.," who married Constance; will proved in 1772 names (114) Robert A., (115) William A., (116) Mary, born December 22, 1765; (117) Judith, not named in will but given in New Poquoson Parish Register, born July 29, 1762.

(113) Aloseley Armistead, son of William6 A., married m 1766 Alargaret, daughter of John Herbert and Judith Curie, his wife, daughter of Joshua Curie and Rosa, his wife, who married second, Anthony Tucker. Issue named in Judith Herbert's will, dated 1777: (120) William, (121) Moseley, (122) Anthony.

William7 A., son of John3 A. and Mary Burbage, was agent for the State providing arms, clothing and other necessaries during Revolutionary War. He was known as William Armistead of "The Neck." He married Susanna Hutching Travis, daughter of Colonel Edward Champion Travis, of Jamestown. He, William A., died June, 1793, leaving a son William8 A. This 'William A. was probably father of Robert A. of "The Neck," who had a daughter, Elizabeth A., who married Robert Christian, brother of Letitia Christian, first wife of President Tyler.

Robert7 Burbage A., son of Colonel John®, of New Kent, married Mary Semple, sister of Judge James Semple. He died in 1811. Issue: (29) John Dandridge Armistead, died, age 17, while a student at William and mary; (30) William®.

(30) William8 A., son of Robert7 Burbage A., born in New Kent, 1797, attended William and Mary in 1816. Married Lucy Boyd, and with his family removed to Alabama in 1833 ; died 1856. Issue: (31) Robert9 A., educated at William and Mary College, where he studied law under Judge N. B. Tucker. Major of Twenty-second Alabama Regiment; killed at Shiloh. He has children living in Texas. (32) William Boyd, student at William and Mary, a physician, married Mrs. Eliza Cantella Knox (*nee* Scott), and had issue Elliott and George. George, born at Snowdown, Montgomery County, Ala., November 18, 1860, married, October 26, 1904, Jennie Judge, daughter of Thomas J. Judge, a brilliant lawyer of Alabama, Judge of the Supreme Court of the State shortly after the war. Jennie Judge Armistead and infant died 1906. He married second. Mary Frobel Raoul, July 5, 1909, the daughter of Thomas Cooper Raoul and Mary Marshall Aloore, his wife. Issue: Elizabeth Boyd A. (3) Rosalie

Virginia married Elmore G. Fitzpatrick, both died, leaving children. (34) Mary A. married Philip Gayle, of Montgomery, Ala.; they have the following children: William Armistead Gayle, Joseph Philips Gayle, Lucy Herbert Gayle, Mary Semple Gayle. William Armistead Gayle married Mary Winn, of Marengo County, Ala. Five children have been born to them, all of whom are now minors and unmarried, being Walter Winn Gayle, Willey Griffin Gayle, Mary Phillips Gayle, William Armistead Gayle, Jr., Norman Winn Gayle. Joseph Philips Gayle died recently. Lucy is living and unmarried. Mary Semple married Dr. William L. Law, a prominent physician of Montgomery, Ala. They have had no children. (35) Lizzie Rowe, married Paul Tucker Sayre and has children. (36) Herbert9 A., lieutenant-colonel of Twenty-second Alabama Regiment, mortally wounded at battle of Franklin, Tenn. (37) Lucy Boyd A., married Robert Goldthwait, and has children.

The following letter is a worthy tribute to the gallantry of Robert Armistead, major of the Twenty-second Alabama Regiment :

"NEAR CORINTH, MISS., April 11, 1862.

"My Dear Mrs. Fitzpatrick — You have doubtless heard of your sad loss in the death of your brother, Major Armistead. I write to claim the privilege of a friend of yours and his; that is sharing in your sorrow. I was with him after he was wounded for some time, giving him all the attention in my power. He was struck by a grape shot in the right side, the shot passing through to the surface on the opposite side. He was conscious that his wound was mortal, but was calm and resigned. Feeling assured that he could survive but a short time, I asked him if he wished me to do anything for him. He said nothing except 'Tell my dear sisters how I loved them, and that my last hours are spent in thoughts of them; I know how they will suffer when they hear this.'

"He frequently reverted to this, and it seemed to be the only thought that troubled him. When the surgeon came to him he said: 'Doctor. I have great confidence in your opinion, examine my wound and give me a candid answer; I do not fear death; I know I must die, but I wish to know how long I have to live.'

"The surgeon examined the wound, but remained silent. major Armistead understood him clearly, but no trepidation was visible,-no alarm expressed. He remained calm as if merely reclining to rest. He frequently spoke of the grief his sisters would feel. He said to me, 'I have died in the right place, I hope at the right time, I know in the right cause.' I am thus circumstantial because I know every word and incident of this final hour will interest you. I did all I could to make him comfortable under the circumstances, while I remained with him.

"Our cause has lost a noble and gallant defender, our State an intellectual man, society a chivalrous and polished gentleman, his friends a true and beloved companion, and his sisters a brother who loved them better than his own life, and who grieved only for them in his death hour.

"I never saw such calm heroism before, and desire to emulate him should it be my fate to die, as he did, in defence of our country.

"I was agitated while he was placid; I wept over his wounds, he sorrowed only for his sisters.

"I hope you may find some consolation in the circumstances attending his end. He died for his country, and in the hour that tries men's souls gave the strongest proof of the nobility of his own. Rest assured that I sympathize deeply with you and yours in this sad bereavement, and only regret that I can do nothing lo palliate your sorrow. may God give you and your sisters the strength to bear your loss with resignation.

"Accept my kindest regards and believe me your friend,

"THOS. W. OLIVER.

"Mrs. E. G. Eitzpatrick, Montgomery, Ala."

Anthony Armistead and Erances Thomson; issue, William and Anne. Issue: William, John, Anthony, Frances.

(1) Anthony[3] A. married Hannah Ellison. Issue: (82) William4, (83) Anthony4, (84) Robert4, (85) Judith4, (86) Hannah.

(84) Robert* A. married first, Miss Booth; second, Katherine Nutting. Issue by first marriage: (212) Elliason5 A., (213) Booth5 A. By second marriage: (214) Robert, (215) Booth5, (216) Angelica5.

(215) Booth5 A. married Miss Stith; will made April 17, 1770. proved June 28, 1770, names (1) Robert, (2) Booth, (4) Betsy A., married Captain William Armistead, son of Gill Armistead, of New Kent.

(212) Elliason, of York County, son of (84) Captain Robert A., was captain, justice and high sherifif of York County. His will, proved

December 19, 1757. He married at least twice. By first wife he had (217) Robert6 Booth, who was at least twenty-one in 1758, when he was guardian of Moss. Children: (218) James6 Brag, who died 1790, leaving property to Diana Wallace Bailey. By second wife, Jane Anderson (daughter of Rev. Chas. Anderson, of Westover, and Frances, his wife), whom he married in 1740, had issue: (219) Elliason6, (220) Charles6, (221) Erances Anderson, who married Nelson, and had only one child, Frances Anderson Nelson, (222) Jane, (223) Elizabeth.

(217) Robert Booth Armistead, son of (95) Elliason5 A., student at William and Mary in 1753, married Ann Shields (born July 31. 1742), daughter of James Shields and Anne Marot (daughter of Jean Marot, a French Huguenot), widow of James Inglis, son of Mungo Inglis, first grammar master of William and Mary College. Issue, one child, (224) Mary Marot Armistead (1761-1797), who married John Tyler, Governor of Virginia (1808-1811), and was the mother of John Tyler, President of the United States (1841-1845).

(219) Elliason6 Armistead, son of Captain Elliason3 A., married Susanna Christian, daughter of Michael Christian of Northampton County, who was grandson of Michael C. and Rose Powell, married in 1722.

(214) Robert3 Armistead, to whom his father (84) Robert4 A. left a plantation on Elk Creek in Hanover County in that part afterwards called Louisa County, married Louisa Westwood, daughter of William Westwood, of Elizabeth City County; will proved in 1701. Issue, four children: (225) Mary Elizabeth A. (born 1740; died February 12, 1824), (226) Catherine A., (227) , (228) Robert A.

(226) Catherine Armistead married James Maury (widower with five children, consul at Liverpool forty-five years. No children by last marriage.

(227) A daughter, married Israel Lacy, of Loudoun County. Issue: (1) Maria L., married William Cooke, and moved to Louisiana; (2) Mrs. Bristow; (3) Mary Lacy, married, 818, Peyton Cooke, brother of William Cooke; (4) Westwood Lacy; Jack L.; (6) Catherine L., married B'rown, a law yer in Tennessee; (7) Robert L., for over thirty years in Postoffice Department in Washington, D. C.

(225) Mary Elizabeth Armistead—"Polly," a great beauty and belle—married Stevens Thomson Mason. "Polly" Armistead's father was (214) Robert Armistead, who married Louisa Westwood, who was the sister of Elizabeth Westwood who married first, James

Wallace; married second, Hon. William Thomson Mason, father of Steven Thomson Alason who married Polly Armistead. Louisa and Elizabeth Westwood were nieces of Elizabeth Westwood who married (83) Anthony Armistead, the direct ancestor of the editor of this record. The women of the Westwood family were famed for their beauty. Mrs. Peyton Wise, of Richmond, Va., possesses an exquisite miniature of her great-great-grandmother, Louisa Westwood. It is the size of a silver half dollar, enameled on gold; on the reverse gold side, the letters R. A. (Robert Armistead), whom she married. Its charming color and graceful design suggest Watteau's idyllic work. In the back ground is a landscape with sheep grazing; in the foreground is seated this beutiful girl in Marie Antoinette court dress—a veritable lady in waiting at La Petite Trianoil. Judges of the painting consider it the work of an expert artist. Although at least an hundred and seventy years old, it has lost none of its purity of color. Louisa's first mentioned child, Mary Elizabeth A. (Polly), was born in 1740. Louisa was married in 1738. At the age, probably, of twenty or eighteen the miniature was painted, making her birth date 1718 or 1720. The beauty of the miniature is best seen under a magnifying glass.

Mrs. Chilton, the mother of Mrs. Wise, possesses a portrait of Mary Elizabeth Armistead (Polly), her grandmother, the daughter of Louisa Westwood and Robert Armistead of "Serenity Hall," Louisa County, formerly Hanover County. This "beauty and belle" seems proudly conscious of her charms.

Colonel George Alason, in 1721, married Anne, daughter of Stevens Thomson, and granddaughter of Sir William Thomson, of England, of the Yorkshire family of that name. Their two sons were "The Bill of Rights" George Alason, of "Gunston Hall," and Hon. Thomson Alason, who married first. Miss Barnes, of Maryland; second, the widow Wallace (*nec* Elizabeth Westwood). ,

NOTE.—Stevens Thomson, Attorney General of Virginia, and Sir William Thomson, born 1658, were sons of William Thomson, of Yorkshire, England, one of the masters of the Utter bar.

By the first marriage was Stevens Thomson Mason the eldest, who married Mary Elizabeth Armistead (Polly), born 1740. Issue: Armistead Thomson Alason, Mary Alason, (Gen.) John Thomson Alason, Catherine Alason, Emily Rutger Alason.

Armistead Thomson Alason lost his life in a famous duel with

William mcCarty. His only child, a son, was killed in the Mexican War. Miss Kate Alason Rowland has an oration by Armistead Thomson Alason delivered when a student, from the rostrum of William and Mary College, July 4, 1807, subject, "The Restriction of Suffrage," printed in Richmond, Va., by S. Grantland, 1807, at the request of the students and faculty of William and Mary College.

General John Thomson Alason married Eliza Baker Moir, of Williamsburg. Issue: (Gov.) *Stevens Thomson M.; Mary,* married General Howard; *Emily Virginia M.; Armistead Mason; Laura M.; Ann M.* Miss Emily Virginia Alason has occupied a most distinguished position in the social and political life of American women. She lived fifteen years in Paris, where her salon was the gathering place for persons of culture and distinction. She was presented at the Austrian court, the most exclusive in Europe. Was a leader in hospital work for wounded and sick Confederates. In 1908, when in her ninetieth year, she traveled to Detroit, Michigan to be present at the unveiling of the monument to her brother, Stevens Thomson Alason, the first Governor of Alichigan, who was another noted member of this family. Born in 1811, he was appointed territorial secretary of Alichigan in 1831; was appointed Governor of the State of Alichigan in 1835; re-elected in 1837; died in New York City, where he was practicing law, in 1843. His remains were taken, by request of the State of Alichigan to Detroit and reinterred in 1905. In 1908 a bronze monument was erected over his last resting place—a replica of the form and face'of this youthful stateman. His face is of the heroic, masterful type, beautiful as well as handsome. The inscription on the monument is as follows:

The Tribute of
Michigan
To the Memory of her
FIRST GOVERNOR -
whose ashes lie beneath.
Called to the duties of
Manhood while yet a boy
He so acquitted himself
As to stamp his name
Indelibly on the history
of the
Commonwealth.

And this honor was paid to him seventy years
after he was first elected Governor.

Catherine Armistead Mason (daughter of General John T. Mason and Eliza Moir, his wife) married Maj. Isaac Rowland. Issue: Kate Mason R., an author of note; Elizabeth Moir R.; Thomas Rowland (on General Ranson's staff), and John Thomson Alason R., who, at the earnest request of his grandfather, General John Thomson Alason, dropped the Rowland, bearing his grandfather's name.

Laura Mason (daughter of General John T. Alason and Eliza Moir, his wife,) married General R. LL Chilton, chief of Gen. R. E. Lee's staff till the last year of the war, when he was, with General Cooper, in Richmond. Issue of above marriage, a son and two daughters—Robert Lee Chilton, Laura C. and Emily Virginia C. Laura, the widow of General Peyton Wise, resides in Richmond. Her mother, Mrs. Chilton, lives with her.

Catherine Armistead Mason (daughter of Stevens T. Mason and Mary Elizabeth Armistead, his wife,) married first, William Barry; married second. Judge Hickey, of Kentucky.

Emily Rutger Alason (daughter of Stevens Thomson Mason and Mary Elizabeth Armistead) married William McCarty, of "Cedar Grove," Fairfax County, Va. Issue: Dr. Jones McC. and Thornton McC. After the death of his first wife, William McC. married Mary Burwell. Issue: Mr. Page McCarty.

There is a splendid portrait of Stevens Thomson Alason, first Governor of Alichigan, a copy of which his sister. Mrs. General Chilton, of Richmond, has. The artist happened in the barber shop where Steven T. Alason was being shaved. As soon as ne caught sight of this gloriously handsome youth, his shirt open and folded back, his throat bare, he begged that he would it for him, and in this way the portrait was painted. The style rather suggests Byron, but far more beautiful.

John Armistead, of Elizabeth City County, married Mrs. Jean Sinclair Bean (*nec* Watts). Issue: (1) John Sinclair Armistead, married Diana Whiting Smith, of Hampton. Issue: Cha.u J. A., who died young. John S. Armistead died, and his widow married Mr. Cumming. (2) Samuel Watts Armistead, married, 1861, Mary Shield Howard. Issue (1) Jean Sinclair A. (2) Kate Howard A. (3) Mary Shield A. (4) Frances Jennings A., who died young.

(1) Jean Sinclair Armistead married, 1888, Woodson S. Venable,

of Danville. Issue: Jean Sinclair V., Mary Howard V.. Paul Carrington V. Armistead V.

(2) Kate Howard A. unmarried.

(3) Mary Shield Armistead married J. Luther Brown, of Danville. Issue : Mary Brown.

The widow Jean Sinclair Bean, who married John Armistead above, had one child — Apphia Whiting Bean — a beautiful girl, who married Dr. William Keaton Jennings. Issue, one child, Jean Frances Jennings, who married, 1872, Thomas Leiper Crouch, of Richmond, Va. Issue, one child, Frances Leiper Crouch, who married Charles Russel Dodson, of Texas, now Virginia.

+242+ TYLER — ARMISTEAD.

John and Henry Tyler, the first of this family in Virginia, settled in 1636 in the middle Plantations between Jamestown and Yorktown, embracing Williamsburg and adjacent country. Henry Tyler settled on the spot where Williamsburg was laid out in 1690. The land upon which the palace of the Royal Governor and the College of William and Mary were built, was acquired from his estate. John settled about four males from Williamsburg, where he built his home, a round brick house — "Warburton" — in James City County. These two, Henry and John, were younger members of an ancient Shropshire family, originally from Wales, represented in Great Britain in the elder line by the late Sir William Tyler, and later Sir Charles Tyler of Parliament and Admiralty.

It is not known whom the first John married. His son, John[2], Esq., married his counsin, Elizabeth Tyler. Their son, John[3], by royal appointment marshal of the colony, married Anne, daughter of Dr. Lewis Contesse, a French Huguenot of high character. Their two sons were John and Lewis Tyler, John[4] Tyler married Mary Alarot Armistead, only daughte(r of Robert Booth Armistead and Anne Shields, his wife, born July 31, 1742. Robert B. Armistead, student at William and Mary 1753, was the son of Robert A. and Aloss Booth, his wife. This last Robert A., the son of Anthony A. and Hannah Elliason, his wife. Anthony A., son of emigrant William A.

"The beautiful Mary Armistead," as she was called by the gallants of Williamsburg (see *Gazette*), was born 1761; died 1797; married John Tyler and went to live at "Greenway," near Charles City C. H. "He was a distinguished Revolutionary patriot." His first born was named Wat. Henry Tyler, at whose christening was Patrick Henry, who, when the child was named, asked "Why that name?" his mother replied, "For the two greatest British rebels, Wat. Tyler and Patrick Henry." John Tyler* was an eminent jurist, and as Judge of Admiralty decided the first prize case after independence was declared, holding his court under a large golden willow on the lawn at "Greenway." He and Thomas Jefferson were great friends. He was governor of the State from 1808 to 1811. Later Judge of United States District Court till he died.

John Tyler5, Jr., the son of John Tyler and mary Armistead, his wife, was a youth of unusual promise. At thirteen was entered at William and Mary grammar school, living at the home of Judge Semple. Graduated at William and Mary just after he was seventeen; studied law under Judge Edmund Randolph, Attorney General of the Washington administration; obtained law license when twenty—no questions as to his age. The second year after he was elected to Virginia Legislature. His winning address, sagacity and eloquence made him a leader for the five consecutive years he was delegate. In 1816, when twenty-six, was elected to Congress; re-elected in 1817 by overwhelming popular majority, and again in 1819; resigned in 1821. Ill .n health, he retired from public life to his home and wife and children. On the 29th of Alarch, 1813, he had married Letitia Christian, daughter of Robert Christian, of "Cedar Grove," New Kent County, Va., both twenty-three years old. She bore him many children, and years afterwards as mistress of the White House, was spoken of as "one of the sweetest matrons ever there." In 1823 he was again sent to the Legislature, and in 1825 was elected by the General Assembly Governor of the State—a second time elected Governor unanimously. In 1827 elected by General Assembly to United States Senate to succeed the illustrious John Randolph; re-elected March, 1833; resigned his seat 1836; was again returned to Legislature in 1838. In 1840 elected Vice-President; Harrison (Tippecanoe) President. The latter lived only one month after inauguration, when Tyler became President. While President he married second time, on 26th of June, 1844, New York City, Church of the Ascension, Julia Gardiner, daughter of Hon. David Gardiner, of Brooklyn, who was killed on ship *Princeton* by the explosion of the gun Peacemaker. Miss Julia Gardiner and other ladies were aboard and detained President Tyler below in the dining-room, when all of his Cabinet and Mr. Gardiner were killed by the explosion of the cannon. She presided at the White House with tact and grace for eight months, when she retired with him to their country home, "Sherwood Forest," in Charles City, where she lived, the mother of many children, for seventeen years till his death, when she went back for a while to her old home on Staten Island, but returned to "Sherwood Forest," which was dear to her .as the home of her husband and the birthplace of her children. They also had a summer home at Hampton.

"The part which Mr. Tyler took in the Peace Convention of 1861 was the most glorious of his life. It alone is a monument worthy of any name." He was by a unanimous election made permanent president, and bis speech at the opening of the Convention, pulsating with all the eloquence and fire of youth, was a clarion voice calling on the country to preserve her unity; but it was soon hushed by the thunderbolt of Lincoln's proclamation.

On the 8th of January, 1862, in Richmond, Va., this patriot and statesman passed from earth. "He fell where he always stood foremost in the ranks, battling for the best interests of the State and country" he loved so dearly. He sleeps in beautiful Hollywood. "By his talents and attainments, his unyielding integrity and devotion to principle, his lofty and ardent patriotism, happily blended with those high qualities of public and personal purity; he has erected in the hearts of his people a monument which will long be cherished as a national treasure."

His son Dr. Lyon Gardiner Tyle)r, man of letters, noted genealogist and author, is president of William and Mary College, of which his illustrious father was rector and chancellor. Dr. Tyler married, 1878, Miss Annie Tucker, daughter of St. George Tucker. Issue: Julia T., Elizabeth T., married Alfred H. Aliles, of United States Navy, and a son, John Tyler.

Mr. Lyon G. Tyler's ancestor on his mother's side was Lyon Gardiner, lieutenant in British army. He bought an island of acres off the eastern end of Long Island, which descended to the family.

NOTE.—The above was mainly gleaned from Governor Wise's *Seven Deeades of the Union.*

228. Robert6 Armistead, son of 214. Robert5 A., of Louisa County, resided at "The Cottage" in Loudoun County, having sold the homestead in Louisa, married first, Margareet Elisey; second. Mrs. Dalrymple (*nee* Fanny Hislop), born at White Raven in England, on February 22, 1763. Issue by first wife: 229. *Elizabeth*, married John McKinley, of Kentucky, United States Circuit Judge. She was born in

1800, and died *sine prole* in 1893. 230. *Mary* married Willis Pope and had three sons and one daughter: (1) William, (2) John, (3) Samuel H. and (4) Elizabeth. The family moved to Columbus, Miss By second wife, Rebert Armistead had five children: 231. Robert7; 232. George Graham; 233. Isabella, who married Dr. Ben. F. Brocchus, of Loudoun County, Va., and had four sons: (1) Robert Armistead, adjutant of a Texas regiment, C. S. A., killed at Mannsfield; John Graham, died in cavalry service C. S. A.; (3) Edmund Eitzhugh, married Mary Allen, of Chester, Illinois, now living at Fort Smith, Ark.; (4) Thomas, married lantha Penn, now living in Huntsville, Ala.; 234. Harriet AL married William H. Nolan, of Alda, V*a*., lieutenant U. S. Navy; both *sine prole*. 235. Nancy Ann married Henry A. Bragg, of Norfolk, Va., February 15, 1832, and lived at Florence, Ala., till 1849, when they moved to Alemphis, Tenn. Issue: (1) Henry T., married Sally Starr; (2) Frank S.; (3) Edward V.; (4) Mary Elizabeth, married Thomas P. Adams; (5) Isabella Graham, married Dr. Fredeick T. Sweet; (6) Fanny Cuthbert, married R. S. Donelson;(7)George G., died infant; (8) Fanny, died infant; (10) Diana, died infant.

231. Robert Armistead, son of 228. Robert, of "The Cottage," married Miss Vaughan, of North Carolina, and had issue one son and four daughters—George G. A., Mary L. A., Neppie A., Fanny L., widow of Dr. Forrester, of Louisville, Ky., Nannie A.

(i) George Graham* Armistead, son of 228. Robert6 A., of "The Cottage," married first, Alice Virginia Fontaine, November 7, 1831, and moved to Florence, Ala. He married second. Jane Forsyth, daughter of James Forsyth. Issue by first wife: Dr. Hislop8 A.; Lewis Carter8 A.; Mary Frances³ A., married Young A. Gray, of Florence, Ala Texas; Alice Fontaine A., died infant. Issue by second wife: A. D. Hunt8 A.; George Graham8 A. Jr.; Ellen Eorsyth8 A., married L. H. Aledberry, of Chicago, 111., and is now a widow; Lizzie Baker A., married Peter Fontaine Armistead, deceased. Issue:(1) Gus. Henry A., (2) James Baker A., (3) George Graham A.. (4) Peter Fontaine A.

Arabella Dobbin, daughter of 232. George Graham Armistead, married her cousin, Frank S. Bragg, of Arlington, Tenn. Issue: (1) Frank S. J. Bragg, (2) Harris Forsyth B., (3) Geo. Graham B., (4) Henry T. B., (5) Hislop B., (6) Ellen B., (7) Elizabeth Fontaine B.

Jane Armistead, daughter of 232. George Graham A., married E. Y. Moore, of Chicago, 111., now living in Cleveland, Ohio. Issue: (1) Sam AI. (2) Janette M., (3) Margaret AI.

Dr. Hislop8 Armistead, son of 232. George Graham7 Armistead, was captain Company H, Fourth Alabama Infantry, C. S. A.; was killed in charge at Alalvern Hill, age twenty-three.

Lewis Carter Armistead, son of 232. George Graham A., was lieutenant in Fourth Tennessee Regiment Infantry, C. S. A.; wounded at Shiloh and Perryville; married Rosalie Dobbin, of Louisville, Ky. Issue: (1) Hamilton, (2) Berkeley, (3) McFarland, (4) Hislop, (5) Jane, (6) Hattie, (7) Mary, (8) Rosalie. Lewis Carter Armistead died at his home in Sumner County, Tenn., October, 1897.

A. D. Hunt8 Armistead, son of 232. George Graham A., married Pattie Eldridge, daughter of Judge Thomas D. Eldridge, of Alemphis. Issue two sons and four daughters: (1) Eldrige A.,(2) A. D. Hunt A., Jr., (3) Mary Eldridge A., (4) Jane Forsyth A., (5) Georgia Graham A., (6) Martha Graham[3] A. George Graham A., Jr., son of 232. George G. A., married Mattie Smith, of Manchester, Iowa. Issue: (1) Hunt, (2) Ellen,(2) Belle.

Mr. Lyon G. Tyler says: "Captain William Armistead was, doubtless, a son of 170. Anthony5, and brother of 204. Anthony6, 205. Robert6, 206. Westwood6, 207. Alexander[3] Carver." Mrs. Margareet A. Lewis, of Texas, a granddaughter of Captain William A., says her grandfather had at least two brothers, both of whom were killed during the Revolution. He saw his brother Westwood killed at the battle of Brandywine. He had two sisters who died young, and mentioned his aunts living in Virginia. Captain William Armistead moved to Randolph County, North Carolina, and married Rebecca Kimball, near Warrenton, N. C.; thence to Alabama in 1819. Children as copied from family Bible as follows: Westwood A., born 1791; John A., born 1792; Elizabeth Lee A., born 1794; Martha A., born 1796. Captain William Armistead married second, Elizabeth, widow of John Morris and daughter of Lewis and Jane Westmoreland, of Halifax County, N. C. She had a son John Morris. Children by second marriage: Robert Starkey A., born 1800; Jane Westmoreland A., born 1802. Captain William A., died in Clarke County, Ala. On his tombstone the following:

"In memory of Captain William Armistead, a soldier of the Revolution, a native of Virginia; departed this life March 1st, 1842, age eighty years."

His son Westwood A. married Elizabeth Borrughs in North Carolina; died in 1845. Issue: (1) James W. A.; (2) Bryan A.;(2)William Westwood A.; (4) Robert S. A.; (5) Emma A., married Cunningham; (6) Elizabeth A., married her second cousin, John Kimball.

The second son of Captain William A., John Kimball A., married Julia Gaines. They lived in Wilcox, Ala.; moved thence in 1840 to Mississippi. Issue: (1) William Henry A.; (2) James A.; (3) General Charles A., C. S. A.; (4) John A., who had a son William and a daughter; (5) Dr. E. R. A., of Prescott, Ala.;(5)a daughter; (7) a daughter.

Robert Starkey, third son of Captain William Armistead, married Anne Carney; moved to Texas in 1835; died 1866.

The eldest daughter of Captain William Armistead, Elizabeth Lee, married his stepson, John Morris. The second daughter married Edmund Waddill, of North Carolina. They have greatgrandchildren in Wilcox County, Alabama. Jane Westmoreland married in Alabama, 1821, Dr. Neal Smith, a native of North Carolina, son of Alalcolm Smith. He and Alalcolm Smith, Sr., were soldiers of the Revolution. Issue: (1) Julia Elizabeth S., born 1822, married in 1840 David White, of Virginia; (2) Sarah Louise S., born 1824, married John B. Savage in 1843 left issue; (3) Margaret Armistead S., born 1825, married in 1845 Kirkland Harrison, of South Carolina, son of Reuben H., who moved from James River, Va., and died in 1850, leaving one son Henry Kirkland Harrison. (3) Margaret Smith married second, Asa Al. Lewis, of Brenham, Texas; native of Tennessee.

4. *Robert A. died a prisoner of zvar on Ship Island, 1864.*

5. Neal, born 1828, married, 1869, Miss Watkins from Virginia, near Hampden-Sidney.

6. Jane Armistead Smith, born 1835, married Jas. D. Bryant, of Wilcox County, Ala.

7. Martha Rebecca S., born 1837, married first, Richard Starkey Jones, of Selma, Ala.; died 1858, leaving two children— Mrs. Sallie Jones Featherstone, of Rome, Ga., and Drury Fair Jones, died unmarried. She married second, Rixie, by whom no issue.

8. Caherine Jeanet S., born 1839, married Dr. H. G. Davis in 1871.

9. Mary Caroline S., born 1841, married Thomas Borrughs, Jr. Issue: Dr. Wm. At. Borrughs, of Pine Hill, Wilcox County, Alabama.

William Henry Armistead, eldest son of John Kimball Armistead and Julia Gaines, his wife, married Mary E. Wilson in Carroll County, Miss, and lived in the town of Shongalo; afterwards moved to Vaiden. Issue: (1) John Armistead, of Shreveport, La.; (2) May A.; (3) A. A. Armistead, a lawyer of Vicksburg, Aliss.; (4) Lula A.; (5) Willie A.

May Armistead married G. W. Baines in Vaiden, Carroll County, Miss They removed to Birmingham, Ala. Their children are: Rosa Baines, William Baines. May A. Baines died 1889.

(3) A. A. Armistead married Lotta Moore in Bolivar County, Miss., in 1899. Issue: Mary Erminie Armistead, born 1901.

(4) Loula Armistead married Eugene Hibbett, of Shreveport, La.; died 1901; no issue.

Willie Armistead married John R. Land, a lawyer, of Shreveport, La. Issue: John R. Land, Jr., and Mary Elizabeth Land.

Anthony Armistead, son of the emigrant, had a son, 83. Anthony, who married Elizabeth Westwood. They had two sons. 169. Westwood Armistead, the ancestor of the editor's line, and 170. Anthony Armistead, whose sons (204) Anthony and William, settled in North Carolina. Mr. Tyler says; "Captain William Armistead was, doubtless, a son of 170. Anthony, and brother of 204. Anthony A., 205, Robert A., 206, Westwood A., 207 Alexander Carver A."

Dr. Lyon Tyler's *doubtless,"* we are persuaded, becomes a certainty when we read the names of Captain William Armistead's children and grandchildren; particularly Captain William's eldest son's children and grandchildren, which line had not come under Dr. Lyon Tyler's observation at the time that he pronounced Captain William A. a son of 170. Anthony A., whose mother was Elizabeth Westwood. The names of both the Westwood and Armistead lines are given by the descendants.

204. Anthony A. married Sarah Archer, of North Carolina. William A. married Rebecca Kimball, near Warrenton, North Carolina. Issue: Westwood, born 1791; John K., born 1792; Elizabeth Lee, born 1794; Martha, born 1796. He married second, Elizabeth, widow of John Morris, daughter of Lewis and Jane Westmoreland, of Halifax County. She had a son John Morris. Issue by second marriage: Robert Starkey A., born 1800: Jane Westmoreland A., born 1802.

Captain William Armistead's eldest son, Westwood, married Elizabeth Borrughs in North Carolina. Issue: James W. A.; Byron A.; *William Westwood A.,* Robert S. A.; Emma A. (married Cunningham) ; Elizabeth A. (married her second cousin, John Kimball).

William Westzwood Armistead left North Carolina when quite a youth and settled at Coushatta, Louisiana.' His plantation, "Cabin Point," is still in the possession of his descendants. He amassed a large fortune. He married Rose Tyler, a cousin of President Tyler, and had five children, viz.: *Franklin A.*, Sumpter A., Laura A., Martha A., Julia A.

After her death he married Mary White, and had by this union Tom, William, Anthony, John Westwood, and Kate.

Franklin Armistead married Virginia Clarke, a descendant of the North Carolina Battles, and had William AI. Armistead, formerly of Alberta, now Philadelphia, and Mrs. John C. Cooke, of Nashville.

We are persuaded that 205. Robert Armistead, son of 170. Anthony4 A., who was son of 83. Anthony[3], son of Anthony[2], son of emigrant William[1], is the progenitor of the line which follows from dates, names, tradition, and facts. Mr. Joseph Robert Armistead, of Alontgomery, Ala., age seventy-two, writes, July 20, 1910: 'T was about eight years old when my grandfather, Robert Armistead, died at the age of ninety-eight. He was an invalid fifteen years, and I delighted to hear him tell of the Revolutionary War. He was a drummer boy; I *know* this from his own lips. Am not sure of the date when he moved from Virginia to Tennessee—think it was about 1816. He brought with him his two sons—Robert and John—and a second wife. His only daughter, Palley, never married. I went from Tennessee to Virginia and brought her to my father's to receive her portion of my father's estate, which was $5,000. She returned to Virginia— Sussex County. My father left three brothers in Virginia. I don't remember their names."

Mr. Lyon G. Tyler says, *Williani and Mary Quarterly*, Vol. XVII., that Captain William Armistead of the Revolution was "doubtless a son of 170. Anthony A., and brother of 204 Anthony, 205. Robert, 206. Westwood, 207 Alexander Carver." Anthony, Westwood, and Alexander Carver would answer to the three brothers that Robert left in Virginia, and would it not be natural that if William A. was a brother and in the Revolutionary War, that his young brother would also be fired with patriotism and enlist, even as a drummer boy? However this may be, Robert Armistead, drummer boy in the Revolutionary War, went from Virginia to Tennessee about 1816 with two sons—Robert and John—and settled in Alontgomery County, Tennessee. Robert married and settled in Alontgomery County, Tennessee. John married and settled near Paducah, Ky. Robert had seven children; William Thomas, died; Joseph Robert; Henry Addison, died; Richard, killed in the War between the States; John; Bryant, lives in Mississippi; Katie.

1.   Joseph Robert Armistead married Susan Darden, of Fayette,

Miss., and had Thomas D., married Lunette Thompson, of Louisville, Ky.

2. Robert S. Armistead married Georgie Reid, of Fort Deposit, Ala.

3. Benjamin P. Armistead married Jessie Brown, of Montgomery.

4. Eugene Douglas Armistead married Mary Moffet, of Knoxville, Tenn.

5. Joseph D. Armistead married Gertrude Sullivan, of St. Louis.

6. Victor D. Armistead married Louise Davout Montgomery.

NORTH CAROLINA BRANCH.

Anthony Armistead, son of the emigrant William Armistead, had a son, 83. Anthony A., who married Elizabeth Westwood. Issue, among others, 170. Anthony A., who married Mary Tucker, daughter of Anthony Tucker and Rosea, widow of Joshua Curie. Issue, among others, 204. Anthony A., married Sarah Archer, of North Carolina. (This statement from a descendant, who says he frequently heard his mother say that Anthony Armistead was persuaded to settle in North Carolina because the parents of his wife Sarah Archer, were so opposed to her living away from them.) Mr: Tyler says. Vol. VII., p. 21, that 204. Anthony married Mourning ———. The following explains this mistake. Starkey Armistead (son of William A., who was the son of 204. Anthony) married Mary Cary Drew, daughter of John Drew and Alourning Brewer, his wife, so that the names of Starkey Armistead's grandmother and his wife's grandmother were confused.

204. Anthony Armistead and Sarah Archer had, among others, William A., born September 19, 1730, who married Sarah Jordan. The following is a copy of their family Bible, made by a descendant, David Wright, of Nansemond County, Va.:

"William Armistead, died Jan. 1791, married Sarah Jordan of North Carolina, daughter of Isaac Jordan, son of Thomas Jordan of Virginia.

"Sarah was born Dec. 13th, 1739. married March 8th, 1756, and had issue; John, born Sep. 2nd, 1757;-Eliza, born Dec. 29th, 1759; William, born March 5th, 1762, died May 13th, 1796; Anthony, born July 26th, 1764, died June 14th, 1789; Sarah, born July 13th, 1770, and died Dec. 1800; Robert, born Nov. 13th, 1767; Jordan, Jan. 19th, 1775, died Dec. 27th, 1799; Mary, bora Sep. 29th, 1777; Starkey, born July 16th, 1780; Thomas and Priscilla (twins), born Nov. 1783. Thomas died Nov. 24th, 1783. William Armistead the father of these children moved to Bertie County, N. C."

NOTE. — Miss Anna Plummer, now of Richmond, has a beautiful old-time miniature of her grandfather, Starkey Armistead.

John Armistead, eldest son of William A. and Sarah Jordan, his wife, married Sarah Cammak (*ncc* Harriman). Issue; (Dr.) William Anthony Armistead and Susan Jordan A.

Dr. Wm. Anthony Armistead married Susan Capehart, of "Avoca," Bertie County. North Carolina, and had issue: (1) Cullen, (2) Meeta, (3) Susan. Cullen and Susan died young. Meeta married B. Ashbourne Capehart, her cousin. Issue; (1) Cullen, (2) Aleeta Armistead, (3) Ashbourne (physician in Washington, D. C.), (4) Armistead, planter at "Ashbourne," Vance County, N. C., and (5) Poindexter. Cullen died in it fancy. Aleeta Armistead married, February 10, 1891, at Christ Church, Raleigh, N. C., Thomas Littlejohn Feild, of London, England, where they now reside. Issue, two sons, Armistead Littlejohn F. and Robert Durant F.

The Feild family is an ancient and honorable one, first of England, later of America. Theophilus Feild was Bishop of the English Church in the seventeenth century. Edward Feild, another prelate, was Bishop of Newfoundland from 1844 to 1876, where he did a glorious work. The founder of the Virginia Feild was Theophilus F., who settled in old Bristol parish early in the eighteenth century, and was one of the founders of Blandford Church, near Petersburg, Va. He is buried under the chancel. The line of Thomas Littlejohn Feild runs thus: Theophilus Feild married Susan Theawtt. Issue, among others, Robert F., who married Nancy Meade, aunt of Richard Kidder AL Issue, among others, George Feild, who married Elizabeth Bolling Stith: Issue, among others, George F., who married first, Sarah Jones; married second, Frances Blunt Littlejohn, both of Warren Co.. N. C. Issue: Thomas Littlejohn Feild, married Meeta Armistead Capehart.

The following notice of this marriage is taken from one of the magazines of that period :

Mrs. Thomas L. Feild.

"Mrs. Aleeta Armistead Capehart Feild, whose portrait is given on this page, ranks as one of the most noted belles and beauties of North Carolina. She is the only daughter of Mr. B.A Capehart, a large planter and prominent citizen of the State, residing at Kittrell, and a gentleman whose home is famed for the refined and elegant hospitality so characteristic of the South. Endowed with wondrous charm of person and manner. Mrs. Feild has held her own in the most exclusive society circles of the South. She is petite, with delicately carved features, absolutely perfect in contour, dark eyes heavily fringed, a complexion of creamy fairness, and wavy auburn hair.

"Mrs. Eeild is a bride of a few months, her husband being Mr. Thomas Littlejohn Feild, a native Carolinian, who has been for several years a resident of London, where he has large business interest. The wedding was a brilliant affair of State-wide importance, attended by Governor Fowle and a great company of distinguished people. The Rt. Rev. Dr. Wingfield, Bishop of Northern California, assisted at the ceremony. The American colony in London will be enriched by the acquisition of this fair daughter of the South."

Susan Jordan Armistead daughter of John Armistead and Sarah Cammak (*nee* Harriman) was born April 23, 1812; died October 17, 1884; educated at Moravian School, Salem, N. C. She married, at eighteen years of age, Augustus Moore (son of Charles Moore, a member of the Continental Congress at Halifax, N. C), who was one of the leading lawyers of North Carolina. At an early age was appointed Judge of the Supreme Court. When quite young she was left a widow, and devoted her life to rearing and educating her children. Her eldest son, William Armistead Moore, suffering from his eyes and unable to read, she gave him his legal education orally and fitted him for the first honors of his law class. He arose to the judicial bench of his native State, as did also her second son, Augustus Minton Moore; and John Armistead, her third son, was also an eminent lawyer in North Carolina. Alfred Moore, her fourth son, was one of the first men in his community.

"Susan Jordan Armistead, a noted woman of her day, was unusually gifted. Her kindness of heart and nobility of nature were such that her children almbst worshipped her."

"Susan Augustus Moore, daughter of Judge Augustus Moore and

Susan Jordan Armistead, married her cousin, Starkey Armistead Wright Righton, November 18, 1856. He was a young man of wealth, fine character, and handsome. Issue: (1) Susan Armistead Moore, born June 2, 1862; died November 27, 1866.(2) Mary Elizabeth Moore, born November 29, 1870; married, October 11, 1892, Patrick Mathew, born October 25, 1853, at Gourdie Hill, Perth, Scotland. No issue."

Starkey Armistead Wright Righton was born January 5, 1829, in Chowan County, North Carolina. Joined the Confederate service at the first of the war; was taken prisoner when ill at home—paralyzed. While in prison and in a pitiable condition, he was offered freedom if he would not go back to the Confederate service. This he would not promise.

February 8, 1887, broken in health and spirit, and bereft of means, he died at the Confederate Soldiers' Home in Richmond, Va., and is buried in Hollywood.

Mary Armistead, daughter of William Armistead and Sarah Jordan, both of Bertie County, N. C., married, June 27, 1795 David Wright, of Nansemond County, Va. (born November 10, 1775; died 7th December, 1813,) son of Nathaniel Wright and Alartha, his wife. David Wright married his second wife, Mary Armistead, before he was nineteen. Issue:

(1) Nathaniel D. Wright, born December 8, 1797. .

(2) **William Armistead Wright, born October 26, 1799.**

(3) Jordan Armistead Wright, born November, 1802.

(4) **John A. Wright, born January 8, 1804.**

(5) Sarah Jordan Wright, born February 19, 1807; married William Righton, March 6, 1827; married second, Peter Hinton. Issue: Sarah Hinton, who married Col. Dennis, of Texas. She only lived a year after this marriage. Was a woman of unusual beauty.

(6) David Minton Wright, born April 21, 1809. Dr. David Minton Wright (1809-1863) married, April 21, 1833, Penelope Margareet Creecy, daughter of Joshua Skinner Creecy and Mary Benbury, of "Benbury Hall," near Edenton, N. C. The said Mary Benbury was the daughter of Richard B. and Penelope Creecy, his wife. Richard Benbury was the son of Thomas Benbury and Thamer Howcutt, his wife. Eor the Revolutionary and State record of Thomas Benbury see *Clarke's Colonial Records of North Carolina*, Vol. IX., 10, 11, and *Wheeler's History of North Carolina*. Joshua Creecy was the son of Lemuel Creecy and Penelope Skinner, his wife.

NOTE. — The Weddells have lovely miniatures of David Alinton Wright and his beautiful wife, Penelope Creecy, painted for each other when he was a medical student in Philadelphia and she was seventeen. They have also a miniature of Mary Armistead, their great-grandmother.

Issue of above marriage (David Alinton Wright and Penelope Creecy) is as follows:

(1) David Alinton Wright, born May 1, 1838; died September 28, 1840.

(2) Penelope Margareet Wright, born February 29, 1840.

(3) Minton Augustus Wright, born December 25, 1841, in Edenton, N. C. Entered Confederate service as ordnance sergeant, Norfolk Light Artillery Blues. Captured at Roanoke Island and exchanged. Lieutenant Fifty-seventh North Carolina Regiment and acting adjutant. Killed at Gettysburg, Pa., July 2, 1863, while leading the charge. He was not quite twenty-one years old.

(4) Elizabeth Alinton Wright, born May 12, 1844 (second of name), married William Henry Talbot, of Norfolk. Issue: Diana, Thomas, Alinton Wright, Elizabeth Wright, Mary Chapman (who married E. Lorraine Ruffin, of Richmond, Va.; issue, Thomas Talbot) and Margareet (died).

(5) Mary Creecy Armistead Wright, born January 21, 1846; died, , 1902. Alarried Rev. Frederick A. Fetter. Issue: Nellie Cox, married Dr. Luther Sapp; Mary Augusta, married Oscar Sapp; Frederick Augustus, married Claude Johnson; Alinnie, married James Webb; Alexander W. Fetter, married Ruth Anderson; Jessie Fetter, married Dr. Ernest De Bordenave, of Franklin, Va.; and Elizabeth Wright, married William Stocks.

(6) Joshua Creecy Armistead Wright, born June 5, 1848. Was a midshipman in the Confederate Navy on the *Patrick Henry*. Died December 5, 1899..

(7) Sallie J. Armistead Wright, born December 9, 1850; married Thomas Davis Warren. Issue: Thomas Wright, Ernest Weddell, married Ruth Worth; Sally Wright, William Plummer, Eugene, David Alinton, Joseph (died in childhood), and Penelope Creecy.

(8) William Armistead Wright, born March 17, 1853; married Sarah S. Coke. Issue: Coke, Sadie, and William Armistead.

(9) Viola Jessica Wright, born March 5, 1856; married Henry De Berniere Hooper. Issue: Penelope De Berniere, May De Berniere, Virginia Wright, Mary T., Joseph (all five died in childhood), Henry

De Berniere, Jr., and Louise Alaclaine.

The above Henry De Berniere Hooper, of North Carolina (who married V. Jessica Wright), was the son of J. De Berniere Hooper and Mary E. Hooper (daughter of Rev. William Hooper and Fanny P. Jones), and great-grandson of William Hooper, signer of the Declaration of Independence, a man whom John Adams mentions as the peer in oratory of Richard Henry Lee and Patrick Henry.

NOTE. — Mrs. Viola Jessica Hooper has a miniature by Sully of her grandfather, Joshua Skinner Creecy, who was the grandson of Thomas Benbury and of William Skinner. For colonial record of the latter *sec Clarke's Colonial Records of North Carolina,* Vol. H-XH, XIII. .

(2) Penelope (Pencie) Margaret Wright, daughter of David Minton Wright and Penelope Creecy, his wife, born February 29, 1840, married Rev. Alexander Watson Weddell, D. D., at "Ashbourne Hall," Granville County, North Carolina, January 31, 1866. He was rector of old St. John's Church, Richmond, Va. Both are buried there, near the entrance. She died January 9, 1901. In the editorial section of the *News-Leader* of that date is the following:

"The death of Mrs. Penelope Wright Weddell renews in the beyond a unity as beautiful as has ever existed between man and woman in this world. She and her husband, the late rector of St. John's Church, left an impress on this community which will never be lost or forgotten. They represented the highest qualities of manhood and womanhood, and together made the ideal combination of them. He was a big, strong, aggressive, lionlike man, a tremendous power for the Master he served, and she was his fitting helpmeet, giving his life the love and tenderness and gentle guidance it needed. She made her influence feit strongly and almost imperceptibly in the wide circle of her friendship, always for the sweetest and best and most womanly way. When her faithful heart ceased to beat her soul went where its affection and hope had long been fixed."

The Rev. Alexander Weddell was the son of James Weddell (of Musselboro, Scotland, later of Petersburg, Va.,) and Margareet Ward, his wife, of Tarboro, N. C. Issue, three sons — John, Virginius, Alexander — who were in the active service of the Confederate army. John and Virginius were killed. After the war Alexander took the law course at the University of Virginia ; later felt called to the ministry. A few years after taking Orders, the degree of D. D. was conferred on him by William and Mary College. .

The children of Alexander Weddell and Pencie Wright: (1) James

Wright (died in infancy). (2) Margaret Ward. (3) Penelope Margaret, married St. George Mason Anderson, son of Col. Archer Anderson, of Richmond, Va.; issue: Penelope Weddell Anderson, Mary Mason Anderson, and Margaret Ward Anderson. (4) William Sparrow. (5) Alexander Welbourne; and (6) Elizabeth Wright.

(5) Alexander Welbourne Weddell was appointed February, 1910, Consul at Zanzibar by President Taft. Prior to his appointment to this consular position. Mr. Weddell served as secretary to Dr. Maurice E. Egan, American minister to Denmark.

NOTE. — David Minton Wright was born in Nansemond County Va., in 1809; educated at Captain Patrick's Military Academy in Middletown, Conn.; studied medicine under Dr. William Warren, of Edenton, N. C., and graduated at the University of Pennsylvania. Removed to Norfolk, where he attended the yellow fever sufferers in 1855, and practised his profession with zeal and success till the war. After the surrender of Norfolk to the Federal authorities in 1862, Dr. Wright became involved in a difficulty with a Federal, Lieutenant Sanborn, which resulted in one of the most heart-rending tragedies of that season of Virginia's martyrdom.

We add the following, clipped from the *Times-Dispatch* Genealogical Column:

"The following generations are proved: William Wright, burgess, born 1668, had at least two sons, William[2] and Stephen[2]. William[2], born about 1690, died in 1750, married Penelope Manley (Vol. II., page 2, *Virginia Historical Magazine*) ; Stephen[2] married Mrs. Mary Thorogood (*nee* Trevethan), January 28, 1728.

"From William[2], son of William[1], comes Dr. Christopher Wright, grandfather of Dr. David Minton Wright, who stands out on the pages of our sacred Confederate history as a martyr and a saint. The mention of his name arouses all the fierce indignation of a past age. His death was 'one of the most tragic, thrilling and pathetic episodes of Virginia history.'

"Dr. Wright, after graduating at the University of Pennsylvania, became the leading physician and the 'most beloved citizen of Norfolk.' He was a Union man and did all in his power to prevent the war. Like many another Virginian, when the die was cast all of his energy went for the South. The story of his valor and his tragic suffering was printed in a Rich-, mond newspaper many years ago, but it stands so distinctly alone in our records and has such a vital interest, that we deem it expedient to print it again:

"'The federal troops occupied Norfolk May 10, 1862. Dr. Wright, recognized as a non-combatant and citizen, and pursuing his usual occupations, was undisturbed and peaceful until July II, 1863. On that day, while he was walking in the afternoon on the sidewalk of Alain Street, having just come from the celebration of his wife's birthday at his home, at a point opposite No. 156, then occupied by Foster & Aloore, he met a column of negro troops occupying the entire walk, and as they moved jostling men, women and children into the gutter.

A FATAL EXCLAMATION.

" 'Dr. Wright stepped aside, and as he did so, in the heat of his indignation, he uttered some sharp exclamation of contempt and disgust. A white lieutenant, A. L. Sanborn, heard this and advanced on Dr. Wright with sword drawn and threatening. Dr. Wright carried no weapon, having always contended, in his own words, that "no man should ever go prepared to take the life of another." A friend standing close to him and seeing his danger hastily passed a pistol into his hand.

" 'Holding the weapon behind him, but facing his foe and sturdily holding his place. Dr. Wright called, "Stand off!"

" 'Sanborn continued to advance, and Dr. Wright, according to the evidence of eye witnesses, fired one shot, striking the officer in the left hand.

" 'Sanborn called on his negro troops to assist him in making the arrest, and there was a short, hot altercation. The feeling against negroes in United States uniform was then intensely bitter, especially among the older men who had been brought up to honor the army and the flag it represented.

MORTALLY WOUNDED.

" 'It is said that several shots were fired, and it has never "been known whether the fatal wound was inflicted by Dr. Wright or some one in the group of citizens around him. Lieutenant Sanborn was struck in the body and clinched with Dr. Wright, who held the pistol to his antagonist's breast a moment and then turned it away without firing again. The negroes rushed in with fixed bayonets, but were turned aside and the officer relaxed his hold, tottered into the store of

Foster & Moore and fell dead.

" 'Dr. Wright was immediately arrested, and in a short time was tried before a military commission. It was at this time, while he was in jail and manalaced, that the City Council of Portsmouth adopted resolutions denouncing "the brutal murder of a Union officer by a ;rabid Secessionist," and calling on "the military authorities to bring to speedy and condign punishment the author of this foul crime and treasonable act to his country and his God." In these same resolutions the military forces are exhorted "to remove from OUT midsts the foul-mouthed traitors who infest the street corners and market places of our city, plotting treason and even contemplating such deeds of bloodshed as we are now called to reflect on."

" 'These are the resolutions adopted July 13, 1863, which have been formally and forever expunged from the record by resolution of the City Council of Portsmouth, May 8, 1901.

Speedily Condemned.

" 'The prisoner was given no chance for his life. Eight days in succession he was led to the place of trial with chains on wrists and ankles. The people of Norfolk who remained in the city showed all the sympathy they dared. They used to stand in groups and silently lift their hats as he hobbled in and out, and he returned the salutation as well as he could with his fettered hands. He knew his fate and wrote his wife: "I suppose the verdict will be the same as that of the provost marshal, made before he had examined the first witness."

" 'The prediction was verified, and the sentence of death was quickly given.

A Daughter's Vain Heroism.

" 'Between the time of sentence and execution. Miss Penelope Wright, the youthful daughter of the condemned man, and afterwards Mrs. Weddell, of this city, was the heroine of an attempt at rescue which was nearly successful, and of which very few of even her most intimate friends were ever told. She went to visit him. in his cell, and in its semi-darkness, although a detective was watching at the door, succeeded in deftly throwing over her father some of her own garments and slipping on his boots, which she thrust below the blankets as she put herself in the cot. Dr. Wright walked out in his disguise, and had actually gone fifty yards from the outer door of his prison and was approaching a carriage which was waiting for him, when a sentry called attention to the unusual height of the departing figure for a woman. Pursuit and recapture were prompt. Dr. Wright accepted his failure with his usual coolness and philosophy. The daughter was not detained or molested.

"'The most powerful influence available were brought to bear. Mrs. Wright, who was Miss Penelope Creecy, of North Carolina, exhausted every effort and appeal. The Confederate authorities protested in vain that Norfolk had been put under civil authority by the Federal troops themselves; that Dr. Wright had fired only after his own life was in imminent danger, and certainly without premeditation, and that he was entitled to civil trial. Beast Butler was in command, and was not then known to his superiors as he subsequently came to be. President Lincoln granted a reprieve for a week, but at the end of that time, on October 23, 1863, Dr, Wright was executed while all the respectability of Norfolk groaned in despair and anguish and shame.

A Brave Man's Death.

" 'He was carried to his death between long columns of troops, and the wails of the people who filled the windows of the houses along the route to call their last good-byes and express their unavailing sympathy. None but the troops, negroes and the lowest riff-raff of the white population attended the execution as spectators, according to the accounts printed at the time. Dr. Wright and had taken his last Communion and bidden farewell to his family and friends with the dignity and serenity becoming a dauntless gentleman, and was attended to the scaffold by three clergymen of the Episcopal Church, of which he was a member He gave the signal for the drop with an unfaltering voice.' "

(7) Nathaniel Alinton Wright (son of Mary Armistead and David Wright), born December 8, 1797, married Huldah Godwin Wilkinson, daughter of John Henry and Martha Wilkinson. Issue: Jordan Armistead Wright,born October i, 1825; Mary Turner Wright, born August 3, 1827, and Alinton David
Wright, born August , 1829. '

(5) Sarah Jordan Wright (daughter of Mary Armistead and David Wright, her husband) married William Righton. Issue: Starkey

Armistead R., born January 5, 1829; Mary Elizabeth R., born September 25, 1832; Jordan Armistead Wright R., born December 16, 1834.

(3) Jordan Armistead Wright married Harriet E. Pugh, July 16, 1832. Their daughter, Virginia Wright, married Dr. Gahnall. Issue: Eelicia Gahnall.

The Weddells of Richmond have an exquisite miniature of their grandfather's brother, (3) Jordan Armistead Wright, set in carved gold frame pendant, with an inset for hair on the gold back. Lafayette pronounced him the handsomest man that he had met in America.

The following, down to Starkey Armistead, is copied from records that Mr. Thomas Stuart Armistead, of Plymouth, N. C., collected:

NORTH CAROLINA BRANCH.

Richard A. married Elizabeth Smith, of New Berne, N. C.; was educated at Wilmington, N. C., 1804. Issue: daughter, married Winthrop; daughter, married Groom, of New York.

Robert, son of William A. and Sarah, his wife, married Mary Stuart, of "Daly's Hill," Roanoke River, N. C., in Mlartin County. Issue: (1) John, died unmarried (drowned at sea whilst en route to West Indies to recover health). At the University of North Carolina he took first distinction alone in all his studies, and left during the vacation between his third and fourth year. Sailed and lost off Hatteras about 1820. The family has a letter from the President of the University saying he was one of the most brilliant scholars ever matriculated at that institution.

Priscilla, daughter of William Armistead and Sarah Jordan, his wife, born Novemlber, 1783, married Joel Thorp, of New Haven, Conn. They lived in Edenton, N. C. Issue: Sarah Jordan Thorp, only daughter, who lived to be more than twenty-one. She married John Martin Saunders, a Alethodist minister. Issue: Sarah Thorp Saunders, married Mr. Key, and Priscilla Armistead Saunders. Priscilla Armistead Saunders married Edmund Nicholas Allen, now Professor of English Language and Literature in University of Alissouri.

Dr. *Robert* A., son of Robert A. and Mary Stuart, married the widow of General P. O. Picot, of France (*nec* Blount). Issue: Thomas Stuart Armistead, married first. Mary De Berniere Jones, of Chapel Hill, January 14, 1868. She died August 24,1868 Second, Mary, daughter of Dr. S. E. Bratton, of Charlotte, N. C.; no issue. Thomas Stuart, died in 1871 unmarried. Anthony, married Miss Ely, of Florida, and died d. s. p.

William, son of William Armistead and Sarah Jordan, married Penelope Stuart, of Daly's Hill. Issue: William J., who married Mary Baker, daughter of Dr. Simmons J. Baker, of "Scotland Neck," Halifax County, N. C. Served in the North Carolina Legislature and moved to Florida. Issue of William J.6 and (Baker) Armistead: (1) Robert7, captain C. S. A.; (2) Anthony7, captain of battery, killed at Sharpsburg, Md.; (3) Thomas Stuart7, lieutenant Eighth Florida Regiment, C. S. A.; (4) William7; (5) Mary7, married a physician of Tallahassee; (6) Anne7, married Dr. Baltzell, of Florida; (7) Sarah7, unmarried. Elizabeth5, married Dr. William T. Turner, of Windsor, N. C., and left issue.

Dr. Robert Armistead6, died August 3, 1857.

Dr. William Anthony Armistead[3] died in 1856 in Virginia. He was born in Plymouth, N. C., October 11, 1808. His sister, Susan Jordan6, daughter of John Armistead®, married Judge Augustus Moore, of Edenton, N. C., and had issue: (1) Judge William Armistead Moore and others.

Starkey Armistead, born 1785, died 1835 (son of William A. and Sarah Jordan, his wife,), married Mary Cary Drew, cf North Carolina. Issue: (1) Dolphin A., died young. (2) Eliza A., married William Plummer, of Warrenton, N. C. William Plummer was a lawyer, the son of Kemp Plummer (also a lawyer) and Susannah Martin, and grandson of William Plummer, of Gloucester County, Va. (3) Mary Cary Armistead, married William T. Sutton, of Bertie County, N C. (4) Starkey A., died unmarried.

Children of William Plummer and Eliza Armistead, his wife: (1) Mary Cary P., married, 1850, Jos. B. Batchelor, North Carolina; (2) Susan P., married, 1861, Rev, Cameron F. McRae, North Carolina; (3) Harriet P., married, 1853, DT. Frank W. Tatem, Virginia; (4) Stark Armistead P., married, 1855, Cornelia Peterson, Virginia; (5) Edward Hall P., married, 1862, Sally D. Fitts, of Virginia; (6) Virginia P., died in childhood; (7) William Turner P., married, 1861, Rebecca Purnell, Norch Carolina; (8) Walter George P., married, 1871, Nannie Cawthorn, North Carolina; (9) Eliza Armistead P., unmarried; (10) Anna Sutton P., unmarried. Edward, William and Walter Plummer served in C. S. Army.

Children of William T. Sutton and Mary Cary Armistead, his

wife; (1) Stark Armistead S., married Henrietta Moore, North Carolina; (2) William Thomas S., married Annie Outlaw, North Carolina; (3) John Mebane S., died unmarried; (4) Plummer S., died unmarried. Stark A., William T., and John AL Sutton served in C. S. Army.

Stark A. Sutton was killed at the battle of Ohancellorsville. He left a son, William T.[3], who married Miss Delia Shultz, and died in Norfolk, Va.

William T. Sutton[2] was surgeon in the C. S. Army. After the war he practiced medicine in North Carolina, and then moved to Norfolk, Va., and died there many years later.

Children of William T. Sutton and Annie Outlaw, his wife: (1) Emily Turner S., married Alan Cameron, of North Carolina; (2) Stark Armistead S., married Lucile Hudgins, of Virginia; (3) Mary Armistead S., married William White, of Virginia ; (4) Annie Peyton S., unmarried.

Children of Jos. B. Batchelor and Mary Cary Plummer, his wife: (1) Wm. Plummer B., married David Ella Chinault, of Kentucky; (2) James Watts B., died in infancy; (3) John Branch B., died in childhood; (4) Edward Armistead B., died unmarried; (5) Joseph Branch B., married Mary Gouge, of New York; (6) Henry Plummer B., died in infancy; (7) Eliza Armistead B.. married Harry Loeb, of North Carolina; (8) Walter Bradford B., died in infancy; (9) Junius Lewis B., died in infancy; (10) Stark Sutton B., married Lula Purnell, of North Carolina; (11) Kemp Battle B., married Ferbe Dewey, of North Carolina: (12) Susan Branch B., died in infancy; (13) Francis Howard B., died unmarried.

Children of Walter G. Plummer and Nannie Cawthorne, his wife: (1) Susan P., unmarried; (2) Walter George P., married Emily Blanton, of Mississippi; (3) Mary Kenan P., unmarried ; (4) Robert Spencer P., married Cornelia Davis, of North Carolina; (5) Edward Hall P., married Agnes Messine; (6) Lurana Blount P., unmarried; (7) Eliza Armistead P., married Prank L. Schofield, of Virginia; (8) Cary Josephine P., married D. McDaniel, of North Carolina; (9) Harry Cawthorne P., unmarried.

Children of Rev. Cameron F. McRae and Susan Plummer, his wife: (1) William Plummer AlcRae, died unmarried; lawyer. (2) Julia Theodosia AlcRae, married, 1899, Algernon S. Hurt, of Virginia; (3) Edward Winslow McRae (4) Cameron Farquhar McRae, married, 1908, Sarah Woodward, of New Jersey.

Children of Frank W. Tatem and Harriet Plummer: (1) Mary Nash T., married John AI. Berkeley, of Virginia; (2) Eliz.a Armistead T., died unmarried; (3) Frank Warren T., unmarried.

John M. and Mary Nash Berkeley had three children who died in infancy.

Children of Stark Armistead Plummer and Cornelia Peterson, his wife: (14 Mary Eliza P., married Sydney M. Green; (2) William P., married Virginia Edwards, of New Jersey; (3) Susan P., married Stephen Urquhart, of Virginia; (4) John Peterson P., married Nannie Strachan, of Virginia; (5) Anna Thweatt P., unmarried; (6) Edward Hall P., married Anita Green, of North Carolina; (7) Louisa Haskins P., married Kirk Seabury, of Virginia; (8) Georgie Campbell P., married Levin Smith, of Virginia; (9) Powhatan Stark P., married Clara Warriner, of Virginia; (10) Stark Armistead P., married Eliza Bond, of Virginia; (11) Kemp P., died in infancy; (12) Bessie P., died in infancy; (13) Herbert P., unmarried; (14) Frank Turner P., married Elizabeth Warwick, of Virginia; (15) Julia AIcRae P., married Neville Henshaw, Louisiana.

Children of Edward H. Plummer and Sally D. Fitts, his wife: Lucy Davis P., died in infancy; (2) Lucy Murrell P., died unmarried; (3) James Fitts P., married Fanny Minor, of Virginia; (4) William Turner P., married Tommie Roan, of Tennessee; (5) Ethel P., unmarried; (6) Charles* Evans P., married Margaret Creel, of Kentucky.

Children of William T. Plummer and Rebecca Purnell, his wife; (1) Ida Campbell P., married J. D. Purcell, of Virginia; (2) Mary Elizabeth P., married R. D. Mcllwaine, of Virginia; (3) Walter P., died in infancy; (4) Cornelia Armistead P., unmarried; (5) Eliza P., unmarried; (6) John Fenner P., unmarried; (7) Willie Rebecca P., unmarried.

Children of Alan Cameron and Emily Turner Sutton, his wife: (1) William C.; (2) Annie Sutton C.

Children of Stark A. Sutton and Lucile Hudgins: (1) Stark Armistead S..

Stark A. Sutton, Sr., is a physician, and lives in Norfolk, Va.

Children of William White and Mary Armistead Sutton, his wife; (1) William W.

Children of James Fitts Plummer and Fanny Minor: (1) James Alinor P.; (2) Charles Cazenove P.; (3) Edward Armistead P.; (4) William Gardner P.; (5) Cameron McRae P.

William Turner Plummer and Tommie Roan, his wife, had one child, who died in infancy.

Children of J. D. Purcell and Ida Campbell Plummer, his wife: (1) Pauline Purcell; (2) Wm. Plummer Purcell; (3) Mary McIlwaine Purcell.

Children of Robert D. AlcIlwaine and Mary E. Plummer, his wife: (1) Mary Plummer Mcd.; (2) William Baird Mcl.; (3) Rebecca Mcl.; (4) Lucy Atkinson Pryor Mcl.

Robert D. AlcIlwaine was a physician, and died in Petersburg, Va., which had always been his home.

Children of Sydney AI. Green and Mary Eliza Plummer, his wife: (1) Sydney G.; (2) Cornelia Armistead G.; (3) Mary G; (4) George G., died in childhood.

Child of John Peterson Plummer and Nannie Strachan, his wife : (1) Richard Armistead Plummer.

Children of Kirk Seabury and Louisa Haskins Plummer, his wife: (1) Kirk S.; (2) Cornelia Armistead S.

Children of Levin J. Smith and Georgie Campbell Plummer, his wife: (1) Bessie S.; (2) Cary S.; (3) Levin J. S.

Children of Neville Henshaw and Julia AIcRae Plummer, his wife: (1) John Marsh H.; (2) Herbert Plummer H.

William Plummer[3] (son of S. Armistead Plummer and Cornelia Peterson, his wife,) and his wife had three children who died in infancy.

Children of Stephen Urquhart and Susan Plummer, his wife: (1) Norfleet U.; (2) Armistead Plummer U.

Children of William P. Batchelor and David Ella Chinault: (1) David B.; (2) Joseph Branch B.; (3) William Plummer B; (4) Anne B.; (5) Mary Shelton B.; (6) Martha B.

Children of Joseph B. Batchelor and Mary Gouge, his wife: (1) Edward Armistead B.; (2) Winifred B.: (3) Dorothy B. This Joseph B. Batchelor was captain in the U. S. Army, and died in the Philippines.

Child of Stark Sutton Batchelor and Lula Purnell, his wife: (1) Carey Plummer B.

Children of Kemp B. Batchelor and Ferebe Dewey, his wife: (1) Elizabeth B.; (2) Kemp B.; (3) Mary Cary B. Kemp B. Batchelor, Sr., was a physician; lived in Baltimore, and died there.

Children of Algernon S. Hurt and Julia AIcRae, his wife: (1) Algernon S. H., born 1900; (2) Susan Plummer H., born 1903.

Children of Cameron F. AIcRae and Sarah Woodward, his wife:

(1) Elizabeth Woodward McRae; (2) Cameron Farquhar AIcRae. This Cameron F. AIcRae is also a clergyman in the Episcopal Church, and a missionary to China.

Children of Walter G. Plummer and Emily Blanton, his wife: (1) Emily P.; (2) son, who died in infancy. This Walter Plummer lives in Jackson, Miss. (1910).

Child of Frank L. Schofield and Eliza A. Plummer, his wife: (1) Frances Armistead Schofield.

Among the names of the vestry of Kingston Parish, Gloucester County, 1677, is Kemp Plummer.

William and Kemp Plummer owned a great many servants, as is recorded in the Kingston Parish Register, Gloucester County.

CARY — ARMISTEAD — SELDEN.

William Cary, Lord Mayor of Bristol, England, who died 1632, had a son John who married Alice, daughter of Henry Hobson, alderman of Bristol, England. They had seven children — Thomas, Anne, Henry, Bridget, Elizabeth, Miles, William. Miles came to Virginia in 1640. Settled in Warwick County, which, in 1659, represented in the House of Burgesses. He married Elizabeth Taylor, and died in 1667, leaving four sons — Thomas, Henry, Aliles and William. Thomas C. married Ann Milner. Henry of "The Eorest" married a daughter of Richard Randolph of "Curies." His five daughters married, respective!)", Thomas Alann Randolph of Tuckahoe, Thomas Isham Randolph of Dungeness, Archibald Bolling, Carter Page of Cumberland, and Joseph Kincade. Archibald Cary "Old Iron" of Revolutionary fame was a son; also Aliles "The Elder."

Henry of "The Forest" was appointed to superintend the building of the Capitol at Williamsburg; also, at a later period, the rebuilding of William and Mary College, which had been burned.

Miles "The Elder," of "Pear Tree Hall," married Hannah Armistead, daughter of 82. William Armistead, son of Anthony A, who was the son of William A. the emigrant.

Issue of Aliles C.4 and Hannah A.; (1) Aliles C., of Southampton County, married Elizabeth Taylor 1752; (2) Richard B, of Warwick, married Mary Cole; (3) Col. John C., of Elizabeth City County, officer in Revolutionary War, married first, Sallie Sclater about 1766, and had Aliles C.; he married second, Susanna, daughter of Gill

Armistead; issue: (1) Aliles C., born 1767, who married a Alallory.

2. John C., of Hampton, born 1770, died 1822, married Anne Sweeny, niece of Chancellor Wythe.

3. Colonel Gill Armistead Cary, of Hampton, born 1783, married Sarah Eliza Smith Baytop, of Gloucester.

4. Robert Cary, unmarried.

5. Hannah Armistead Cary married Horatio Whiting.

6. Judith Robinson C., married Henry Howard.

7. Susan Cary, unmarried, born 1791, died 1873, Betsy Cary, unmarried.

Issue of Col. Gill Armistead Cary and Sallie Baytop: (1) John Baytop Cary; (2) (Dr.) Nathaniel Robert Cary; (3) Richard Miles Cary; (4) Gill Armistead Cary.

1. Col. John Baytop Cary, of Hampton, married Columbin Hudgins, of Mathews County, 1844. Issue: Gilliena Armistead Cary; John Baytop Cary, Jr., died young; Elizabeth Earle Cary; Effie May Cary; Sallie Campbell Cary, Thomas Archibald Cary.

Gilliena Armistead Cary, unmarried.

Elizabeth Earle Cary married William Travers Daniel. Both husband and child died two years after marriage.

Effie May Cary married John Lewis White, of "The Old Mansion," Bowling Green, Caroline County. Issue: John Cary White and Anne Maury White.

Cammie Cary (Sallie Campbell) married Louis P. Knowles, of Pensacola, Fla.

Thomas Archibald Cary married Maria Barry Abert, of Columbia, Miss Issue: John Barry Cary, Patty Abert Cary, Sallie Campbell Cary, George Abert Cary, Thomas Archibald Cary.

John Baytop Cary was colonel of the Thirty-second Virginia Regiment, C. S. A. After the war he settled in Richmond, where he was prominent in the business, literary, social and religious interest of the city. He died in 1898. Shortly afterwards there was endowed and established in the University of Virginia "The John B. Cary Bible Chair" as a memorial to him:

Dr. Nathaniel Robert Cary, son of Col. Gill Armistead Carv and Sallie Baytop, his wife, married Sue Fisher, of Eastern Shore, Va., about 1855. Lived in Pensacola, Fla., where he stood at his post during yellow fever scourge and died of the dread disease. Issue: (1) Sallie Cary, married Wm. S. Gravc.s, of Bedford City. She was soon left a widow with four children—Cary, Kenneth, Junia, Jean. (2) Juliet

Fisher Cary, married Herbert Sitwell, of England, first cousin of Countess of Warwick (Lady Brooke), and Duchess of Sutherland. Issue: Evelyn Fay Sitwell, Herbert FitzRoy Sitwell.

Richard Aliles Cary (son of Col. Gill Armistead Cary and Sallie Baytop, his wife,) married Hannah Elizabeth Whiting, of Hampton, Va. Issue: (1) Sallie Baytop Cary, married Edwin Abercrombe, of Pensacola,, Fla., and had Cary Abercrombe, Richard Whiting Abercrombe, Lelia Abercrombie. (2) Richard Aliles Cary, Jr., married Daisy Wright, of Pensacola, Fla., and had Richard Aliles Cary and Margareet Cary. (3) Lelia Cary, married Henry Hall, of Mobile, and had Lelia Cary Hall, Henry Hall, Jr., Elise Hall. (4) Martha Armistead Cary, unmarried. (5) Clara Whiting Cary, unmarried.

Gill Armistead Cary-, Jr. (son of Col. Gill Armistead Cary and Sallie Baytop, his wife,), married, about 1857, Jane Ladston Alston Smith, of South Carolina. Her mother, when a widow, married Dr. McCabe, of Hampton, rector of old St. John's Church, and father of Colonel Gordon AlcCabe, of Richmond, one of Virginia's and of the South's noted literati. Issue of Gill Armistead Cary and Jane, his wife: Belle Gordon Cary and Martha Armistead Cary. Belle Gordon Cary married Gordon Macdonald and had Olive Cary Macdonald.

Patsy Vail, the old colored mammy, has lately died, and Col. Gordon AlcCabe has placed a monument *over her grave* in memory of her faithfulness and love to three generations whom she nursed and cared for.

In the garret of the old Back River home of the Carys were bags of engraved book plates marked Aliles Cary that had been sent from England to the American descendants. This fact was known and told by Miss Susan Cary, who lived until 1873, and her nephew. Colonel John B. Cary. Gillie Cary, of Richmond, has several of these. It is the Cary Arms: Argent on a bend, sable, three roses of the field silver. Alotto : *Sine Deo Careo.*

NOTE.—The Back River farm descended to the Carys through Judith Armistead (wife of John Robinson, Jr.,), who was a sister of Hannah Armistead who married Miles Cary of "Pear Tree Hall."

At the close of the Baytop genealogy, which appeared and was continued in several issues of the Sunday *Tiines-Dispatch* Genealogical Column by Mrs. Sallie Nelson Robins, is the following :

(The Mrs. Catlett spoken of was a sister of Sally Baytop who married Col. Gill Armistead Cary, of Hampton, where she afterwards lived and died, leaving her fortune to her sister, Sallie Baytop Cary. Our earliest recollections are interwoven with this charming old lady who was Wheeled to our home (she was lame) to spend a day in every week or two with our mother. They were firm friends. The whispered tragedy invested her, in our childish mind, with a mysterious glamer that set her apart as something wierd and uncanny.)

" 'James Catlett murdered when a young man by a favorite slave.' This was perhaps the most intensely dramatic situation ever felt in Gloucester County.

"James Catlett was the only son of his mother, who was a widow. He was just returned from college, brilliant, handsome and rich, with life in its fulness spread out before him.

"His bodyservant, a mulatto fellow, promising, too, and apparently faithful, was present when he read his will to a friend. To this bodyservant he left the priceless boom of the human soul — freedom.

"Soon after this incident James Catlett one bright morning started with this man to a distant plantation. He was to return that evening, but he did not. The servant did return, and announced that his master was detained. The master's prolonged absence created suspicion, and when the negro was gravely required to tell what he knew he lost courage and fled to the woods. The men of the whole countryside started in pursuit; the women stayed at home filled with a despairing dread.

"Dogs were let loose and fell in with spirit for the ghastly chase. A favorite dog of James Catlett led to the discovery of his body near his home, where it was covered deep with earth, brushwood and leaves.

"Days passed before the murderer was trapped, desperate, weak and famished in the woods.

"A trial ensued, and he was condemned to death. Old residents have told us of the hanging; how the negroes from all the plantations, and many white citizens, too, filed in garrulous lines from the various plantations to the courthouse to watch a pitiful and tremendous tragedy."

In 1852 John Baytop Cary, of Hampton, Va., eldest son of Colonel Gill Armistead Cary and Sallie Baytop, his wife, founded and built the Hampton Military Academy, the grounds of which, fronting on the "Creek," adjoined his residence. Co-education being a local necessity, there was a department for girls, with a woman of high education and refinement in charge. These school buildings were by far the best equipped south of Boston. The various class rooms and auditoriums were spacious, flooded with light and sunshine, slate blackboards, hard-wood desks with nickleplated ink wells, and revolving chairs. In the faculty, besides Mr. Cary, who was headmaster, were an A. AI. of the University of Virginia, a degree man from Heidleburg or Leipsic, a graduate of V. AI. I. at the head of the military department, and the lady teacher.

This high-grade, classical school, numbering an hundred and forty students just before the war, attracted the patronage not only of adjacent counties in Virginia, but of far Southern States, its alumni bearing the hall-marks of thoroughness, culture and high ideals.

The Cary Family of Gloucester County, Va.

Mrs. Eliza Cary, of Gloucester, age eighty-nine, September, 1910, gives the following data:

"The father of John Reid Cary came from England and settled in Cloucester County, John Reid Cary had four sons — *John Reid C.*, Thomas C., Samuel C., Edward C. Thomas C. married twice, but there were no children. Samuel C. married and settled in Nottoway County. Edward Cary never married; died in Bermuda.

"John Reid Cary married Harryann Beverly Whiting Pryor. Issue, nine children—Samuel Beverly C., John Reid C., Edward A S. C., Thomas C., Charles Grymes C., William H. C., Elizabeth Courtney C., Catherine Clayton C., Julia Pryor C." (Mrs, Eliza Cary's data ends here.)

Edward B, S. Cary married Eliza Smith, of Gloucester, whose mother, Lucy Armistead, was descended from the Ralph Armistead line, which will follow this Cary line,

Samuel Beverly Cary was a successful and much loved physician of Gloucester County, Va.

William Cary (son of Edward B. S. C. and Eliza Smith, his wife,) married Miss Eield, of Gloucester. Charles C., another son, married Miss Willis. Samuel C., a third son, married Mahlon Bagby, of Richmond, daughter of Bagby and Mildred Goodman, his wife. Mr. Samuel Cary and wife Mahalon A have two sons. They ireside in Roanoke, Va.

It is said that this family of Carys and the Aliles Cary line are not related, though the parent stock in England may have been the same.

The Armistead line of Mrs. Eliza Cary has been gathered from Kingston Parish register and *William and Mary Quarterly*, Vol. VI.

Ralph Arniistead, who patented land in Gloucester County, 1678, was evidently a member of the emigrant's family — brother, nephew, or cousin. He had Francis A. and Ralph A. Ralph's son Francis married Dorothy Reade, February 2, 1766. Issue: George Reade Armistead, who married Lucy (?), Their son Francis Armistead married, 1798, Elizabeth Buckner, niece of Armistead Smith, granddaughter of Thomas S. (Mrs. Eliza Cary states this). Issue of this marriage ten children. Four of the sons were Thomas Buckner A., George Reade A, John Patterson A., Francis A. Their daughter, Lucy Armistead, was the mother of Mrs, Eliza Cary.

SELDEN.

Samuel Seiden married Rebecca, and had among others: Joseph Seiden, married Mary Cary, daughter of Col. Aliles Cary and Mary Wilson, his wife. Issue: (Rev.) Aliles Seiden, married Rebecca Cary, daughter of Hannah Armistead, wife if Aliles Cary4. Issue: Col. Aliles Seiden, married Elizabeth (Betty) Armistead, daughter of Colonel Gill Armistead. She (Betty) died 1833, age eighty-two. Issue eleven children.

Rev. Aliles Seiden as ordained in London, and minister of Henrico Parish (St. John's, Richmond, Va.,) 1752 to 1776; died 1785- ,

Issue of Col. Aliles Seiden (grandson of Hannah Armistead and Aliles Cary, of "Pear Tree Hall,") and Betty Armistead, his wife, married at Mr. John Lewis', Williamsburg, Va., 27th Alarch, 1774: (1) Betty, (2) Aliles, (3) Mary, (4) Gill Armistead, (5) Cary, (6) Joseph, (7) Patsey, (8) Samuel, (9) James M., (10) Martha.

(5) Cary Seiden, born February 16, 1783, married Miss Jennings, of West Indies. Issue, among others: (Dr.) Wilson Cary Seiden, married a daughter of Charles Armistead. Dr. Wilson Cary Seiden and Armistead, had Elizabeth Armistead Seiden, who married John I. Lloyd. Issue, among others: Rebecca Lloyd, first wife of Rev. Alelville Jackson, and Arthur S. Lloyd, who married Elizabeth Blackford. Arthur S. Lloyd is Bishop Coadjutor of Virginia.

ARMISTEAD — DANDRIDGE — RANDOLPH — WILLIAMS — RICHARDSON.

Anthony Armistead, of Yorkshire, England, and Frances Thomson, his wife, had William A. the emigrant, who married Anne, and had issue, among others, Anthony A., who married Hannah Elliason. Their son John, of New Kent County, married Miss Gill, an heiress. Issue, among others, Major William Armistead, married Mary, niece of James Nicholas, widow of Baker. Their only child, Susannah Armistead, married William

Dandridge5 (John D.4, Bartholomew D.³, Col. William D.², Dandridge¹, of London,). William Dandridge's sister Martha married George Washington.

Sianna Dandridge, daughter of William D. and Susanna Armistead, his wife, married John Williams. Issue: (1) Robert Armistead Williams, married Elizabeth Marshall Colston. (2) Susanna Elinor W., unmarried. (3) William Langbourne W., married Isabella Reid. (4) Margareet S. W., married Patrick G Gibson. Issue, among others, Henry G., married Nannie Higginbotham. Issue: Susan G., died; George Armistead G., married Alice Winona A'IcChmg in 1903. Issue: George Patrick G., Elizabeth AlcClung G., Patrick Armistead G.

(5) John Langhorne Williams married Maria Ward Skelton. Issue: (1) John Skelton W., married Lila Lefebvre Isaacs; two children — John Skelton and Herbert LeF. (2) E. Randolph W., married Aland Stokes. (3) Langbourne W., married Susie Nolting. (4) Lancaster W., married Rebecca Watkins. (5) Dr. Ennion W., married Anne Lassiter. (6) Berkeley W., married Hulda Steel. (7) Sianna W., married E. L. Memiss. (8) Maria Ward W., married Lewis C. Williams. (9) Charlotte W., died young.

The grandchildren of John L. Williams and Maria Ward Skelton, his wife, are thirty-one — perhaps more.,

Alfred Brokenborough Williams, Virginia's brilliant editor and man of letters, is the son of Robert Armistead W. and Elizabeth Marshall Colston, his wife. A. B. Williams, in 1882, married May Young Brice, of South Carolina. Issue: Margareet and A. B. W., Jr.

Elizabeth (daughter of Robert Carter and Judith Armistead, his wife,), widow of Nathaniel Burwell, married Dr. George Nicholas. Their son, Robert Carter Nicholas, had a daughter Elizabeth, who married .Edmund Randolph, first Attorney General United States in

1790; Governor in 1786-'8; in 1794 succeeded Thomas Jefferson as Secretary of State. Issue among others (of Edmund Randolph and Elizabeth Nicholas) : Peyton Randolph, who married the beautiful Maria Ward. Their daughter, Elizabeth Randolph, was the first wife of Dr. John Gifford Skelton. The daughter of this union married John Langbourne Williams. Thus were united two descendants of the Armistead brothers, John and Anthony,

The Langbourne and Dandridge families were very intimate. Colonel John Dandridge, whose son married Susanna Armistead, was a close friend of William Langbourne, who was aid to LaEayette and much attached to him. He visited LaEayette in Trance; married Ann Claiborne. In King William County is the tombstone of this first Langbourne, son of Robert and Mary L., of Eetter Lane, London, England, and bears the Langbourne Arms.

George Nicholas came to this country as a physician. His son, Robert Carter Nicholas, was distinguished at the bar in Williamsburg, in the House of Burgesses in the Council, as Treasurer of the State, and as a patriot in the Revolution; but he had higher honor than all these offices could give him—he was a sincere Christian and a zealous defender of the Church of his fathers at a time when the writings of Erench philosophers, so-called, were corrupting the minds of the Virginia youth.— (Meade).

He married Anne, daughter of Col. Wilson Cary, of Hampton. A portion of a letter written to her son, Wilson Cary Nicholas, on entering public life, will give a glimpse into the character and ideals of this Christian mother:

"WILLIAMSBURG, 1784.

"Dear Wilson,— I congratulate you on the honor your country has done you in choosing you their representative with sc large a vote. I hope you have come into the Assembly without those tramels which some people submit to wear for a seat in the House. I mean, unbound by promises to perform this or that job, which the many-headed monster may think proper to chalk out for you * * * from long observation I can venture to assert that the man of integrity, who observes one equal tenor in his conduct, who deviates neither to the one side or the other from the proper line—has more of the confidence of the people than the very pliant time-server, who calls himself the servant— and indeed is—the slave of the people. * * *

The children of Robert Carter Nicholas and Anne, his wife, were: George, who moved to Kentucky; Lewis lived in Albemarle; John moved to New York; *Wilson Cary,* of U. S. Senate and House of Representatives, and Governor of Virginia; and Philip Norbourne. Their daughter Elizabeth married Edmund Randolph.

William Armistead, son of Col. John Armistead, of New Kent County, was major in 1772 and 1775, and a vestryman of Blissland Parish. He married Mary, widow of Baker. She was niece of James Nicholas, who left her a legacy of one thousand pounds. Issue of this marriage, Susanna, an only child, who married first, William Dandridge; married second, about 1805, David Darrington. Major William Armistead died before 1784. .

Issue of William Dandridge and Susanna, his wife: Robert Dandridge, d. s. p. Sianna Dandridge, married John Williams and had issue. Eleanor Dandridge, married Charles C. Richardson, d. s. p. Lavinia W. Dandridge, married John Blair Richardson, and had John Harvie Richardson, married Margaret Hodges, and had issue: Charles Richardson, married Charlotte Blain, daughter of Samuel Wilson Blain and Susan Isham Harrison, and had issue: William Dorrington R., Samuel Blain R., and Lavinia Dandridge R. Susanna Armistead Richardson married Edward H. Norvell, and had issue.

1.   Anthony[1] A. married Frances Thompson. Issue: 2. William[2] A.

2.   William A. married Annie. Issue: 3. William[3], 5. Anthony®, 6. Frances.

5. Anthony[3] A. married Hannah Ellison. Issue: 82. William, 83. Anthony, 84. Robert, 85. Hannah.

82. William4 A. married first, Hannah Hinde. Issue: 87. Anthony5 A., 88. William[3] A., 89. John[3] A., 90. Hinde[3] A.

82. William4 A. married second, Rebecca Aloss. Issue: 91. Robert[3] A., 92. Aloss[3] A., 93. Edward[3] A., 94. Hannah[3] A., 95. Judith[3] A.

87. Anthony5 A. married Margaret Benit. Issue: 96. John[3] A., 97. Anthony[3] A., 98. Benit[3] A.

96. John[3] A. married first, Anne; second, Elizabeth Jones; died 1791. Issue by second wife: 100. Starkey7, 101. John7 (102) Robert7, (103) a daughter.

101. John6 Armistead (John6, Anthony4, William[3], Anthony[3],

William[2], Anthony[1], of Yorkshire, EngLand,) owned 1,000 acres in Northampton County, North Carolina, and negroes. He bought land from Francis Bracie in Lunenburg, afterwards Mecklenburg County, Virginia.

101. John Armistead married Elizabeth Royster, of Granville County, N. C. Issue: (1) John Clayton8 Armistead, born January 12, 1782; died April 11, 1832; (2) Robert Alexander8; (3) Marcus Aurelius8; (4) Eabian8, born December 25, 1794; (5) Leander[8]; (6) Ajax8; (7) Latinus8; (8) Lycurgus8; (9) Stella.6.

John Clayton[3] Armistead married Lucy Ann Eanny Harrison, December 20, 1814, daughter of the Rev. William Harrison, rector of Blandford Church, Petersburg, V'a. Issue: (1) Adelia Harrison Armistead, born April 21, 1816; (2) John Royster Armistead, born April 12, 1818; (3) William Harrison Armistead, born February 8, 1820.

Adelia Harrison Armistead married John E. Johnson, of Richmond, Va. Died August 12, 1834. Issue: William R. Armistead Johnson, who died in San Erancisco about 1900, leaving no children.

John Royster Armistead married Elizabeth Edmondson Edloe, of Williamsburg, Va., December 11, 1837. Issue: (1) John Royster Armistead, Jr.; (2) Lucy Harrison Armistead; (3) Willie Anna Armistead; (4) Elizabeth Allen Armistead; (5) Clayton Armistead; (6) Henry Edloe Armistead. The four last named are living at the old home, "Tomahund," Charles City County, Va.

(1) John Royster Armistead, Jr., was married to Gertrude Hooff, of Alexandria, Va., November 28, 1883, in Alabama. He died childless at Newbern, Ala., January 7, 1897. He joined the Petersburg Rifles, Twelfth Virginia Regiment, C. S. A., April, 1861, aged eighteen, and remained with the company until *h* surrendered at Appomattox, having been twice a prisoner; was severely wounded at the battle of the Wilderness. Though physically weak, he was a brave soldier, and the record of his captain is, "There was no truer man in the Army of Northern Virginia than John R. Armistead."

(2) Lucy Harrison Armistead married John Emory Welbourn, of Baltimore, Md., December 18, 1873. Issue; (1) Rev. John Armistead Welbourn (missionairy in Tokyo, Japan,) ; (2) Edward Hambleton Welbourn; (3) Elizabeth Edloe Welbourn.

(5) Clayton Armistead married Emms Lacy, of Charles City, County, Va. No surviving children.

(2) William Harrison Armistead married Sarah Henry, daughter

of Edward Winston Henry, of Charlotte County, Va., youngest 'son of Patrick Henry, April 23, 1844.

(3) William Harrison Armistead, born February 8, 1820, died in Halifax County, Va., December 6, 1895. Sarah Henry Armistead, his wife, died May 25, 1899. Of a large family there survived three children, viz.: (1) Grattan Henry Armistead, born April 6, 1851; died October 31, 1883. (2) Adeha Harrison Armistead, married Fletcher Yuille. (3) Edward Winston Armistead, married Annie Hobson Clarke, April 22, 1890. Issue: (1) William Harrison Armistead; (2) Mary Isabella Armistead; (3) Annie Winston Armistead.

Edward Winston Armistead now owns, at Wolf Trap, Halifax County, Va., a part of the large estate of John Clayton Armistead, his grandfather.

Marcus Aurelius Armistead married Mary Ann C. Harrison, daughter of the Rev. William Harrison, rector of Blandford Church, Petersburg, Va. He died in Florida, and his widow died near Petersburg, May 1, 1857, aged sixty-four years. Issue: (1) Marcus Latinus Armistead, AI. D., surgeon in the U. S. A.; died at Vera Crus, Mexico, of yellow fever while on duty in the army. (2) Latinus Armistead, AI. D., died in Tallahassee, Fla., about 1900, leaving three children. (3) Ann Elizabeth Harrison Armistead, married first, Peter Batte Jones; no surviving children; married secondly. Dr. Austin Watkins, of Nottoway County, Va Issue: (1) Aurelius Augustus Watkins, lieutenant S. A.; killed at Gettysburg, July 3, 1863, aged twenty-four years. (2) Ann Elizabeth Watkins, married George W. Robertson. Issue: Charles Blankenship Robertson. Alarried thirdly, Marcus Latinus Robertson, died in Petersburg June, 1878, aged twenty-four. (2) Peter Branch Robertson, married Alattie Campbell Jones; no children. (3) James Fletcher Robertson, married Loula Dyerle. (4) Mary Catherine Robertson, married Micajah J. Oliver; no children.

Ann Elizabeth Harrison Robertson died March 3, 1875, aged sixty-two years.

(4) Eugenia Armistead, daughter of Marcus A. and Mary A.C Armistead, married in Florida; left no children.

(5) George Armistead, son of Marcus A. and Mary A. C. Armistead, died in Florida; unmarried.

(6) Mary Virginia Armistead married Rogers, of New Orleans. Issue: Mary Eugenia Rogers, married William E. Bradley, of North Carolina. Issue: (1) William Harrison Bradley,(2) John Rogers

Bradley, (3) Jesse Bradley, (4) Thomas Bradley, (5) Grover Cleveland Bradley, (6) Marcus Aurelius Bradley, (7) Mary Virginia Bradley, (8) Elsie Bradley.

(7) Lucy Fanny Armistead, daughter of Marcus A. and Mary A. C. Armistead, married Robert Tucker, of Dinwiddie County, Va. Issue: (1) Evelyn Tucker, (2) Clarence Tucker, (3) Anna Harrison Tucker.

Fabian8 Armistead, born December 25, 1794, died September 16, 1865, married Virginia Harrison, daughter of the Rev. William Harrison, of Blandford Church, Petersburg, Va., who was born January 10, 1805, and died August 24, 1881. Issue: (1) John Clayton Armistead, (2) Fabian Harrison Armistead, (3) Anne Harrison Armistead, (4) William Harrison Armistead, (5) Robert Alexander Armistead, (6) Mary Virginia Armistead, 7George Ajax Armistead.

(1) John Clayton Armistead married Mary L. Keen, daughter of the Rev. Thomas G. Keen, of Philadelphia, Pa.; no surviving issue. He died October 14, 1901, aged sixty-six years.

(2) Favian Harrison Armistead married Annie Spencer, of Farmville, Va.; died June 7, 1901, aged sixty-four years. Issue:
(i) Virginia Harrison Armi.stead, (2) Fabian Spencer Armistead.

(3.) Anne Harrison Armistead married her first cousin, Richard W. PAnson, M. D. Issue: Robert Armistead I'Anson.

(4) William Harrison Armistead died 1893, aged forty-one years; unmarried.

(5) Robert Alexander Armistead married Marcella Eugenia Herron, of Memphis, Tenn. Issue: Robert Alexander Armistead, Jr.

(6) Mary Virginia Armistead married John Monroe Banister, of Petersburg, Va.; no issue.

(7) George Ajax Armistead married Mary Bland, daughter of Dr. Theodorick Bland, of Jordan's Point, James River. Issue:
(1) George Clayton Armistead; (2) John Clayton Armistead, married Estelle Ruffin Marks; no issue; (3) Mary Jeffery Armistead; (4) Sallie Bland Armistead.

(6) Ajax8 Armistead moved to Georgia and married. He died there in Petersburg, Ga. Issue: John Armistead.

EDLOW FAMILY.

Mathew Edlow (spelled also Edlowe and Edloe) came to Virginia in 1618, and in 1623~'24 was living at ye Colledge Land in Henrico. In 1629 he was a member of the House of Burgesses "for the plantation at the Colledge."

(2) Lieutenant-Colonel Matthew Edlow, son and heir of Alatthew Edlow, dec'd, had a grant of 1,200 acres on the north side of the James River over against Chippoak creek, July 12, 1637. He was a member of the House of Burgesses for James City 1658-'59. Charles City, in which was his grant, was at that time included in James City. He married Tabitha, probably a Minge, and died in 1668.

(3) John Edlow, son of Lieut.-Col. Mathew Edlow, was born about 1661. He married first, Rebecca, daughter of Alathew Hubard, of York County, and secondly, in 1699, he married Miss Martha Hatcher, of Henrico County. Henry Edlow, son of John Edlow, who was living in 1734, married Rebecca Browne, daughter of Henry Browne, of Surry County, son of Colonel William Browne, of "Four Mile Tree." That is an old estate on the James River opposite to "Tomahund." The square brick colonial house is still standing. Henry and Rebecca Edlow left several children, among them Henry, who died in Charles City County about 1750, leaving an infant son John, who was probably the father of John Edlow, born 1777, who married Ann Armistead Allen, of Claremont, Va., where both of them are buried. This last John Edlow was brother to Henry Edlow, whose children were William, Henry and Anne Cocke. William was the son of first wife, Elizabeth Edmondson, and Henry and Anne Cocke were the children of his second wife, Sally Lamb.

William Edlow married Elizabeth Laury Allen, and their daughter, Elizabeth Edmondson Edlow, married John Royster Armistead, of Petersburg and "Tomahund."

Thomas Barrett Allen married Virginia Armistead, mother of Elizabeth Barrett, of Barrett's Ferry, James City County . Owned lands on both sides of Chickahominy at the mouth. The public road from Richmond to Williamsburg went by Barrett's Ferry. Thomas Barrett Allen was brother of Elizabeth Laury Allen, who married William Edloe, of Williamsburg, grandfather of Lucy Harrison Armistead.

(9) Stella Armistead married Mackie I'Anson. Issue; Richard W. I'Anson.

Leander, Lycurgus and Latinus Armistead, sons of John and Elizabeth Royster Armistead were unmarried.

In 1756 Francis Bracie and Elizabeth, his wife, sold land in Lunenburg County to John Armistead, of Elizabeth City County. John Armistead and his tithes were added in May, 1773, to the list of tithes in Mecklenburg County between John Armistead of the one part and his children — John Clayton, Robert Alexander. He had other children later — Fabian, Ajax, etc. There is a tradition in the family that 101. John A. became involved in some feud with his family or kin, and vowed he would never give another child a family name. With Spartan determination he kept his vow. Therefore the old Roman names that have descended in his line.

A descendant of 101. John Armistead sends the following from a copy of a deed of John Armistead, of Elizabeth City, lo his son John, of Mecklenburg County, for 1,000 acres of land on Butcher's Creek, the same land he had purchased from Francis Bracie in 1756. The deed was dated 1773. In 1790 the son John deeded the same land to his sons Robert Alexander, John Clayton, Latinus, Marcus Aurelius, and Leander. He gave each three or four negroes, several horses, cattle, sheep, wagons and gear, and to each a feather bed and furniture. (This was before the birth of his children Fabian, Ajax, and Stella.) In 1792 he gave to Stella two negroes, forty hogs, a riding chair and harness, and other personal property. In 1803 Robert Alexander Armistead sold to John Clayton Armistead 170 acres of the Butcher's Creek land, and to Sir Peyton Skipwith 21½ acre.s. Later, John Clayton Armistead, of Petersburg, sold the land he bought to George Feild. In 1810 there was an appraisement of the personal property of Elizabeth, widow of John Armistead, value £244; Marcus Aurelius Armistead administrator. In June Marcus Aurelius A. sold to Clarke Royster several negroes, the money to be paid to his mother Elizabeth, sister Stella, and brothers Fabian and Ajax. In 1818 Robert Alexander Armistead and his wife Anne, of Norfolk County, deeded the Butcher's Creek land of 805 acres to John L. Ravenscroft.

Robert Alexander Armistead, M. D., son of John and Elizabeth Royster Armistead.

A copy of the Delphin edition of *Vergil*, in the possession of Mrs. Mary Woodbridge (*nee* Stubbs), of Atlanta, Ga., shows that R. A. Armistead was a student of William and Mary College in 1798. There are portraits of him and his wife in Mrs. Woodbridge's hands. He was a physician and author of a work on English grammar. He died in Florida. He was married in 1820 or 1821 to Mrs. Ann Myers (or Meyers) (*nee* Wright). There were born of this marriage:

Elizabeth, born at Portsmouth, Va., 1822; married to Stephen Cowley.

Stella Louisa Hodges, born at Portsmouth, Va., April 21, 1824; married to John S. Stubbs, May 15, 1845.

Children of Stephen Cozvley and Elizabeth Annistead.

(1) Annie, Alargaret, born January 24, 1840; married Capt. Thomas F. Pettus (captain Co. H, Twentieth Mississippi Regiment, C. S. A.) at Somerville, Ala., December 17, 1861. She died of apoplexy in China (her husband being U. S. Consul at Ningpo), January 18, 1888. Buried in foreign cemetery at Ningpo.

(2) Stephen Armistead, born 1842. Inspector on Generrd Quarles' staff, rank, lieutenant-colonel (C. S. A.). Killed at battle of Franklin, Tenn.; buried in the Confederate cemetery at Franklin.

(3) Eugenia Armistead, born in Portsmouth, Va., 1841; married to Horatio Overton Pettus, at Morton, Miss., March 10, 1869.

(4) Elizabeth, born in Portsmouth, Va., September 1, 1843; married Captain John Hart (C. S. A.), in Somerville, Ala., in 1867. Her husband died near Hot Springs, Ark., in 1885. She was married the second time, September 1, 1890, to her brother-in-law, Captain T. F. Pettus. She died in Albany, Texas, April 12, 1902. She had no children.

(5) Robert Armistead, born in Portsmouth, Va.; was never married. Died at Friers' Point, Miss., in 1895, and was buried there.

Children of Thomas F. Pettus and Annie M. Cowley.

(1) John Jones, born October 19, 1862, in Morton Miss.; married Rose Lillard in 1894. Children: Thomas Wanren, Margaret, John J., Jr., and Thurmond. They reside in Sweetwater, Texas.

(2) Bessie Louise, born in Morton, Miss., August 9, 1865; married in China, Ningpo, December 5, 1888, to J. W. Bu'rke, of China service. Died in Meridian, Miss., November, 1901. Mr. Burke died in Boston, Mass., April, 1899. Children: Louise, born in Newchwang, China, 1889, and Mary, born in Shanghai, 1891. ,

(3) Stephen Winston, born October 15, 1867, in Morton, Miss.;

married Lylie Currie, at Kerens, Texas, December 8, 1902 ; died October 4, 1903. Had one child, Stephen Winston, born October 15, 1903.

(4) Thomas F., Jr., born in Morton, Miss., December 12, 1869; married Leota Bradfield, October 3, 1901. Children: Rose and Bessie. Reside in Moran, Texas.

(5) Annie Madge, born in Morton, Miss., December 2, 1871 ; married W. C. Sanders, of Texas. Two children — Annie Madge and Willy. Reside in Galveston, Texas.

Children of Horatio 0. Pettus and Eugenia Armistead Cozvley.

(1) Mary, born in Morton, Miss; married John Loughridge, M. D., 1893. Two children.

(2) Cowley Armistead, M. D., married Mrs. Kirkland, of Forest, Miss., in 1899.

(3 and 4) Eugenia and Lizzie, unmarried. All these reside in Eldorado, Arkansas.

Children of John S. Stubbs and Stella L. H. Arniistead.

Ten children were the fruit of this marriage, only three of which reached maturity.

(1) Robert Armistead, born 1847; November, 1883; unmarried.

(2) Annie Wright, born July, 1848; died November, 1883: married W. H. Stewart (lieutenant-colonel C. S. A.). To them was born Robert Armistead, March 9, 1877; A. B., A. M., Ph. D., University of Virginia.

(3) Mary Stella, born in Portsmouth, Va., August 3, 1850; married, February 10, 1880, the Rev. W. G. Woodbridge. To them three children were born, only one reaching maturity — William Witherspoon, born September 15, 1883, in Warrenton, Va. These live in Atlanta, Ga.

COATS OF ARMS.

Gu — blood red — means courage.

Az. argent — silver — means purity, honor, truth.

Sable — black — means wisdom, constancy, affection.

Conquefoil — an agriculturist.

Star — honor — shone in learning or virtue, means also to steer s course.

The whole means "the bearer a gentleman, esquire," and that the gentleman had been knighted.

The shield, crest, helmet, wreath, external ornamentation and motto constitute a Coat of Arms.

HALL AIARKS ON SILVER.

These marks were started in 1180.

London mark — A leopard's head, within a shield, crowned or uncrowned.

Lion passant denotes true metal.

Birmingham, England, mark — An anchor within a shield or oblong.

Sheffield — A crown within an oblong with corners cut off.

When sent to the Hall by the silversmith, it is stamped, if satisfactory, with the Hall mark — a lion, if silver — next to the maker's stamp — the letter indicating the year.

In 1784 the sovereign's head was added to the London mark.

A very heavy soup ladle belonging to Robert Augustine Armistead has the sovereign's head — London mark — made 1789. Hester Bateman, maker.

Spoons belonging to some, made in London 1792 by G. G.

Sugar tongs, very primitive in design, made in 1634. This must have been brought over by the emigrant, who came in 1635.

These descended from R. A. and E. Smith, his wife, marked R. E. A. in monogram.

So many Virginians have St. Memin's portraits that a sketch of the artist and his methods may be interesting:

Charles Balthazar Julien Fevre de Saint Memin was of an ancient family of Dijon, France, born in 1770. Was a member of the royal army during the French Revolution. When the army was disbanded, he fled to America in 1793.

A Frenchman, Chretien, had invented a machine which he called physionotrace, by which the human profile could be traced with mathematical accuracy. St. Memin constructed such an implement with his own hands and also made a pantograph by which to reduce the design. His life-size portraits on pink paper, finished in black crayon, could be reduced to a circle two inches in diameter. The physionotrace only gave the outline, the finishing being done in one case with the crayon, in the other with the graver and roulette. One-fourth of the eight hundred portraits done in America were Virginians. The artist sold the drawing and engraved plate, with a dozen proofs, to the sitter for thirty-three dollars. — *William and Mary Quarterly*, Vol. IX.

APPLICATION FOR MEMBERSHIP.

(This application may be used whether the applicant desires to claim eligibility from one or more ancestors.)

This paper for the Anthon)' branch of the Armistead family has been used three times — twice in joining Virginia Sons of American Revolution, and once in joining Colonial Dames of Tennessee.

I, the undersigned, herby apply for membership in the Society by right of lineal descent from

1. William Worlich,   Christopher
6.   Calthorpe.
2. Robert Ellison.   7-   Armiger Wade.
3- Colonel John Tabb.   8.   John Howard.
4- Anthony Armistead.   9-   Col. Erancis Howard.
5 Anthony Armistead.   10.   Humphrey Tabb.

ANCESTOR No. 1.

The said William Worlich was born in England on ——— 16 ———, and resided in the Colony (or Province) of Virginia from 1622 to 1659. He died after 1659 Elizabeth City County. Member of House of Burgesses for Elizabeth City Co. 1644-'49-'54"59 (See *William and Mary Quarterly*, Vol. IX., p. 131.)

ANCESTOR NO. 2.

The said Robert Ellison was born in England on ——— 16 ———, and resided in the Colony (or Province) of Maryland from 1643 to 1663. He died in Virginia after 1663, at ———. Member of House of Burgesses 1656, 1659-'60, 1660-'61, 1663.

Ancestor No. 3.

The said Colonel John Tabb was born in Elizabeth County on ——
— 16——, and resided in the Colony (or Province) of Virginia from
16—— to 1761. He died —— 1761, at Eliza beth City Co., Va.
Burgess from Elizabeth City. (*William and Mary Quarterly,* Vol. VII., p.
46.)

Ancestor No. 4.

The said Anthony Armistead was born in Virginia before 1676,
and resided in the Colony (or Province) of Virginia from 1676 to 1705.
He died after 1705, at Elizabeth City Co., Va. Was one of Sir Wm.
Berkeley's court martial to try Nathaniel Bacon, and member of
House of Burgesses 1693, 1696, 1699. (See *William and Mary Quarterly,*
Vol. VI., p. 227, and *Virginia Colonial Register,* p. 91.)

Ancestor No. 5.

The said Anthony Armistead was born in Virginia before 1700,
and resided in the Colony (or Province) of Virginia from 1700 to 1728.
He died after 1760 at Elizabeth City Co., Va. Lieutenant-colonel of
militia in 1724 (*William and Adary Quarterly,* Vol. VII., p. 19) ; Burgess
in 1720, 1722. See *Col. Va. Register,* p. 103.)

Ancestor No. 6.

The said Christopher Calthorpe was born in England on ——,
16——, and resided in the Colony (or Province) of Virginia from
1635 to 1662. He died ——, 1622, at ——. Member House of
Burgesses for York Co. in 1659. (*William and Mary Quarterly* Vol. II.,
p. 160.)

Ancestor No. 7.

The said Armiger Wade was born in England on ——, 16——,
and resided in the Colony (or Province) of Virginia from 1644 to 1708.
He died in Virginia 1708 at York Co. Member House of Burgesses in
1657. See *Hayden's Va. Genealogies,* p. 571, and *William and Mary
Quarterly,* Vol. II., p. 165; also York Records at Yorktown, Va.)

Ancestor No. 8.

The said John Howard was born in England on ———, 16————, and resided in the colony (or Province) of Virginia from 1635 to 1661. He died in Virginia, 1661, at James City Co., Va. Member House of Burgesses in 1654.

Ancestor No. 9.

The said Colonel Francis Howard was born in Virginia on May 15, 1700, and resided in the Colony (or Province) of Virginia from 1700 to 1747. He died March 14, 1747, at Virginia. Member House of Burgesses. (See *William and Mary Quarterly*, Vol. II., p. 167.)

ANCESTOR NO. 10..

This said Humphrey Tabb was born in England on ———, 16————, and resided in the Colony (or Province) of Virginia from 1637 to 1661. He died before 1662, at Elizabeth City. He was Burgess for Elizabeth City in 1652. (*William and Mary Quarterly*, Vol. VII., p. 45.)

(Signature of Applicant)...

(Address)...

....

Pedigree OF Ancestor No 1.

.... being duly sworn, says:

1. That the applicant was born in...
and is a resident of ....

2. That she is the daughter of...
and .... his wife

3. That the said George W. Armistead was the son of Robert Armistead and Martha Savage, his wife.

4. The the said R. A. Armistead was the son of Robert Armistead and Elizabeth Smith, his wife.

5. That the said Robert Armistead was the son of Westwood Armistead and Mary Jenkins, his wife.

6. That the said Westwood Armistead was the son of Westwood

Armistead and Mary Tabb., his wife.

7. That the said Westwood Armistead was the son of Anthony Armistead and Elizabeth Westwood, his wife.

8. That the said Elizabeth Westwood was the daughter of Worlich Westwood, and Elizabeth Naylor, his wife.

9. That the said Worlich Westwood was the son of James Westwood and ———— Worlich, his wife.

10. That the said ———— Worlich was the daughter of William Worlich and ————, his wife.

PEDIGREE OF ANCESTOR No. 2.

1. The said George W. Armistead was the son of R. A. Armistead and Martha Savage, his wife.

2. The said R. A. Armistead was the son of Robert Armistead and Elizabeth Smith, his wife.

3. The said Robert Armistead was the son of Westwood Armistead and Mary Jenkins, his wife.

4. The said Westwood Armistead was the son of Westwood Armistead and Mary Tabb, his wife.

5. The said Westwood Armistead was the son of Anthony Armistead and Elizabeth Westwood, his wife.

6. The said Anthony Armistead was the son of Anthony Armistead and Hannah Ellison, his wife.

7. The said Hannah Ellison was the daughter of *Robert Ellison,* his wife.

PEDIGREE OF ANCESTOR No. 3.

1. The said George W. Armistead was the son of R. A. Armistead and Martha Savage, his wife..

2. The said R. A. Armistead was the son of Robert Armistead and Elizabeth Smith, his wife. -

3. The said Robert Armistead was the son of Westwood Armistead and Mary Jenkins, his wife.

4. The said Westwood Armistead was the son of Westwood Armistead and Mary Tabb, his wife.

5. The said Mary Tabb was the daughter of *Col. John Tabb* and — ——, his wife.

1. The said George W. Armistead was the son of R. A. Armistead and Martha Savage, his wife.

2. The said R. A. Armistead was the son of Robert Armistead and Elizabeth Smith, his wife.

3. The said Robert Armistead was the son of Westwood Armistead and Mary Jenkins, his wife.

4. The said Westwood Armistead was the son of Westwood Armistead and Mary Tabb, his wife.

5. The said Westwood Armistead was the son of Anthony Armistead and Elizabeth Westwood, his wife.

6. The said Anthony Armistead was the son of *Anthony Armistead* and Hannah Ellison, his wife.

7. The said Anthony Armistead was the son of the emigrant *William* and , his wife.

PEDIGREE OF ANCESTOR No. 5.

1. The said George W. Armistead was the son of R. A. Armistead and Martha Savage, his wife.

2. The said R. A. Armistead was the son of Robert Armistead and Elizabeth Smith, his wife.

3. The said Robert Armistead was the son of Westwood Armistead and Mary Jenkins, his wife.

4. The said Westwood Armistead was the son of Westwood Armistead and Mary Tabb, his wife.

5. The said Westwood Armistead was the son of *Anthony Armistead* and , his wife.

PEDIGREE OF ANCESTOR No. 6.

1. The said George W. Armistead was the son of R. A. Armistead and Martha Savage, his wife.

2. The said Martha Savage was the daughter of Teackle Savage and Martha J. Wade, his wife.

3. The said Martha J. Wade was the daughter of Chidley Wade and Ann Kirby, his wife.

4. The said Ann Kirby was the daughter of William Kirby and Margaret Howard, his wife.

5. The said Margaret Howard was the daughter of John Howard and Ann Shield, his wife.

6. The said John Howard was the son of Col. Henry Howard and Frances Calthorpe, his wife.

7. The said Frances Calthorpe was the daughter of Elimelech Calthorpe and Mary Robinson, his wife.

The said Elimelech Calthorpe was son of James Calthorpe and his wife Mary ———.

The said James Calthorpe was the son of Col. *Christopher Calthorpe*. (See *William and Mary Quarterly*, Vol. II., p. 163, *et seq.)*

PEDIGREE OF ANCESTOR No. 7.

1. The said Martha Savage was the daughter of Teackle Savage and Martha J. Wade, his wife.

2. The said Martha J. Wade was the daughter of Chidley Wade and Ann Kirby, his wife.

3. The said Ann Kirby was the daughter of William Kirby and Margaret Howard, his wife.

4. The said Margaret Howard was the daughter of John Howard and Ann Shield, his wife.

5. The said John Howard was the son of Col. Henry Howard and Frances Calthorpe, his wife.

6. The said Frances Calthorpe was the daughter of Elimelech Calthorpe and Mary Robinson, his wife.

Mary Robinson was the daughter of John Robinson and Frances Wade.

Frances Wade was the daughter of Armiger Wade. (See *Hayden*, 571, and *William and Many Quarterly*, Vol. II., p.165.)

PEDIGREE OF ANCESTOR No. 7.

1. The said George W. Armistead was the son of R. A. Armistead and Martha Savage, his wife.

2. The said Martha Savage was the daughter of Teackle Savage and Martha J. Wade, his wife.

3. The said Martha J. Wade was the daughter of Chidley Wade and Ann Kirby, his wife.

4. The said Ann Kirby was the daughter of William Kirby and

Mlargaret Howard, his wife.

5. The said Margaret Howard was the daughter of John Howard and Ann Shield, his wife.

6. The said John Howard was the son of Henry Howard and Frances Calthorpe, his wife.

7. The said Henry Howard was the son of Col. Francis Howard and Martha ———, his wife.

Col. Francis Howard was son of Henry Howard and Elizabeth, his wife.

Henry Howard was son of *John* Howard. *(See Williaim and Mary Quarterly,* Vol. II., p. 167, and York Records.)

PEDIGREE OF ANCESTOR NO. 9.

1. The said George W. Armistead was the son of R. A. Armistead and Martha Savage, his wife.

2. The said Majrtha Savage was the daughter of Teackle Savage and Martha J. Wade, his wife.

3. The said Martha J. Wade was the daughter of Chidley Wade and Ann Kirby, his wife.

4. The said Ann Kirby was the daughter of William Kirby and Margareet Howard, his wife.

5. The said Margareet Howard was the daughter of John Howard and Ann Shield, his wife.

6. The said John Howard was the son of Henry Howard and Frances Calthorpe, his wife.

PEDIGREE OF ANCESTOR NO. 10.

1. The said George W. Armistead was the son of R. A Armistead and Martha Savage, his wife.

2. The said R. A. Armistead was the son of Robert Armistead and Elizabeth Smith, his wife.

3. The said Robert Armistead was the son of Westwood Armistead and Mary Jenkins, his wife.

4. The said Westwood Armistead was the son of Westwood Armistead and Mary Tabb.

5. The said Mary Tabb was the daughter of Col. John Tabb and Mary Sclater, his wife.

6. The said John Tabb was the son of Thomas Tabb and

Elizabeth Moss, his wife.

7. The said Thomas Tabb was the son of Thomas Tabb and Martha , his wife.

The said Thomas Tabb was the son of *Humphrey Tabb. (William and Mary Quarterly,* Vol., VII., pp. 45, 46.)

For the verification of the within statements we beg leave to refer to the Armistead Family, by R. A. Brock in the *Richmond Standard;* also to the able genealogical work of Dr. Lyon G. Tyler in Vols. VI. and VII. of the *William and Mary Quarterly,* p. 227 of the former and p. 19 (VII.) of the latter. This proves descent of Armisteads as stated in this paper; also official position of each ancestor mentioned herein. Reference may be also given to the *Virginia Colonial Register,* by W. G. and Mary Newton Standard for every office claimed by the first five ancestors.

The Armisteads of England and America have been honorable and useful men; in Virginia they have intermarried with the "Carters," "Burwells," "Wormeleys," "Pages," "Grymes," "Taylors" and "Lees."

The Armistead blood has helped to make presidents, councillors, burgesses, clergymen, and generals.

The famous Harrison family had an Armistead ancestress, as, indeed, had most of the makers of the "Old Dominion."

The first Armistead who came to Virginia had three sons and one daughter. The sons were William, John and Anthony; the daughter, Frances. William died young, John and Anthony were both members of the House of Burgesses, and John was also member of the Council, and was dropped for refusing to take the oath after the accession of William and Mary. (See *Lee of Virginia,* p. 532.)

The family lost none of its prestige as the years went on, for upon the Committee of Safety, in 1775-'6, were Robert Armistead, of Louisa; John Armistead, of Caroline; Henry Armistead, of Charles City; John Armistead, of New Kent, and *Westwood Armistead,* of Elizabeth City, ancestor of George W. Armistead.

The fact of Martha J. Wade being the daughter of Chidley Wade is proved by enclosed letter from D. B. Wade, who deposes that his grandfather was brother of Martha J. Wade, and that they were children of Chidley Wade, etc., etc.

Prepared by SALLY NELSON ROBINS,
Asst' Libr. in Va. His. Soc'y, Richmond, Va.

Mrs. Virginia Garber:

Dear Madam,—Your letter in regard to the Wade family received. From your letter I conclude you are a niece of Mr. Ned Savage, of Hampton; if so, your grandmother was sister to my grandfather, and they were children of Chidley Wade, of James City Co., who married Ann Kirby, of York Co.

Their marriage license is recorded in the clerk's office in Yorktown. I have my grandfather's Bible, but that has only the records of his own family, except his mother's birth.

(A copy of his mother's birth:)

"Ann Kirby, daughter of William Kirby and Margaret, his wife, was born August 30th, 1760."

This is the only record we have of our family.

Very respectfully,

D. B. WADE,
Grafton, Va.

RICHMOND, Va., *October* 24, 1903

I hereby certify that the within writing is a true, literal and correct copy of the letter written by D. B. Wade to Mrs. Virginia Garber, dated at Grafton, Va., June 20, 1903, original and copy read and examined by me.

Witness my hand, A. C. HARMAN,

Notary Public.

THE WILL OF WILLIAM WESTWOOD, NEPHEW OF ELIZABETH WESTWOOD WHO MARRIED COL. ANTHONY ARMISTEAD, AND BROTHER OF LOUISA WESTWOOD WHO MARRIED COL. ROBERT ARMISTEAD, OF LOUISA COUNTY.

In the name of God. Amen.

I, William Westwood of the County of Elizabeth City, do make this my last Will and Testament in manner and form following—

Imprimis, I give and bequeath to my Son William Westwood all the Land I possess between the two roads, adjoining the Land Merritt Westwood gave between him and John Stith Westwood, containing by estimation fifty acres more or less to him and his heirs forever.

Item. I give unto my Son John Stith Westwood twenty-five acres Land adjoining the Land his Grandfather gave him, which I have purchased of Edward Parish to him and his Heirs forever.

Item. I lend unto my Wife twelve thousand pounds to purchase a House and plantation for the benefit of Her and my Children during her life; and at her death, it is my Will and desire that the said Land and House be sold for the most money they will fetch and divided among all such of my children as my Wife shall judge most in want of it.

If my Wife should be now with child it is my Will and desire that if the child should live that, he or she as it may happen to be shall receive the same benefit from my Lstate as my Daughters, which are already Born shall receive. -

It is my Will and desire that should Child die before it comes of Age, or marries, ye said child's part shall be divided between all my Daughters as my Wife shall think proper.

Item. It is my Will and desire that in case my Wife should die before she makes a purchase of a House and plantation that ye whole money I lend her to purchase ye same, shall be equally divided between my Daughters.

Item. It is my Will and desire that the further sum of Three Thousand pounds be added to the above mentioned twelve Thousand pounds to purchase a House and plantation for ye above purpose and use.

Item. It is my Will and desire that my Wife shall make use of as much of my remaining money as will purchase ye necessary provisions for ye ensuing year.

Item. It is my will and desire that the remaining part of my money shall be put out at interest, as long as my executors hereafter named, shall think proper, and that the interest of ye said money, shall be towards the support of my Wife and Daughters.

Item. It is my will and desire that if either of my Daughters come to a Lawful age Marriage, my Wife or Lxecutors, hereafter mentioned, shall pay off such Daughter or Daughters their proportional part of my Estate —

Item. It is my further will and desire that my Wife have the care and management of my children until they come of age or marry.

Item. I give unto my Wife all my Household and Kitchen furniture.

Item. I give one Negro Woman named Rachel and her future increase to her and her Heirs, — that is to my said Wife and her Heirs forever.

Item. I give to my Wife two yoke of oxen, cart, &c., one Black Horse, then to Her and her Heirs forever —

Item. It is my Will and desire that my present crop shall be kept for ye use of my Wife and Children.

Eastly. I appoint my Wife, Ann Westwood, John Tabb, Worlich Westwood, and Stith Hardiman to be my Executrix and Executors of this my last Will and Testament, in witness whereof I have hereunto set my hand and affixed my seal this 24th day of December, 1780.

The word Wife was interlind over the third line at the bot-of ye first page before ye signing.

WILLIAM WESTWOOD.

Signed, sealed published and declared in the presence of —
JAMES BRAY ARMISTEAD
ERANCES ARMISTEAD
JOHN BRODIE

THE WILL OF CAPTAIN WESTWOOD ARMISTEAD, SON OF LIEUT-COL. ANTHONY A., WHO WAS SON OF THE EMIGRANT.

In the name of God. Amen.

I, Captain Westwood Armistead, of the County of Elizabeth City do hereby in order to dispose of my worldly Estate make this my last Will & Testament in manner following.

Imprimis. I give and bequeath unto my loving wife the use & property of these five Negroes named Ceasar, Jeffery, Coffe, Davie, & Rachel, during her natural life, with full power at any time, while she is living, or by will at her death, to give and dispose of them as my said wife pleases to any one or more of my three Children or to either of their heirs.

Item, I give to my Said Wife one Feather Bed and furniture at her choyce, also my Grey Horse & Black Mlare.

Item, I give to my Said wife the use of my Land and Plantation I purchased from my Brother Anthony, with full power to cutt down and sell timber for the payment of all my debts and after that is done, then further to cut down and sell ye said Timber until she has raised two hundred pounds current money of Virginia, which said two hundred pounds I give to my wife and my two Daughters Elizabeth and Mary.

Item. My Will and desire is that all the negroes that I shah hereafter give my two Daughters shall work and be employed with those I have given my wife in getting and carrying the said Timber to market, and that for the time they are employed, in raising the money sufficient to discharge my debts, that my said wife or any Guardian to my said Daughters shall not be accountable for any profits from the said slaves.

Item. I give and bequeath unto my son Westwood (after my said wife has made and raised the above sums of money) all that Tract and Plantation of Land I purchased of my brother Anthony containing four hundred and sixty and eight acres, and to the heirs of his body lawfully begotten forever.

Item. I give and bequeath to my said son these following Slaves named Minne, Andrew, Pompey, Jeffery, Ben & Peter to him and his heirs forever.

Item, I give my said son my silver watch.

Item. I give to my said son six heiffers six Ewes and two Mares.

Item. I give my said son twelve silver spoons.

Item. I give my Daughter Elizabeth these slaves named Lucy, Frank, Jack, Nan, Phoebe, and Tom, and to her heirs forever.

Item. I give my said Daughter my largest looking Glass.

Item. I give to my daughter Mary these Slaves named Judy, Will, Charles, Beck, Nelly, to her and her heirs forever.

Item. My will and desire is that if either of my Daughters should die before they come of age or marry, that then the slaves & other estate of that child so dying and heretofore given them by this will shall be equally divided between each of my surviving children.

Item. I give the use of all my remaining plate to my wife and full power to her to dispose of it to my children as she thinks proper.

Item. My will and desire is that all the remaining part of my estate not given by this will, shall be equally divided between my wife and two daughters.

Item. I do hereby constitute and appoint my loving wife Executrix to this my will & Colonel John Tabb & Anthony Armistead Executors.

In witness whereof I have hereunto set my hand and seal this ninth day of Eebruary Anno Domini 1756.

Sealed, & Delivered Published & Declared in the Presence if
JOHN TABB
HANNAH TABB
JOHN ERAZIER.

THE WILL OF WESTWOOD ARMISTEAD, SON OF CAPTAIN WESTWOOD ARMISTEAD AND MARY TABB, HIS WIFE.

In the name of God Amen. I Westwood Armistead of the County of Elizabeth City do hereby in order to dispose of my Worldly Estate make this my last Will and Testament in manner & form following

Imprimis. I give unto my son Robert Armistead the plantation where on 1 live lying on Back River containing four hundred and fifty acres, to him & his Heirs forever.

Item. I give to my Son Robert Armistead the Plantation lying on Back River which adjoins the Lands of Thomas Kirby and Charles Miles Collier, Orphans — containing by Estimate two hundred and sixty acres to him and his Heirs forever.

Item. I give and bequeath unto my Son Robert Armistead my young black mare.

Item. I give unto my son Robert Armistead six young cows & two yoke of Steers to be at his on choice.

Item. I give to my son Westwood Armistead four hundred and sixty & eight acres of Land lying on Sawyer's Swamp & known by the name of Ridge Land to him & his Heirs forever.

Item, it is my desire that the following negroes be equally divided between my sons Robert Armistead & Westw'ood Armistead to wit Pompey, Nat, George, Peter, Abram, Jeffery, Charles, Nanny, Rachel, Dolly, Lucy, Grace, Sukey, with their increase.

Item. The remaining part of my Estate not given by this Will, it is my desire that the same be sold to the best advantage & after my just debts are paid off, the remaining money arising from the said sale be equally divided between my Sons Robert Armistead and Westwood Arniistead.

Item. If my sons Robert Armistead & Westwood Armistead should either of them die before they come of age or marry it is my will and desire that the survivor take the Estate of the deceased & I give the same to the survivor and his Heirs forever.

Item. I do hereby appoint my wife Mary Armistead Executrix & my Son Robert Armistead Executor of this my last Will & Testament in Witness whereof I have hereunto set my hand and Seal this 18th day of January one thousand seven hundred & eighty two.

WESTWOOD ARMISTEAD.

[SEAL.]

Signed, sealed and delivered in presence of
EDWARD ALLEN
ROBERT KIRBY
JAMES DIXON.

THE WILL OF ELIZABETH WESTWOOD, WIFE OF 83. ANTHONY WESTWOOD.

In the name of God Amen. I, Elizabeth Armistead of Elizabeth City County, being sick and weak in body but of perfect sense and memory, thanks be to Almighty God for the same, do constitute and appoint this to be my last will and Testament in manner and Form as Follows; and after my Just Debts and Funeral Charges are paid, I give the Remaining Part of my Estate as Follows—

Imprimis. I give unto my loving Son Westwood Armistead my negro man named Sampson, my Copper Kettle & my Large Looking Glass, to him & his Heirs for ever.

I give unto my loving son Anthony Armistead my Silver Tankard, Silver Salt*and Brandy Still, to him & his Heirs forever.

I give unto my Grand Daughters Elizabeth and Mary Allen, Daughters of Jolm Allen all the Remaining part of my Silver plate to be equally Divided Between them. To them and their Heirs forever.

I give unto my aforesaid Grand Daughters Elizabeth Allen Six black Cain chairs & Walnut oval Table To her and her Heirs forever.

I give unto my daughter Sarah Smelt, Ten pounds Current money to be paid her when she comes to Lawful age or married & in case she dies before, my will is that it be divided Between my loving Son Anthony Armistead & my Daughter Hannah Allen. And lastly I give my Remaining part of my Estate (viz) negroes. Household goods. Stock, money & what debts are due to me to be equally Divided Between my Loving Son Anthony Armistead and my Loving Daughter Hannah Allen. To them and their heirs for ever.

I constitute and appoint my Loving Son Anthony Armistead and Mr. John Allen to be my Executors of this my Last will & Testament. In Witness whereof I have hereunto Set my hand & seal this the 28th day of September 1750.

ELIZABETH ARMISTEAD.

Signed, sealed, and acknowledged in presence of
MARGARET HUNTER
JUDITH ROBINSON
R. A. ARMISTEAD

THE WILL OF ROBERT ARMISTEAD, SEN.

In the name of God Amen, I Robert Armistead Sem of Elizabeth City County being sick and weak in body, but of sound and disposing mind do make and ordain this to be my last Will Sc Testament in manner & Eorm following;

Imprimis. I give & bequeath unto my Daughter Elizabeth Armistead the following slaves to wit—Yellow Bob, Jeffery, Sucky, Wocly, Mildy, Jack, Big Beck & her child Phillis, little Eanny, Sal & Milly—the said negroes to be hired out annually by my Executors hereafter named and the money arising from the Hire of the said slaves to be paid to my loving mother Elizabeth Armistead during her life for the especial Purpose of supporting herself and my Daughter Elizabeth Armistead.

Item, my will and desire is that all my Lands—Slaves and personal Estate of every Kind excepting the slaves above named be kept together during my mother's life and during the Widowhood of my loving Wife Ann Armistead for their mutual Benefit and Advantage and after my mother's Death and the Marriage of my Wife, I give and devise my lands in the County and my lands Iying in York County to my son William Armistead to him & his Heirs for Ever; but in case my Wife Should marry I lend unto her during her natural life one third part of my lands and one Third Part of all my negroes except those above named.

Item. I give unto my son William Armistead ten negroes of those that may remain after my Wife's one Third is taken out, to be hired out for his Benefit and Advantage, and the Remainder of the negroes to be equally divided between my said Son William and Elizabeth Arniistead, and it is my further will and Desire that after my Mother's Death and the Death of my Wife, that all my negroes including those given to my daughter Elizabeth Armistead and those given to my son William Armistead should be equally divided between my said Son & Daughter to them and their heirs for Ever.

Item. It is my Will and Desire after the death of my Mother and the marriage of my wife that my Stock of every Kind & Household and Kitchen Furniture and Plantation utensils be sold and the money arising from the sale thereof together with all the money due me in the State of North Carolina, I give and bequeath all said money to my Daughter Elizabeth Armistead. The money due me in North Carolina I devise may be collected immediately — all the aforesaid money I request that it may be placed in the Treasury of Virginia and the Interest there of to be applied to the support of my said Daughter Elizabeth until she comes of age or marries and then she is to draw both the principal and interest.

Item. I devise that all the money due me in this County or as much of it as shall be suffcient be supplied in the first place to the payment of my Just Debts and the Balance that may be remaining I give unto my son William Armistead.

In case my Daughter Elizabeth Armistead should die before she comes of age or marries then & in that case I give unto my son William Armistead all the property that I have already devised to her and in case my son William Armistead should die before he arrives to the age of twenty one years it is my Desire that all the property which I have given to him should be given to my said Daughter Elizabeth Armistead and to their Heirs for Ever.

Si Lastly I nominate and appoint Col. Jno. Cary, Mr. Robert Armistead Son of William Armistead, Sheldon Moss & Johnson Tabb to be Executors of this my last Will and Testament In witness whereof I have hereunto set my Hand and Seal this 12th Day of November 1792.

ROBT. ARMISTEAD.
[RED SEAL.]

Signed, sealed, published and declared to be the Testator's last will in Presence of

JOHNSON TABB

THOS. BAKER ARMISTEAD
WILLIAM ARMISTEAD
MILES KING -
1000 lbs. Bond as security.

It is supposed that son William named in above will married Priscilla (d. 1825) and had Robert Henry Armistead of Williamsbprg, Va.

THE WILL OF ROBERT ARMISTEAD, FATHER OF ROBERT AUGUSTUS ARMISTEAD.

In the name of God amen I Robert Armistead of the County of *Eliz th* City being in perfect health and of sound disposing mind and memory do in order to dispose of Estate make and ordain this Instrument of writing to be my last will and Testament in manner and form following:

I lend to my wife Elizabeth Armistead during her natural life all my Estate both real and personal, except as hereinafter excepted to be kept together and employed for the purpose of supporting herself and my unmarried children, and to assist in clearing my estate from Debt. I also authorise my said wife to take from the plantation called the Ridge Land which descended to me by the death of my Brother, any Timber for Staves or to have cut up, at the Saw Mill or otherwise for the purposes aforesaid: the exceptions above alluded to are that my Said Wife is not to have any right or interest in the Slaves hereby given to my Son Westwood S. Armistead to my son Thomas S. Armistead and to my daughter Maria Crawford, nor in the one third of the fifty acres of Land given to my Son Westwood S. Armistead: or the Bay Tree Tract of Land given to my Son Thomas S. Armistead —

I give to my Son Westwood S. Armistead Two negroes named Charley & Lockey now in his possession also one third part cf the fifty acres of Land purchased from the Trustees of the Hampton Academy to him and his Heirs for Ever.

I give to my Son Thomas S. Armistead my Plantation lying in the County of York Known and Called by the name of the Bay Tree Tract of Land, containing three hundred and thirteen acres more or less; also a portion of my Lott in the Town of Hampton having a front on Kings Street of Eighty feet bounded on the north by the Lot of his

Brother Westwood S. Armistead, and Southerly by the remaining portion of my Lot hereafter given to his Brother Robert Augustus Armistead, & running back westerly the full Depth of my Said Lot, and one third of the fifty acres of Land purchased from the Trustees of the Hampton Academy together with a negro man named Manuel and a Boy named Yellow Charles, to him and his heirs for ever.

I give to my Son Robert Augustus Armistead a Tract of Land called the Ridge Land lying in the County of *Eliz th* City which descended to me by the Death of my Brother, also my Mill Seats and their improvements together with my House and the remaining undivided portion of my Lot in the Town of Hampton, bounded north by the Lot hereby given to his Brother Thomas S. Armistead. Easterly on Kings Street & Southerly by Queen Street, *riming* back the full Depth of my Lott also one third of the fifty acres of Land purchased from the Trustees of the Hampton Academy and the piece of Land divided & assigned to me under a Decree of the Court of Elizabeth City: out of the Land formerly belonging to the Estate of Henry Jenkins Dec'd and a negro Boy named Tom to be put to learn a Trade & accounted for at Such valuation in the general division of my Estate. The aforesaid Property is given to my Said Son Robert Augustus Armistead and his Heirs forever, provided and on the express condition that he permits his single and unmarried Sisters to have use and enjoy a Decent and Convenient portion of the House & Lott in Hampton, hereby given to him during the term of their remaining Single and unmarried:

I hereby give to my Single and unmarried Daughters namely Louisa Y. Armistead, Hellen S. Armistead, Emilly S. Armistead & Harriet Armistead the undisturbed right & privilege to use and enjoy during the term of their remaining Single and unmarried, a Decent & convenient portion of the House & Lott in Hampton hereby given to their Brother Robert Augustus Armistead, and in order to prevent any misunderstanding as to Such portion of the House & Lot my Executors are to decide & make if necessary Such assignment.

I give to my Daughter Maria Crawford a Negro Boy named Randolph and a Girl named Clary, valued by me at five hundred Dollars, to be accounted for at such valuation in the general division to her and her Heirs forever.

I give to my Daughter Emilly S. Armistead a negro woman named Rachel and her Daughter named Rose, to be valued and accounted for in the general division to her and her heirs forever If my Said Daughter Emilly Should die before She arrives to Lawful age or marries I desire my executors to permit the Said Two Slaves to make choice of Such of my Daughters as they may want to belong to to be valued and accounted for.

In all cases where a valuation is to be made, I authorise my executors if they are alive or either of them, to make Such valuation.

My further will and desire is that whereas it may so happen that at the Death of my Said Wife Elizabeth Armistead Some of my Daughters may at that time be Single and unmarried and my two youngest children not Educated and thereby left too suddenly unprovided for, having regard to their peculiar situation, Should a general division of my Estate take place at that time, and in order to provide for Such an event the following Slaves to wit. George, by Trade—Blacksmith and Negro Girl named Liza with her future increase be considered, and is hereby given as a Specific Gift and Legacy to my Single and unmarried Daughters before mentioned : To wit, Louisa Y. Armistead, Helen S. Armistead, Emily S. Armistead & Harriet Armistead, so long, and during the term of their or either of their remaining Single & unmarried; this Gift being considered a conditional one, it is understood to be my will that, in the event of all my Daughters marrying or after the Death of Such of them as do not marry, that then the Slaves aforesaid with the increase are to be equally divided between my Daughters & their Heirs and my Son Robert Augustus Armistead and his Heirs forever and whereas it may happen that my Daughters that are now single may wish when ever a Division of the Slaves aforesaid takes place to make a choice among themselves of those Slaves or their Increase, my will is that they or either of them be permitted to make Such selection by accounting for a fair Valuation, giving the priviledge of Such selection to my oldest Single Daughter Louisa first and So on according to age, among the rest of my Said Daughters—

My will and desire is that if my wife Elizabeth Armistead Should die before my two youngest children are Educated and my Estate clear of Debt, that my Surviving Executor do keep my Estate together for the purpose of raising funds to pay off my Debts, and finishing the Education of my Said two youngest children, or So much of my Estate as may be Sufficient for that purpose.

After the death of my Said wife & my Debts paid off & a Suitable revenue or provision made for the Education of Two Young Children aforesaid: I desire & it is my will that all my Personal Estate not otherwise appropriated and disposed of, be equally divided between all my Daughters & their Heirs & my Son Robert Augustus Armistead; to them and their Heirs forever.

I do hereby appoint my wife Elizabeth Armistead and my Son Westwood S. Armistead Executors to this my last will and Testament, Revoking all others heretofore made and, I earnestly request of the Court that they will not compell my Said Executors to give Security for their Executorship.

I do hereby appoint and assign my Executors aforesaid to be the Guardians of my infant Children untill they arrive to the age of Twenty one years. In witness whereof, I have hereunto Set my hand and affixed my Seal this first day of May, 1817: in order that the proper Construction to this my will may be made as to the life estate of my wife Eliz Armistead.

It is understood to be my will and meaning that she has her life Estate in the Boy Yellow Charles given to my Son Thomas S. Armistead: also to the Lot & portion of the fifty acres of Land also given to my Said Son Thomas, also her life Estate in the Slaves hereby given to my Daughter Emilly S. Armistead— in addition to the life Estate in the property mentioned and expressed in the first clause of this my will to my said wife. In further Testimony & In witness whereof I have hereunto Set my hand and affixed my Seal this first day of May 1817.

ROBERT ARMISTEAD [Seal].

Signed Sealed published & declared in the presence of
ELIJAH SMITH
THOS. T. YOUNG
HENRY H. ELLIOTT
WM. FACE.

NOTE.—He died suddenly August 31, 1817, age fifty-one years and twenty-two days. His youngest child, Robert Augustus Armistead, was nine years old.

* September 28, 1752, Francis Jordon, of Yorktown, wrote to your good friend Mr. Commissary Dawson died about 20th of July, about ten days after he married the widow Bassett. It is generally said that it was happy for him that he did not live to experience the unhappiness it would have created for him."

*William Armistead Braxton was named by his father for his friend–. Dr. William Armistead, who studied with him at the same college in Philadelphia.

* Landon Carter's (Robert W.4 Landon[3], Robert[2], John[1]) mother was Winifred Beale. Landon C.'s wife, Mary Burwell Armistead, was left a widow in 1846, at Alexandria; was buried at Shooter's Hill.

* Humphrey Gwynn owned and occupied Gwynn's Island in 1776, when Lord Dunmore made it his temporary home.

* "Darcy South all had issue Col. Turner Southall, of the Revolutionary War, prominent in Church and State. He succeeded to his father's estate in 1759; was appointed vestryman in the place of John Randolph in 1770; warden on December 8, 1772."

* Mrs. Emily Gordon Batte, great-granddaughter of Lord Lewis Gordon, of Scotland, gave the following account of the Grampus: Mrs. Batte's cousin was lost on the Grampus- Her uncle, William Lewis Gordon, was midshipman on the Constitution^ and promoted for bravery to first lieutenant.

In 1821 the Grampus, a twelve-gun schooner, was commissioned as one of a fleet for the destruction of pirates. Lieutenant Francis Hoyt Gregory commander (George Magee McCreery was promoted from mid- shipman to lieutenant, U. S. N., 1839).

The capture of various notorious pirates and cargoes were accomplished by the fleet. On one of the ships coming in, the commander discovered a plot to mutiny and take possession of the ship. The ringleader was promptly executed- He was later found to be the brother of a notorious pirate, who, with his ships, was at the Isle of Pines awaiting the expected captured vessel. When he heard of the miscarriage of his plans and execution of his brother, he vowed he would capture and destroy the first ship out from Norfolk, which proved to be the Grampus. This ship was the only one of the navy that carried a peculiar kind of sail or sails; such sails were afterwards seen on a pirate ship.

Bushrod Washington Hunter, whose place Lieutenant McCreery

took, had a very ill wife at the time of the sailing of the Grampus, and, meeting McCreery. was told his trouble. McCreery promptly offered to take his place. Their daughters afterwards went to school together at Lefebvre's.

* Issue of Colonel Anthony Armistead and Elizabeth Westwood, his wife: (169) Westwood A., married Mary Todd; issue, (172) Westwood A., (173) Elizabeth A., (174) Mary A. (172) Westwood A. married Mary Jenkins; issue, (178) Robert A., (179) Westwood A., died unmarried. (178) Robert A. married Elizabeth Smith; issue, among others, Robert A. Armistead, born May 7, 1808.

*Elizabeth Westwood, daughter of William W and Anne Smith, his wife (who married first, James Wallace), "was remarkable for her beauty, accomplishments, strength of intellect and piety." She had eleven children, six of whom attained maturity—two sons and four daughters— who were noted for their beauty. One, Euphon Wallace, married first, Baily Washington, brother of Colonel William Washington of the Revolution ; married second, Daniel Carroll Brent of Winsor Forest, Stafford County, Va.

*William S. Harrison, of Farmington, Charles City County, Va., was a descendant of an old Scotch family.

* There *is* a quaint old brick house near the Pianketank, the early residence of the Cookes. Mordecai Cooke patented eleven hundred and seventy-four acres at the head of Ware River on Mob Jack Bay.

* Augustine Smith (son of Major Lawrence Smith, great-uncle of Thomas Smith, of York,) was one of the Knights of the Golden Horseshoe. He married Susanna Darnell; had a son Thomas, a son John, and daughter Mary, who married Robert Slaughter. His will proved in Orange County; lived in St. Mary's Parish, Essex County.

* Robert Smith, son of Colonel Lawrence Smith, married Afary Calthrope, born February 17, 1733. Issue: Robert S. Calthrope S., born September 14, 1767; Lucy and Ceorge S., *twins*. Robert Smith sold the land at the mouth of Wormeley Creek, 1769, for 1,200 pounds to Augustine Aloore, who married his sister Lucy. On his death, in 1788, without issue, Moore left the estate to his "ever worthy friend, Cen. Thos. Nelson," subject to the life estate of his wife.

Augustine Moore occupied the Smith mansion (Temple Farm, Moore House) when the articles of surrender were signed in 1781.

General Thomas Nelson appears as guardian of Augustine and Thomas Smith, orphans of Robert Smith, deceased. In General Nelson's will in 1789, "Dr. Augustine Smith was not to be called upon to repay one shilling that I have expended on his maintenance or education." Dr. Augustine Smith married Alice Page, daughter of Governor Page, and died 1805. His widow married Dudley Diggs. The above Robert Smuh and Thomas Smith, of York, were half brothers.

* As far as we can prove Nicholas Martian was the first owner of the land upon which Yorktown stands. This Nicholas was a French Protestant, who went to Fngland for religious liberty perhaps; however that may be, he obtained denization in Fngland and could "hold any office or employment in Virgima." He was born in 1591, and was a Burgess in Virginia in 1623. Martian, the first owner of the land lying upon the York, now called Yorktown, was the ancestor of George Washington, to whom Cornwallis surrendered on the spot once owned by his great-great-great-grandfather. This Nicholas Martian married three times. By his first wife, Flizabeth, he had three daughters — Flizabeth, Mary and Sarah. Flizabeth married George Reade Mary married John Scarsbrook, and Sarah married Captain William Fuller Governor of Maryland. No son carried on the name; but this man Alartian is a very real character. He has steered many an inspiring lady into the sacred privileges of "Colonial Dameship." He died in 1656 and left a good estate.

The oldest Martian girl made an excellent match for George Reade, Secretary; of the Colony,Burgess and Councillor; was of very noble descent. He was son of Robert Reade and Mildred Windebank, and the fair maiden was daughter of Sir Thomas Windebank and Frances Dymoke — and these Windebanks and Dymokes make all sorts of praiseworthy genealogical turns, landing „afely at last in the bosom of Alfred the Great. George Reade, when he first came over stayed with Governor Harvey at Jamestown, but after he married Martian's daughter he went to live in York.

† Sir Edmund Dymoke was a descendant of Sir Robert Marmyum, Lord of Castle Eontenage in Normandy, and of Lamborth and Schrivelsby Castles in England. This Lord Marmyum was a descendant of "Rollo the Dane," and was "hereditary champion" to his kinsman William, Duke of Normandy, afterwards William the Conqueror.

At the battle of Hastings King William gathered his principal retainers — one of whom was Lord Marmyum — on a hill the site of the most desperate fighting, and vowed to bulit the great Battle Abbey, which was done.

From the above will be seen that Battle Abbey is a misnomer for any other memorial building.

227*John Bell Bigger was Clerk of the Virginia House of Delegates for thirty-five years. He married Annie Burnley Muse, and had twelve children.

*This silver salt was a solid silver cross, nine inches long by six inches wide and a half inch thick, with silver cups on the four ends for salt. It descended to Robert Augustine Armistead.

Made in the USA
Columbia, SC
23 September 2021